MW00632815

Bucking the Buck

Bucking the Buck

*US Financial Sanctions and the International
Backlash against the Dollar*

DANIEL McDOWELL

OXFORD
UNIVERSITY PRESS

Oxford University Press is a department of the University of Oxford. It furthers
the University's objective of excellence in research, scholarship, and education
by publishing worldwide. Oxford is a registered trade mark of Oxford University
Press in the UK and certain other countries.

Published in the United States of America by Oxford University Press
198 Madison Avenue, New York, NY 10016, United States of America.

© Oxford University Press 2023

All rights reserved. No part of this publication may be reproduced, stored in
a retrieval system, or transmitted, in any form or by any means, without the
prior permission in writing of Oxford University Press, or as expressly permitted
by law, by license, or under terms agreed with the appropriate reproduction
rights organization. Inquiries concerning reproduction outside the scope of the
above should be sent to the Rights Department, Oxford University Press, at the
address above.

You must not circulate this work in any other form
and you must impose this same condition on any acquirer.

Library of Congress Control Number: 2022060608

ISBN 978–0–19–767988–3 (pbk.)
ISBN 978–0–19–767987–6 (hbk.)

DOI: 10.1093/oso/9780197679876.001.0001

Paperback printed by Marquis, Canada
Hardback printed by Bridgeport National Bindery, Inc., United States of America

For the "Crazy Crew"
(Luella, Eileen, and William)

Contents

Figures

Tables

Preface and Acknowledgments

At the time of this writing, Russia's brutal and unprovoked war in Ukraine is in its seventh month. Thousands of civilians have been killed. Tens of thousands of soldiers, on both sides, have lost their lives. As the shock of war in Europe unfolded on television screens around the world, the United States and its allies in Europe and Asia were compelled to respond. Though direct military intervention was quickly ruled out, the leaders of these countries reached for one tool of foreign policy early and often: economic sanctions. Chief among the sanctions employed were those measures that denied targeted Russian individuals, businesses, and government institutions access to the global financial system. Within a few months' time, the Central Bank of Russia, many powerful Russian oligarchs, Vladimir Putin himself, and even his longtime girlfriend and his daughters had all been placed on a fast-growing financial blacklist.

As these events played out in real time, public awareness of such measures grew almost as quickly as the long list of sanctions themselves. Cable news networks and opinion pages of major newspapers openly discussed the nuances of the cross-border payment messaging system known as SWIFT, a communication network unknown to even the most astutely informed citizens prior to February 2022. Experts unpacked for audiences arcane elements of the international financial system to explain how international dependence on the US dollar provided the basis for the West's swift and punitive economic response. Some observers openly questioned whether cutting off Russia's access to the dollar—or "weaponizing" the currency, as it has come to be described—would backfire and hurt the greenback's global standing in the months and years to come.

When I started developing the idea for this book in 2017, I had no idea that the subject would be so salient five years later. Neither did I know that I would write most of this book during a pandemic while splitting time with my wife as teacher to our three, suddenly homeschooling, kids. Many pages of this book (though, I cannot recall which ones) were put to page while an energetic four-year-old entertained himself on my home office floor. Reaching this moment was something that, on many occasions and for long stretches,

I doubted I would ever achieve. In fact, I kept this book a secret from everyone but my closest friends and family for four years because I lacked the confidence that it would ever be finished. Completing a long project brings with it many emotions, but the two that I feel most acutely now are relief and gratitude. Though the feelings of relief will quickly recede as the busyness of life overtakes the present moment, my gratitude will endure. I could have never finished this book were it not for the many people who contributed to its development.

At my home institution, the Maxwell School of Citizenship and Public Affairs at Syracuse University, I am indebted to several colleagues. Brian Taylor shared sage wisdom with me about the process of writing a second book. Dennis Rasmussen and Shana Gadarian helped me think through the publishing process and what comes after. Dimitar Gueorguiev provided critical feedback on survey question design. Several graduate students at the Maxwell School assisted with research. Olga Boichak, Michael McCall, and Nikiti Selikov each performed critical tasks at various stages of the project's development. Two research assistants—J. Michael Dedmon and Jingding Wang—worked with me over the long haul, dutifully and carefully collecting data, analyzing foreign-language media reports, and digging through government documents for information. I am thankful for each hour that these individuals worked on behalf of this book. Generous research support for this book was provided by the Andrew Berlin Family National Security Research Fund at the Institute for Security Policy and Law (ISPL) at Syracuse University. I personally thank Mr. Berlin, his family, and all of the people at ISPL for funding this project from its earliest stages until the final steps of the editing process. Your commitment helped make this possible.

Outside of my home institution, I thank two longtime friends and mentors—Jerry Cohen and Eríc Helleiner—who each provided feedback in the early days of the project. Thomas Oatley gave me the opportunity to present and receive feedback on my unfinished manuscript at Tulane University in 2019, for which I am grateful. I thank my good friends and frequent co-authors David Steinberg and Steven Liao for being patient with me as I worked on the book and for providing periodic advice along the way. I am indebted to Eddy Malesky for allowing me to place several questions on the 2019 Provincial Competitiveness Index survey at no cost. Eddy's commitment to providing public goods for the academy is well known, and this is yet another example of his generosity. At Oxford University Press, I thank my editor Dave McBride for his support and enthusiasm for this project. I am deeply indebted to the three anonymous reviewers who provided exhaustive, invaluable advice for me as I revised the manuscript. The book is so much better for having their collective input. I hope they see their ideas reflected in the final product. I am also indebted to Kelley Friel who skillfully copyedited every line of this book and vastly improved the quality of my language and the clarity of my ideas.

Finally, I thank my family for their enduring support and for keeping me connected to what matters most while working on this project. I am grateful for supportive parents, in-laws, and my creative brother. To my three children—Luella, Eileen, and William—I am sorry that this book often took me away from you, especially during the summers. Your energy and light made the most grueling periods of completing this book bearable. For that, I dedicate this book to each of you. To my incredible wife, Sara, I know that this project caused you to endure many life moments with a grumpy, distracted husband and co-parent. Yet, over the span of five years you cheered me on and supported me through the most challenging and frustrating moments, as you always have. You listened to my anxieties and provided unyielding encouragement. You selflessly put my needs before yours. Thank you for being my co-author in this life. Without your steadfast love and support, neither the book nor my sanity would have made it to the finish line. I love you.

Abbreviations

BCV	Central Bank of Venezuela
CBR	Central Bank of Russia
CHIPS	Clearing House Interbank Payment System
CIPS	Cross-Border Interbank Payment System
INSTEX	Instrument in Support of Trade Exchanges
JCPOA	Joint Comprehensive Plan of Action
OFAC	Office of Foreign Assets Control
PBOC	People's Bank of China
SDN	Specially Designated National
SPFS	Financial Messaging System of the Bank of Russia
SREO	Sanctions-related Executive Order

Introduction

In the last week of April 2018, French president Emmanuel Macron and German chancellor Angela Merkel made back-to-back trips to Washington in an effort to convince US president Donald Trump not to withdraw from the Joint Comprehensive Plan of Action (JCPOA), the multilateral nuclear arms agreement his predecessor had signed with Iran. Then-UK foreign minister Boris Johnson timed his US visit to coincide with an op-ed he wrote for the *New York Times* urging Trump to stay in the deal. Johnson even appeared on *Fox & Friends*, the president's favorite news program, to plead Europe's case.[1] In the end, none of it worked. On May 8, Trump announced that the United States was pulling out of the Iran nuclear deal. The condemnation from Europe was swift. Major German newspaper *Die Zeit* pulled no punches, tweeting the day after: "Trump destroys the liberal world order."[2] Merkel more gently echoed these sentiments, saying the move put the multilateral global order in a "real crisis."[3] Macron warned that the move would only make the world a more dangerous place, adding, "I regret the decision of the American president. I think it's an error."[4] A joint statement from the British, French, and Germans soon followed, condemning the decision.[5]

That Europe was directing its anger and disappointment at the Trump administration after its controversial decision came as no surprise. However, several prominent European policymakers soon turned their ire toward what might seem like unlikely targets: the US financial system and the currency that underpins it. German Foreign Minister Heiko Maas was the first to speak up. Writing in *Handelsblatt*, a German newspaper, in August 2018, Maas characterized the Trump administration's decision as a "mistake," adding that Trump's move made it "essential that we strengthen European autonomy by establishing payment channels independent of the US [financial system]."[6] French finance minister Bruno Le Marie quickly backed Maas's position, saying, "I want Europe to be a sovereign continent, not a vassal, and that means having totally independent financing instruments [from the United States]."[7] European Commission president Jean-Claude Junker was also frustrated by

Bucking the Buck. Daniel McDowell, Oxford University Press. © Oxford University Press 2023.
DOI: 10.1093/oso/9780197679876.003.0001

Trump's decision and used his 2018 State of the Union Address to express his displeasure.[8] Speaking before members of the European Parliament, Junker stated that more needed to be done to "allow our single currency to play its full role on the international scene." Noting that Europe paid for 80 percent of its energy imports in dollars rather than euros, he called this "absurd" and challenged members to support a united effort to promote the common currency as an "instrument of a new, more sovereign Europe."[9]

Why did the Trump administration's decision regarding the Iran nuclear deal trigger anti-dollar rhetoric from so many prominent European policymakers? The American withdrawal from the agreement led to the reinstatement of harsh financial sanctions against Tehran, which had been suspended when the United States signed the JCPOA in 2015. These direct measures blocked the Iranian regime from accessing the global dollar-based financial system, but this is not what irritated the Europeans. The United States also reimposed "secondary sanctions" that went beyond the targeted regime. Secondary sanctions cut off, from the dollar and the financial institutions through which those dollars flow, any third-party individual or firm doing business with designated Iranian targets. This was a problem for many European firms that had reentered the Iranian market after the JCPOA was signed. They were now faced with a Hobson's choice: continue business with Iran (and be blacklisted by the US Treasury) or write off all past investments in their Iranian business relationships. Because of the dollar's centrality in the global financial system, which includes its use in the settlement of international trade, European companies involved in Iran chose the second option. While losing the potential to develop Iranian business was a blow, losing access to the dollar would have been infinitely more costly. European policymakers' frustration with the United States was based on a stark reality: the dollar's global dominance allowed Washington to wield its currency as a weapon of foreign policy. This motivated European countries to discuss how to promote the euro's global role to minimize future injury.

During the JCPOA negotiations in 2015, then-president Barack Obama foreshadowed Europe's reaction to backing out of the agreement. He warned that the failure to reach a deal would result in new US sanctions that would "raise questions internationally about the dollar's role as the world's reserve currency."[10] Secretary of State John Kerry offered a more alarmist take, asserting that walking away from the nuclear deal and unilaterally imposing sanctions was "a recipe . . . for the American dollar to cease to be the reserve currency of the world."[11] Critical observers characterized their statements as breathless, hyperbolic rhetoric. One popular business television personality asked in a tweet, "Does the secretary [John Kerry] know anything about the dollar?"[12] Another critic opined that there was no "less convincing argument" for the Iran deal than "fear-mongering" about the dollar.[13] Others claimed any assertion that the dollar would lose its top global position due to "geopolitical" forces was "laughable"; they maintained that only economic forces could weaken the currency's dominance.[14] Obama's and Kerry's claims were both exaggerations—as political rhetoric often is. Yet criticizing their political hyperbole by jumping to the conclusion that the dollar's status as the world's pre-eminent and most widely used currency is divorced from politics is misguided.

In a speech the year after the JCPOA was signed, Jack Lew, then secretary of the US Treasury, offered a more nuanced take on the link between financial sanctions and the dollar's status, warning of "sanctions overreach." While Lew explained that financial sanctions are a powerful tool of US foreign policy made possible by the dollar's global dominance, he cautioned that their overuse could, over time, weaken the Treasury's ability to employ them effectively. "The more we condition use of the dollar and our financial system on adherence to US foreign policy," he detailed, "the more the risk of migration to other currencies and other financial systems in the medium-term grows."[15] Careful to avoid the apocalyptic tone of his colleague at the State Department, Lew offered a measured explanation of why the dollar's dominance depended not just on economic factors but on political ones as well. According to the memoir of a high-ranking Trump administration official, Lew's successor Steven Mnuchin also worried that relying on sanctions could damage the dollar's reserve currency status and push more cross-border transactions into euros.[16]

Financial sanctions again gained prominence as a key tool in the West's response to the unprovoked Russian invasion of Ukraine in February 2022. Days later, the Central Bank of Russia, many Russian oligarchs, and even Putin himself were cut off from their dollar-denominated assets and blocked from transacting in the dollar-based financial system.

As before, questions about potential blowback from sanctions emerged. Influential economist and first deputy managing director at the International Monetary Fund, Gita Gopinath, warned that Washington's measures could fragment the international monetary system. Certain economies, she predicted, might gradually move away from the dollar in their trade and investment activities.[17] Strategists at major global banks also weighed in. Credit

Suisse's Zoltan Pozsar called the sanctions a turning point for the dollar's global dominance. Dylan Grice of Société Générale forecast via a tweet that the moment marked "the end of USD hegemony & the acceleration towards a bipolar monetary order."[18] Renowned journalist and associate editor at the *Financial Times*, Martin Wolf, predicted a "currency disorder" in which the dollar's dominance is increasingly challenged.[19] State media in China gleefully published commentary on the subject with headlines like "Biden takes victory lap over Russia sanctions but US dollar hegemony shows cracks."[20]

In public debates, the notion that politics influences the international appeal of currencies has become *nouveau chic*. Among scholars of international political economy (IPE), such ideas have deeper roots. In her pathbreaking 1971 book *Sterling and British Policy*, Susan Strange argued that the pound was able to extend its reign as a top global currency largely due to Britain's political relations with former dependencies.[21] The IPE literature on the political underpinnings of international currencies has since grown considerably (despite being mostly ignored by economists).[22] Yet the current public debate about sanctions differs from how the field of political economy has modeled the relationship between politics and a currency's international popularity.[23] Prior work in IPE has generally emphasized how political variables either help a currency move up the international money hierarchy or help it maintain dominance. Such research points out that currencies issued by states with large militaries and extensive alliances benefit from enhanced market confidence. States with these qualities can also use geopolitical leverage to pressure friends and allies to continue to back their currencies. The current debate about sanctions and the dollar suggests that politics may also work in the opposite direction. Political factors need not only propel or reinforce a currency's cross-border use; they may also undermine it. The scholarly debate on international money has only very recently started to seriously consider the possibility that financial sanctions might eventually "trigger a politically motivated diversification away from . . . the dollar."[24]

The European response to President Trump's decision to withdraw from the Iran nuclear deal provides anecdotal evidence in support of this proposition. If this were the only example of such a reaction, we might easily dismiss it as meaningless bluster. After all, the Europeans have a decades-long history of complaining about the dollar and the "exorbitant privilege" that comes with it.[25] Yet, there are many other examples of backlashes against the dollar in response to financial sanctions. The US Treasury has blacklisted targets in Iran, Russia, Turkey, and Venezuela in recent years. Each retaliated by lambasting the dollar's grip on the global financial system and took steps to promote the use of alternative currencies in their international business dealings. Some reduced their holdings of dollar assets and invested in other currencies or assets like gold.

The Argument

The book's central claim is that US financial sanctions generate *political risk* in the international currency system. In this context, political risk is related to, but distinct from, its meaning in the study of foreign investment.[26] I define political risk as *the potential for a political act to raise the expected costs of using a currency for cross-border transactions or as a store of value*. Over time, the accumulation of political risk in the system creates incentives for governments to adopt *anti-dollar policies* that promote the use of currencies or assets other than the dollar for investment and cross-border transactions. Of course, anti-dollar policies may fail. Thus, on their own they do not imply that the dollar is playing a diminishing role in a country's international economic relations. They merely indicate that the government is attempting to bring about such a shift. When sanctions-induced anti-dollar policies *do* successfully reduce reliance on the dollar, it signifies *de-dollarization*—the intentional reduction of the dollar's role in a nation's cross-border economic activities.

The book explores this argument with a series of empirical chapters that examine the first two decades of the twenty-first century, a period in which the United States steadily increased its use of financial sanctions against foreign adversaries and pariah states. As subsequent chapters will show, in some cases the link between US financial sanctions and anti-dollar policy reactions from targeted governments is undeniable. Other cases are suggestive, though less conclusive, of a link. The evidence that sanctions provoke anti-dollar policies is strongest for countries that have already been targeted by the United States. There is even limited support for the claim that the risk of being sanctioned provoked pre-emptive efforts to reduce dollar dependence. On the whole, the illustrations in this book support its central claim: sanctions generate political risk, provoke anti-dollar policies among targets, and in some cases correlate with de-dollarization.

What does this mean for the dollar's status and for US power more generally? Will we look back on this moment in a few decades and identify sanctions as the cause of the dollar's "suicide" and the end of American financial might?[27] While extreme predictions get "clicks" (and perhaps sell books), that is not what I conclude. Despite growing complaints about how the United States wields the dollar as a weapon, the currency retains considerable economic (and political) advantages over all potential rivals. Those circumstances are unlikely to change anytime soon. Many of the anti-dollar policy responses identified in this book were implemented out of necessity. Targeted states dump the dollar not because they *want* to, but because they have no other choice. Most would rejoin the dollar-based system if they could. Moreover, where anti-dollar policies have been tried, some have failed to produce the intended result. And when de-dollarization has occurred, it has been marginal, rather than transformational. Dollar dependence remains the reality, even for sanctioned regimes.

Though this book stops short of doomsday predictions, the implications of its conclusions should not be dismissed as meaningless. As the United States increasingly used its currency for coercive means in the early twenty-first century, discontent with the use of the dollar for political reasons rose. Spurned governments responded with measures designed to insulate their economies from US financial pressure. The responses were overwhelmingly ad hoc, haphazard, uncoordinated, and devoid of leadership. But that could change. If US reliance on sanctions continues to grow with the same level of intensity and frequency over the next twenty years, the number of anti-dollar states will continue to grow—especially if the United States employs financial sanctions unilaterally. The larger the pool of discontents—both in the total number of states and the group's aggregate economic size—the more attractive it becomes for US rivals to pounce. As the potential "user base" of an alternative financial network grows, there will be greater incentives to build that network. Coordination among exasperated capitals will become easier, reducing the transaction costs of cooperation. Who might step in and attempt to meet the needs of this underserved market? Europe and China are possible challengers.

Brussels and Beijing are both keenly aware of the growing frustration with the dollar. While they are unlikely to dislodge the dollar from pre-eminence, a less transformative outcome could still impact American financial power. Smaller steps could chip away at the dollar's dominance in ways that limit the effectiveness of financial sanctions as a tool of statecraft. The global financial system could fragment: countries that maintain fraught relations with Washington could conduct more of their business in less efficient (but politically safer) currency networks, and central banks would become more likely to invest surplus reserves in assets like gold and alternative, less traditional reserve currencies. These changes would make US financial sanctions less effective. Coercive threats of sanctions would be far less successful. The US capacity to cripple adversaries' economies and, indirectly, degrade their military capabilities would shrink. Thus, we are left with Jack Lew's policy paradox: while dollar primacy gives the United States a powerful foreign policy weapon, its overuse might cause its disarmament.[28]

Plan of the Book

Chapter 1 presents the theoretical and conceptual framework that guides the rest of the book. Until recently, most research on the link between politics and international currency status has emphasized how US foreign policy promotes and sustains the dollar's global appeal. Scholars have only recently begun to consider how US foreign policy, including its use of sanctions, might tarnish the dollar's shine by creating expectations of costs associated with its use. The chapter also more fully introduces the concept of political risk in the international currency system and describes the main argument that is illustrated in subsequent chapters.

Chapter 2 explains how dollar dominance gives the United States the unrivaled capacity to cut foreign actors off from their dollar-based assets and from the global dollar-based financial system. It unpacks the mechanics of the correspondent banking system in which US financial institutions serve as intermediaries in most cross-border financial transactions. It then describes the critical role played by presidential executive orders and the US Treasury's Office of Foreign Assets Control in overseeing and enforcing the US financial sanctions regime. Finally, the chapter presents original data documenting how the United States has used its financial sanctions capabilities with increasing frequency in the first two decades of the twenty-first century, targeting states with specific characteristics. I use these data to illustrate how political risk associated with the dollar varies across countries and over time: the risk of facing sanctions is not equally distributed.

Chapter 3 examines the dollar's position as the world's leading store of value. This enables the United States to freeze foreign actors' dollar-based assets, effectively cutting off adversaries from their financial wealth. Washington has employed such measures in concentrated efforts to pressure politically connected elites in target countries and as part of broad strategies to topple authoritarian regimes. The chapter then presents empirical case studies of Russian and Turkish reactions to US sanctions. Though the evidence is strongest in the Russian case, both countries responded with heightened anti-dollar rhetoric, suggesting Washington's actions generated political risk concerns in both countries. This rhetoric was accompanied by a suite of anti-dollar policies designed to reduce dependence on the currency. The aim was ostensibly to reduce both countries' vulnerability to US financial pressure in the future.

Building on these case studies, Chapter 4 presents additional analyses exploring the link between US financial sanctions and the buildup of physical gold reserves. After documenting how central bank gold purchases have increased since the global financial crisis of 2008, the chapter explains how gold operates as a form of insurance against potential US sanctions. The case of Venezuela's embattled Maduro regime illustrates this point, revealing why investments in gold can be understood as an anti-dollar policy. The chapter then presents a statistical model demonstrating the link between US sanctions and increases in gold holdings. Gold reserves grew faster among sanctioned states as well as those facing an elevated risk of sanctions compared to non-sanctioned and low-risk states. Additional illustrations show that sanctions are associated with a decline in foreign holdings of US Treasury bonds, suggesting that they provoked actual de-dollarization of reserves.

Chapter 5 examines the dollar's grip on cross-border payments, including its position as the world's most widely used trade settlement currency. It recounts how the United States used sanctions to cut targets off from the dollar-based payments system—a move that had punishing consequences for targeted individuals, firms, and governments. These consequences are demonstrated in three case studies on Russia, Turkey, and Venezuela. Targeted governments' perceptions of the political risk associated with the dollar grew after sanctions were imposed. Each responded with policy measures designed to reduce dependence on the dollar as a payments and trade settlement currency, with varying degrees of success. These examples demonstrate that while de-dollarization may remain elusive for targeted regimes, sanctions can (and do) elicit clear anti-dollar policy responses.

Chapter 6 presents statistical analyses indicating that US sanctions provoked anti-dollar policy responses and may have led to modest de-dollarization in cross-border payments. First, it considers whether a specific policy designed to reduce dollar dependence in payments—local currency–central bank currency swap agreements—correlates with US sanctions. Such swap agreements can facilitate cross-border trade settlement in non-dollar currencies, making the deals potentially useful for countries concerned about being cut off from the dollar system. The evidence suggests that sanctions, though not the *risk* of sanctions, are related to the propensity to sign such swap deals. Moving beyond anti-dollar policies to measures of de-dollarization, the chapter demonstrates that sanctioned countries, and those at greater risk of facing sanctions, rely less on the dollar as a trade settlement currency—which suggests a link between sanctions and de-dollarization. The chapter concludes by exploring experimental data from a survey of over 1,000 multinational firms in Vietnam. The data illustrate that information about the growing use of US sanctions increases firm managers' interest in learning about cross-border payments systems based on the euro or the renminbi.[29]

Chapter 7 explores whether US sanctions incited potential rivals to further internationalize their national currencies, focusing on the two economies that present the greatest possible challenge to the dollar's pre-eminence: the European Union (EU)/the euro, and China/the renminbi. Historically, the EU has done little to actively promote the euro's global popularity. China has pursued contradictory policy paths, implementing some measures aimed to internationalize the renminbi alongside others that stunted its international appeal. Yet, as Washington enacted sanctions more frequently, both economies developed a new perspective on the value of issuing international currencies. The calculus they use to determine the costs and benefits of currency internationalization expanded to include the political risks of dollar dependence. That may tip the scale in favor of a more robust set of policies designed to weaken the dollar's grip on their economic relations and, in turn, the world economy.

Our attention turns in Chapter 8 to China's efforts to create an alternative payment system based on its own currency. While the Cross-border Interbank Payment System, or CIPS for short, remains far behind the dollar system, it picked up steam quickly after its introduction in 2015. As elites in China grew more aware of their country's vulnerability to US financial pressure, interest in building this system increased. Yet for this new financial network to be effective at insulating China and its economic partners from Washington's coercive tools, Beijing will have to "close the loop" by disconnecting it not only from the dollar but also from existing financial and communication networks. This is an extraordinary challenge, and it remains unclear whether China's leadership is willing or able to take the steps to pull it off. Outside of China, US sanctions appear to be creating interest in CIPS as autocrats who worry about the long arm of the US Treasury look to Beijing to build a system that will protect them.

The book concludes by considering how US policymakers should respond to the challenges identified in these chapters. While the increased use of financial sanctions is unlikely to jeopardize the dollar's status as the world's preeminent global currency, targets are adapting to the tool. In time, these adjustments can weaken the effectiveness of US financial coercion, diminishing Washington's capacity to achieve its aims during international crises. There are methods that can be used to achieve foreign policy objectives that do not politicize the dollar and provoke countervailing currency measures. Other tools that do not present the same risks to the future exercise of US power exist and can be used in place of financial coercion. Policymakers should adopt a more circumspect approach to financial sanctions with an eye toward preserving the efficacy of the tool for the moments where coercion really counts.

1

Financial Sanctions and Political Risk in the International Currency System

The study of international relations now needs a political theory of international currencies.

Susan Strange[1]

States impose financial sanctions on individuals, firms, governments, and other entities that restrict the target's international financial activities, including participating in cross-border transactions and accessing assets held abroad. While other countries also use sanctions as a tool of economic statecraft, the United States employs them more than any of its peers. And its use of sanctions has steadily increased over the past twenty years.[2] There is a long-standing, fierce debate among scholars and policymakers about whether economic sanctions "work." Many experts maintain that they are ineffective tools of coercion that rarely get the target government to bend to the sanctioning state's will.[3] Others assert that critics wrongly focus on *imposed* sanctions, ignoring the effect of the *threat* of sanctions, as it can often deter bad state behavior.[4] Yet nearly all observers agree that financial sanctions are effective tools for imposing economic pain on their targets.[5] US financial sanctions have been described as having a "crippling" effect.[6] One recent target, the head of a Russian aluminum company, described America's sanctions capability as a "devastating power."[7] What is the secret behind the punch that US financial sanctions pack? According to former treasury secretary Jack Lew, the United States owes these capabilities to "the predominant role that the US financial system plays in global commerce."[8] It is precisely because the world economy relies so heavily on the dollar, and the American financial institutions through which those dollars flow, that US sanctions are so potent. Yet despite—or perhaps because of—this potency, overusing

Bucking the Buck. Daniel McDowell, Oxford University Press. © Oxford University Press 2023.
DOI: 10.1093/oso/9780197679876.003.0002

sanctions incentivizes targeted and at-risk governments to reduce their dependence on the dollar-based financial system. This suggests two important implications for consideration. First, the more the United States uses its devastating power, the less devastating it will become in time. Second, politics—not just economic fundamentals—is central to the dollar's appeal as an international currency.

This chapter establishes the theoretical and conceptual framework for the rest of the book, further developing the notion of political risk in the international currency system and presenting a general theory of how US foreign policy influences foreign governments' policies toward the dollar. The theory considers how politics impacts the appeal of the dollar in simple terms. It identifies the full range of US political actions that affect expectations regarding the benefits *and* costs associated with the dollar's international use in two steps. In the first step, the theory incorporates established ideas about how US foreign policy increases the attractiveness of the dollar. In the second step, it explores the often-overlooked observation that US political behavior (in this case, imposing financial sanctions) can also turn states and market actors against the currency.

A Theory of US Foreign Policy and the International Use of the Dollar

Few national currencies are used outside their country of issue. A small number function as international currencies, used as much outside their nation's borders as within. The world economy tends to rely on just a few select currencies due to economies of scale and network effects. The transaction costs associated with cross-border economic activity are greatly reduced when parties on each side of an exchange use the same currency to set prices and to make the payment.[9] What determines whether a national currency becomes widely used outside a country's borders? The most important factors are the "two C's": *confidence* and *convenience*.[10] First, for a currency to gain widespread global appeal, markets must be *confident* that the money's value will be stable over the long run. Second, global currencies must also be *convenient* for markets to use. Investors, traders, and governments are drawn to currencies that are widely available and broadly accepted in the global marketplace. The dollar meets both criteria, underpinning its position as the world's pre-eminent global currency. Yet the international political economy literature has long recognized that a purely economic explanation of international currency status is incomplete.[11]

The theory underpinning the book's argument builds on the insights of previous work on the politics of international money and proposes a new and unified framework for understanding the political determinants of international currencies. The theory maintains that *US foreign policy influences foreign governments' calculations of the expected costs and benefits associated with the dollar's international use which, in turn, affects governments' policies toward the currency.* Using the analogy of a ray of light, I characterize these politically generated costs and benefits as either *diffuse* or *direct.* When light scatters, we refer to it as diffuse light; when US foreign policy generates a utility gain (loss) that is distributed, or scattered, across a group of states, we can describe the benefits (costs) as *diffuse.* When light has a well-defined path, we call it direct light; *direct* benefits (costs) are generated when US foreign policy produces a utility gain (loss) that is captured by a specific target state.

The Traditional View: US Foreign Policy and the Benefits of Dollar Use

Many scholars have argued that political factors can *promote* and *sustain* a currency's global appeal. Such arguments generally contend that US foreign policy generates expectations of *diffuse benefits* of dollar use among certain foreign governments, and these contribute to its global popularity. States that support America's activist role in world affairs stand to gain, if only indirectly, by supporting the dollar's global role. A common argument from this perspective points out that official investments in dollar assets, especially Treasury bills, function as loans to the US government. Supporting the dollar's reserve role, then, enhances Washington's ability to pursue an assertive global military posture by financing US government defense spending.[12] As Jonathan Kirshner explained, the dollar's reserve currency role has "made it easier for [the United States] to pursue an ambitious and often costly grand strategy."[13] Governments that view US military preponderance and broader foreign policy goals as indirectly serving their own national interests should, all else equal, adopt pro-dollar policies. In particular, they should hold higher shares of their foreign exchange reserves in US dollars. Consistent with this argument, numerous studies point out that US military allies tend to be strong supporters of the dollar, ostensibly because of the positive security externalities of holding dollars.[14]

Past research has also drawn attention to a second mechanism where US foreign policy can create expectations of *direct* benefits associated with dollar use. Unlike the diffuse gains discussed above, direct benefits flow from an explicit or implicit quid pro quo between the United States and a foreign government. In this case, US foreign policy is crafted to fortify the dollar's pre-eminent global position by securing a deal with a critical partner government. The United States may obtain foreign support for the dollar's international role in exchange for security assistance, like military aid or permission to station troops in the partner's territory, or economic concessions like special market access and economic aid.[15] The best-known example of this sort of political arrangement is Saudi Arabia's 1974 commitment to invoice and accept payment for oil exclusively in dollars in exchange for US military aid and equipment.[16] Another is the 1961 "offset agreement" in which the United States pledged to maintain a significant troop presence in West Germany in exchange for German investments in dollar-denominated assets.[17] Other reserve currency issuers have also engaged in similar behavior. For example, to sustain the pound's international role after World War II, Britain made these types of bargains with its dependencies. Today, there is emerging evidence that China dangles "carrots" to entice foreign governments to support the internationalization of its currency.[18]

Most of the studies in this strand of the literature focus on how US foreign policy contributes to dollar pre-eminence. This book advances the emerging body of work that explores how Washington's approach to foreign affairs could do the opposite and damage the dollar's global appeal.

A New Perspective: US Foreign Policy and the Costs of Dollar Use

US foreign policy can bolster *or* jeopardize the international attractiveness of the dollar. Washington's choices may at times *undermine* political support for the currency, even if only among a subset of states. US foreign policy may lead some governments to conclude that the continued use of the currency will prove costly in the future. What has been missing from debates about the link between foreign policy and dollar status is the concept of *political risk*. In this context, political risk is understood as the *potential for a political act to raise the expected costs of using a currency for cross-border transactions or as a store of value.* As the political risk associated with the dollar's use increases, governments will seek to implement policies that reduce their dependence on the currency.

US foreign policy can generate expected costs of dollar use that are scattered across a group of like-minded states that oppose or resist American influence in the world. In this way, Washington's policy decisions produce expectations of *diffuse costs* linked to dollar use that push governments to adopt anti-dollar policies. In the same way that foreign policies that serve US allies' interests may encourage them to support the dollar, the opposite should hold for US adversaries. One study on Russia's international currency policy explains how Moscow's opposition to US foreign policy after the 2003 invasion of Iraq contributed to the Kremlin's de-dollarization efforts during that decade. A pamphlet distributed at a 2006 anti-dollar rally in Moscow warned that buying dollars "finances the war in Iraq [and] finances the construction of US nuclear submarines."[19] In this case, the dollar's appeal was diminished in Russia not because of any targeted costs from US foreign policy but rather due to *indirect* costs. Investing in the dollar promoted a series of US policy measures that were out of step with Russia's broad interests. Other governments that oppose US foreign policy may also seek to reduce their use of the dollar since this would mean that "the United States would have greater difficulty debt-financing its security projects and expansive military budget."[20]

Finally, US foreign policy can also generate expectations of *direct costs* for states with economies that depend on the dollar, pushing them to adopt policies that reduce their reliance on the currency. As I detail in Chapter 2, global dependence on the dollar is the foundation of US sanctions capabilities. As a key instrument of foreign policy, financial sanctions are political measures that impact targeted foreign actors' access to the dollar and the US financial system. In this case, the costs of dollar use are concentrated and direct, with a clear target in Washington's sights. Sanctions can prohibit the target from using dollars to conduct cross-border trade or investment, impacting the currency's usefulness as an international medium of exchange. Sanctions can also freeze a target's dollar-denominated assets, affecting the currency's appeal as a store of value. For those targeted by US sanctions, the dollar will lose its aura of "convenience," a fundamental component of its appeal as a global currency; dependence on the dollar becomes quite *in*convenient for targeted states. Existing debts in dollars may become difficult or impossible to repay, resulting in default. Assets held abroad in dollars may be frozen, effectively nullifying their value to the target. Foreign economic partners that prefer to use dollars to settle cross-border deals may cut off economic ties, further isolating the target. Thus, governments that have been hit with US sanctions—and potentially those that worry they may soon face such measures—should perceive high *direct costs* associated with dollar use. This, in turn, should prompt them to pursue anti-dollar policies in an attempt to reduce their dependence on the currency.

The Theory in Brief

According to my theory, US foreign policy (the explanatory variable) affects governments' expected cost-benefit calculations related to dollar use (the causal mechanism), which shapes their policies toward the dollar (the outcome to be explained). Employing the categories introduced above, Figure 1.1 presents a set of expectations regarding how US foreign policy is likely to influence foreign governments' policies toward the dollar.[21] When US policies generate expectations that dollar use will produce diffuse or direct benefits (rows 1 and 2 in Figure 1.1), governments should be more likely to adopt pro-dollar policies such as holding more dollar reserves or promoting the use of the dollar as an international medium of exchange (or, at least not working to undermine its dominant role). Alternatively, when a US policy action generates beliefs that political risk is rising due to expected diffuse or direct costs of dollar use (rows 3 and 4 in Figure 1.1), governments should be more likely to adopt anti-dollar policies. If these policies are successful, we would observe a reduced role for the dollar in foreign exchange reserves and cross-border payments—a process called de-dollarization.

To be clear, my theory does not purport to explain the full scope of governments' international currency policies. In most cases, the economic appeal of the dollar—based on confidence in its value and the convenience of its use—outweighs governments' political reservations about using it. The theory merely claims that considering the political costs and benefits associated with dollar use is one factor among many that influence governments' international currency policies. So, while a government may strongly oppose US foreign policy, it is unlikely to pursue total de-dollarization due to the economic benefits of dollar use. However, the theory predicts that a government

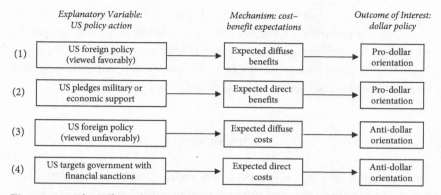

Figure 1.1. The Effect of US Foreign Policy on Dollar Policy Orientation. The figure presents a summary of four testable claims derived from the book's theory linking foreign policy to national policy orientations toward the dollar. This book is focused on testing row 4.

in this position should, all things equal, be more likely than others to take steps to reduce its reliance on the dollar.

This book tests the claim, presented in row 4 of Figure 1.1, that Washington's use of financial sanctions leads to political risk in the international currency system by generating expected *direct costs* of using the dollar. Such expectations should be concentrated among states targeted by sanctions and those that perceive themselves to be at risk of facing sanctions in the future. These governments should be more likely to adopt anti-dollar policies. If those policies succeed, we would also expect to observe de-dollarization in those countries' foreign economic activity.

The theory suffers from at least two limitations. The first relates to questions of *capability*. Some governments may want to pursue anti-dollar policies but lack the capacity to do so. Consider a hypothetical country that has been harshly sanctioned by the United States. While the targeted government may want to reduce the dollar's share in its foreign exchange reserves, if it is a small, poor economy with few reserves, there is little it can do. In this case, we would not observe a de-dollarization of reserves despite the government's real interest in implementing such a policy.

The second limitation is that the theory aims to explain how US foreign policy influences governments' policy orientations toward the dollar, but not whether such policies will *succeed*. It offers clear predictions about how US foreign policy should impact a government's propensity to implement anti-dollar policies but is less clear about why some such policies translate into actual de-dollarization while others do not. While analyzing the reasons why anti-dollar policies achieve de-dollarization (or not) is beyond the scope of the book, Appendix A presents a brief discussion of three potential factors that influence the chances that an anti-dollar policy will succeed.

Conclusions

Theories about the political foundations of international currency status have typically emphasized the ways in which foreign policy helps a currency climb up the global currency hierarchy or maintain dominance. My theory seeks to unify these ideas with a set of emerging claims informed by unfolding events in world politics. The notion that political factors have a universally positive impact on a currency's international appeal is misguided. The policy actions of the issuing state may enhance the attractiveness of its currency for international use or harm it by influencing expectations about the future costs or benefits associated with the currency. When the United States wields the dollar as a weapon against its adversaries, this weakens its appeal as an international reserve currency and cross-border medium of exchange. And the more it uses financial sanctions, the more non-sanctioned states with interests in conflict with Washington are likely to worry that they will face similar measures in the future. Over time, a subset of states may seek to minimize their reliance on a currency that leaves them vulnerable to coercion.

2

The Source and Exercise of American Financial Power

First you get the money, then you get the power.

Tony Montana[1]

It's all about the Benjamins.

Puff Daddy[2]

International currencies are those that are regularly used to perform the three basic roles of money—store of value, medium of exchange, and unit of account—at the global level. While multiple national currencies can claim "international" status, no other currency is more widely used in the world economy than the US dollar.[3] The first two of the three roles mentioned above are the most important for understanding America's coercive financial capabilities. The dollar is the world's most popular currency in which financial assets are held (store of value), as well as the most used currency for cross-border payments, like settling trade or repaying debts (medium of exchange). Its dominance in these two roles places the American financial system, which operates under US legal jurisdiction, at the center of most cross-border financial transactions. To adapt a famous phrase coined by former US secretary of state Madeline Albright, it is the "indispensable currency" of global finance and commerce. If Washington wishes to prevent a foreign entity from accessing its dollar-denominated assets or block it from completing a cross-border transaction using dollars, it can do so with little more than the stroke of the president's pen.

Few states have ever held this much power. Great Britain pioneered modern financial sanctions by wielding its primacy in global banking against its enemies during World War I with great effect.[4] But the US dollar soon supplanted the pound.[5] While London remains a critical financial hub, the

Bucking the Buck. Daniel McDowell, Oxford University Press. © Oxford University Press 2023.
DOI: 10.1093/oso/9780197679876.003.0003

United States controls the plumbing of most cross-border transactions and investments, thanks to the dollar's centrality. Currency supremacy is the source of American financial power. And to the great displeasure of some, Washington has exercised this power with increasing frequency in the twenty-first century.

King Dollar

A popular legend in US history is George Washington's refusal to become America's first king as the Continental Army was about to defeat British forces in the American Revolutionary War. Though Washington never became an American monarch, his appearance on the US one dollar bill has made his likeness a symbol of financial royalty. The dollar is often described as the "king" of all currencies, and rightly so. Its function as an international medium of exchange and as a store of value are two arenas in which the dollar's royalty is unquestioned.

The Dollar as an International Medium of Exchange

Money is a widely accepted token for settling debts and purchasing goods and services. It makes economic exchanges more efficient than, for example, a barter system. International currencies are monies that are broadly accepted for the *cross-border* transfer of value between individuals, firms, or other entities. Cash is one way that value can be transferred, but it typically requires that both parties to an exchange are present in the same physical location. Since this is not realistic for international transactions, value is instead transferred via payments systems that allow parties to exchange claims on accounts held by banks. Such exchanges can be transacted using checks and credit cards, but electronic wire transfers are the most common way to execute international payments. They enable firms and financial institutions to move large sums of money at high frequency.[6]

The world economy depends on a functioning international payments system. Cross-border investment requires effective payment solutions that allow investors to transfer funds in exchange for foreign assets like real estate, equities, or debt securities. International debt markets depend upon debtors' ability to regularly make payments by transferring money from their own accounts to their foreign creditors' accounts on a timely basis. Even international trade is highly dependent on a functioning international payments system: 80 to 90 percent of global commerce depends on trade finance, and financial institutions play a critical role in ensuring that importers and exporters can make secure cross-border payments.[7]

To understand how cross-border payments are executed, it helps to use a heating, ventilation, and air conditioning (HVAC) system as an analogy. An HVAC moves warm or cold air from a building's furnace or air conditioner to where it is needed. A thermostat communicates with the furnace via an electrical signal that warm or cold air is needed in a particular room or zone, and the duct work routes the air from its starting point to its destination.

The cross-border payment system uses a similar division of labor that relies on three basic components. The first is a *communications network*. Just as the HVAC relies on the thermostat to communicate to the furnace that warm or cool air is needed, banks need a reliable and secure communication system to send payment instructions.[8] Nearly all cross-border financial messaging now relies on SWIFT (the Society for Worldwide Interbank Financial Telecommunication), a private corporation located in Brussels, Belgium. SWIFT is the industry standard; it dwarfs all other cross-border messaging systems. Since its founding in 1973, it has developed a telecommunications network through which more than 40 million daily payment orders are sent between financial institutions, directing banks to debit one account and credit another[9]—totaling roughly $5 trillion in *daily* payment orders.[10]

The second component of the cross-border payment system is the *medium of exchange*. While the HVAC's thermostat sends a signal requesting the delivery of warm or cold *air*, SWIFT sends messages requesting that *money* be moved from one bank account to another. The money requested is usually denominated in one of a small number of major currencies functioning as international mediums of exchange. The elevation of a few national monies for this purpose results from network effects: the more that other market actors make or accept payment in a currency, the more useful and efficient it is for other market actors to do the same. As Figure 2.1 shows, from 2014 through 2020, the US dollar was used as the medium of exchange for roughly 40 to 45 percent of all international payments processed by SWIFT.[11] The only other currency that comes close is the euro, at 27 to 38 percent. The remaining 2 to 30 percent of international payments is divided among nearly twenty other currencies.

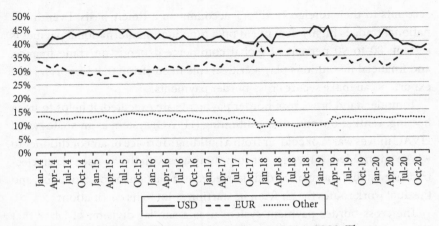

Figure 2.1. Cross-Border Payments by Currency, 2014–2020. The "other" category includes only British pound sterling, Japanese yen, and Chinese renminbi. Lesser currencies are not included or shown. Payments data presented are from the Society for Worldwide Interbank Financial Telecommunication (SWIFT).

Though the dollar is the most widely used medium of exchange for international payments, most of these transfers do not directly involve a US individual or firm on either side of the transaction. While the United States is involved as an importer or exporter in only about 10 percent of global trade, roughly half of all international trade is settled in dollars.[12] In the same way that English has emerged as the dominant language for scientific research, even for non-native English speakers, the dollar is the dominant currency for cross-border payments, even for non-US individuals and firms. The dollar is the global payment system's *currency franca*.

In addition to SWIFT's communication system and the dollar's dominant role as the preferred medium of exchange, the global payments system requires a third component—a *mechanism through which money can be moved from one account to another*, often across borders. In the same way that a thermostat can request air, but cannot move it, SWIFT can send payment instructions, but it cannot wire money from one account to another. Payments are now largely cleared through correspondent banking relationships, which act as the financial "duct work" of the international payments system. A brief example helps illustrate the process.

Figure 2.2 visualizes an imaginary transaction involving the Argentine Widget Corp. (the "originator"), which wishes to transfer $100,000 from its account at Banco Patagonia to the account of Midwest Industrial LLC (the "beneficiary") at Intrust Bank in Wichita, Kansas. Because Banco Patagonia and Intrust Bank hold no accounts with each other, they cannot directly wire funds. However, if both banks hold correspondent accounts with a third-party institution like JP Morgan Chase in New York, then that third-party bank can act as an intermediary between the smaller institutions. After receiving instructions via SWIFT, JP Morgan debits Banco Patagonia's account $100,000 and credits the account of Intrust Bank. Intrust Bank then credits the account of Midwest Industrial $100,000 to complete the process.

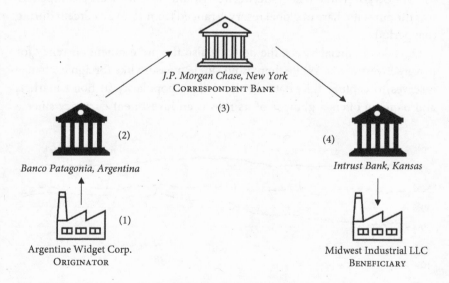

Figure 2.2. A Typical International Payments Transfer. The stages of the payment transfer are as follows: (1) Argentine Widget Corp. instructs its bank to make a payment in US dollars to Midwest Industrial; (2) Banco Patagonia sends a payment message via SWIFT to J.P. Morgan Chase; (3) J.P. Morgan Chase debits the account of Banco Patagonia, sends a payment message to Intrust Bank, and credits the account of Intrust Bank; (4) Intrust Bank credits the account of Midwest Industrial LLC.

The Dollar as an International Store of Value

Beyond improving the efficiency of economic exchange, money is also a technology designed to preserve purchasing power, protecting it from spoilage and depreciation over time. Individuals, firms, and governments have myriad options to choose from when selecting a store of value. Despite its archaic origins, gold remains a popular asset for such purposes. New digital assets, like Bitcoin and other cryptocurrencies, have gained a foothold as an investment class all of their own. Yet most global wealth (or "value") is stored in state-backed monies. Because most sovereign nations issue their own currency, there are scores to choose from. Once again because of network effects, a select few play oversized roles as international investment currencies. At the official level, governments allocate most of their financial assets in the US dollar.[13] As Figure 2.3 illustrates, the dollar comprised roughly 60 percent of all foreign exchange reserves (much of this held in the form of US government debt) between 2010 and 2020. Its nearest competitor was the euro: its share of global reserves ranged from 19 to 27 percent during that period.

Outside of official assets, the dollar is also the pre-eminent currency for private investments. While there is no single measure like foreign exchange reserves to capture this, data on the dollar's popularity in bond markets and banking offers a glimpse of its role as an investment currency since a

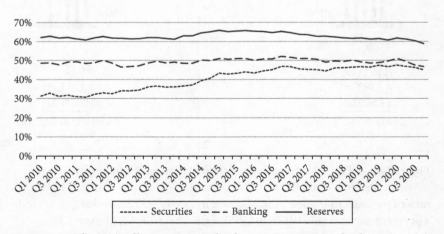

Figure 2.3. The US Dollar as a Store of Value, 2010–2020. Author's calculations using data from the International Monetary Fund and Bank for International Settlements.

significant portion of global wealth is stored in securities or held in banks. Alongside the reserve data, Figure 2.3 presents the dollar's share among the outstanding stock of international debt securities and outstanding bank liabilities.[14] About half of all global banking liabilities were denominated in dollars between 2010 and 2020. Though not pictured, the euro came second, accounting for 32 to 44 percent of worldwide bank liabilities during this time. Turning to international debt securities (known as bonds), the dollar's share is somewhat more modest, accounting for 36 to 49 percent of the global market from 2010 to 2020. The euro took the top position until 2014, when the dollar regained its pre-eminence in global bond markets. While not pictured in the figure, the dollar also dominates global equity markets: the value of American stocks accounted for over half of all equities held worldwide as of 2019.[15] In sum, across multiple measures, the dollar outcompetes its rivals as the world's most popular investment currency.

Dollar Dependence and US Financial Centrality

As a result of the world economy's reliance on the dollar as an international medium of exchange and store of value, the US financial system operates as the epicenter of global finance.[16] On the payments side of the ledger, due to the world economy's preference for dollar-based transactions, American banks play an outsized role in the mundane, but essential, financial operations needed to keep global business moving. Nearly all dollars used to make international payments (about 96 percent) are cleared through banks associated with the Clearing House Interbank Payments System (known as CHIPS).[17] CHIPS is a private corporation owned by the financial institutions that use its services. A small, elite group of banks are selected to operate as CHIPS' participant correspondent banks, including institutions like JP Morgan from our example above. The number of financial institutions in this select group varies somewhat over time, but is typically less than fifty. In 2019 there were forty-four,[18] eighteen of which were US banks. Foreign institutions associated with CHIPS must have American operations and are therefore subject to US law. In 2020, CHIPS participant banks transferred an average of $1.8 trillion dollars per day between institutions, totaling over $417 trillion for the year.[19] In much the same way that a handful of major airport hubs connect thousands of smaller airports, this elite group of major global banks facilitates nearly all international dollar payments through their role as CHIPS correspondent institutions.

The dollar's central role as an investment currency for private and official actors means that the United States is the geographic (and legal) home of many foreign investors' assets. Dollar-denominated securities issued in New York are subject to US law, and dollar-denominated bank accounts held in financial institutions with American operations are under US legal jurisdiction. Foreign governments' dollar-denominated assets are especially close to American power: the Federal Reserve Bank of New York holds roughly half of the world's foreign exchange reserve assets.[20] Investors in US Treasuries often hold their securities in accounts maintained by the US Treasury itself.[21]

Dollar Dominance as a Power Resource

In their seminal study of the weaponization of economic interdependence, Henry Farrell and Abraham Newman explain how states that control key hubs in global networks gain "considerable coercive power." Such privileged states can cut adversaries out of the network by limiting their access to the hub. This "chokepoint effect" levies serious costs on its targets.[22] The dollar's pre-eminence as an international store of value and medium of exchange is the foundation of the United States' capacity to employ chokepoint effects against foreign adversaries by applying financial sanctions. As noted above, 40 to 45 percent of all cross-border payments involve the US dollar, and 96 percent of cross-border, dollar-denominated payments involve a CHIPS participant institution as an intermediary. While not all CHIPS participants are American banks, they are all required to have a US branch.[23] Thus the select group of CHIPS correspondent banks, which effectively facilitate the clearing of all dollar payments in the global financial system, are collectively subject to US law. This jurisdictional control over the flow of dollars in the global economy gives the United States the immense power to levy crippling sanctions against its adversaries. In the remainder of this section, I discuss the two main types, primary and secondary sanctions.

Primary Sanctions

Most financial sanctions can be categorized as *primary sanctions*. These measures are designed to cut the targeted individual, firm, or government off from the dollar-based financial system. Oversight and enforcement of

US financial sanctions generally falls to the Office of Foreign Assets Control (OFAC) at the US Treasury Department. OFAC's most important tool is the Specially Designated Nationals (SDN) list, which contains the names of individuals, firms, or other entities that the United States wishes to "blacklist" or isolate from the global financial system. All financial institutions subject to US law (including all CHIPS correspondent banks) are prohibited from facilitating cross-border transactions on behalf of any SDN. Banks may also be asked to freeze an SDN's assets, thereby prohibiting the target from accessing its dollar-denominated wealth.

Individuals working in the financial industry who are found to be involved in a transaction that violates OFAC's demands face steep penalties, including up to thirty years in prison and fines as high as $20 million.[24] Financial institutions can also be fined billions of dollars for violations. For example, Standard Chartered was fined $1.1 billion in 2019 for processing transactions for SDNs from numerous countries targeted by US financial sanctions.[25] French banking giant BNP Paribas was hit with a $8.9 billion fine in 2015 for similar infractions.[26] Institutions found to be in violation of US sanctions also face reputational damage.[27] Such severe penalties encourage banks to self-monitor and self-report. If a financial institution receives a payment request involving an SDN as an originator or beneficiary, the bank is required by law to freeze the funds in question and report the request to OFAC.[28] Most banks use specialized software to screen all payment orders for SDN violations to avoid running afoul of OFAC. Experts have described this as a "public-private feedback loop" in which the Treasury Department effectively mobilizes the financial sector, by threat of penalty, to independently enforce US laws.[29]

Treasury has access to a trove of data on cross-border financial transactions that it can assess to identify violations if banks fail to identify or report them. This control over information is another core component of US coercive capabilities in finance. It exemplifies what Farrell and Newman call the "panopticon effect":[30] states that control critical network hubs have unrivaled access to information flows within the network, which gives them valuable insights into their adversaries' behavior and tactics.[31] Treasury's control over information flows is a function of US banking regulations. As a result of the so-called Travel rule,[32] all financial institutions operating in the United States are required, on penalty of steep fines, to keep detailed records on all transfers of $3,000 or more involving a foreign bank.[33] Until 2010, these records were available to Treasury at its request. Since 2010, banks have been required to report information about all such transfers to Treasury in real time.[34] Additional rule changes in recent years have placed the onus on financial institutions to "obtain, verify, and record the identities" of the "ultimate beneficial owners" of any entity involved in a transaction.[35] This relates to what is known as the "50 percent rule," which declares that "any entity owned in aggregate, directly or indirectly, 50% or more by one or more blocked persons is itself considered to be a blocked person."[36] This rule effectively blacklists any business where an SDN, or group of SDNs, holds at least half of the ownership stake. Under these rules, it is not enough for a bank under US jurisdiction to record and report that the Argentine Widget Co. is involved as an originator in a payments request. It must also verify and report that neither the firm itself, nor its majority ownership, is an SDN. These regulations make it very difficult for a target to evade US financial sanctions.

Any entity designated an SDN will find it nearly impossible to locate a bank with US operations willing to conduct business on its behalf. This includes all CHIPS participant banks, which are involved as correspondent institutions in nearly all cross-border dollar clearing operations. Thus, being placed on the SDN list results in near total isolation from the dollar-based financial system; SDNs will find it very difficult to service foreign debts, purchase or sell foreign assets, or finance cross-border trade using dollars. If an SDN holds dollar-denominated assets at an institution with US operations, Treasury can also compel the bank to freeze those funds, effectively taking possession of the SDN's wealth. The economic costs of being designated a target by OFAC are enormous.

Secondary Sanctions

Despite the severity of primary US financial sanctions, they are not always enough to fully isolate a targeted SDN from the global financial system. For instance, targets may seek refuge by moving their dollar-based transactions to a small number of dollar clearing centers that are not on US soil.[37] While these centers handle only a small fraction of dollar clearing, correspondent banks operating in these jurisdictions that do not have a US branch are not legally obliged to enforce Treasury's requests. In addition, SDNs might seek safe haven by transacting in alternative currencies like the euro or pound sterling. Foreign banks without US operations can facilitate non-dollar transactions on behalf of SDNs without penalty.

Despite these apparent loopholes, Treasury has developed methods to further curtail a target's access to cross-border financial services. Following the attacks of September 11, 2001, the United States reached an agreement with SWIFT and the European Union that gave Treasury access to its payment communication records.[38] Recall that SWIFT is the primary communication network through which payment requests are sent in the world economy. This is true for dollar-based payments as well as payments in other currencies. Access to SWIFT's communication records is critically important, as it allows Treasury to determine whether an SDN is making or receiving payments in dollars or other currencies outside the US financial system. If Treasury wishes to further cut a target out of global financial networks, it may employ *secondary sanctions*. These measures provide an extraterritorial means of punishment that further exploits global dollar dependence and the centrality of the US financial system.

Secondary sanctions enforce an additional degree of separation between any financial institution operating in the United States and an SDN. Such measures require banks with US operations to not only refrain from conducting business with OFAC targets; they must also end all correspondent banking relationships with any non-US financial institution that conducts business on behalf of an SDN. Non-compliance incurs severe financial and legal penalties. Figure 2.4 illustrates the difference in scope between primary and secondary sanctions. Panel A depicts a primary sanctions regime in which OFAC prohibits all financial institutions with US operations from conducting business on behalf of the target. In this scenario, foreign banks without US operations are free to maintain business ties with the SDN, and US banks can maintain their correspondent accounts with those foreign banks. Panel B illustrates the impact of secondary sanctions, which not only block US banks from having ties with the original target; US banks are also prohibited from conducting business with any third-party foreign institution that maintains a relationship with the target. Panel C represents the typical outcome of a secondary sanctions regime. Once foreign financial institutions recognize that continuing to do business with the original target will result in losing their correspondent accounts with US banks, they cut off ties with the target because preserving those correspondent relationships is far more important than the SDN's business. Secondary sanctions are designed to be "extraterritorial" in nature. They magnify the effect of primary sanctions outside US territory by imposing significant costs on non-US banks, bringing

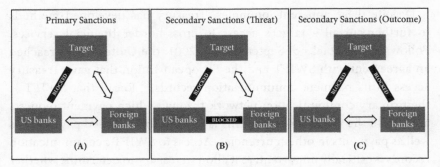

Figure 2.4. Primary and Secondary Financial Sanctions. Secondary sanctions further isolate targets by threatening extraterritorial penalties on foreign banks without US operations, which are not subject to primary sanctions.

them into compliance with US law even though they operate outside its jurisdiction.

Secondary sanctions can have a chilling effect. Imagine a hypothetical scenario in which the Persian Gulf Petrochemical Industries Company (PGPIC)—an Iranian company designated an SDN by OFAC in 2019—seeks to conduct cross-border financial business in euros with Norisbank, a German bank that does not have a US subsidiary. If PGPIC were targeted by primary sanctions alone, Norisbank could conduct euro-denominated payments operations on behalf of the firm and still maintain relationships with CHIPS correspondent banks. Yet under secondary sanctions, Norisbank's financial operations on behalf of PGPIC would place the bank on the Treasury's blacklist of financial institutions conducting business on behalf of an SDN. CHIPS participants would begin to cut off their correspondent banking relationships with Norisbank to avoid stiff financial and reputational costs. Anticipating this kind of reaction from US-based partners, Norisbank would have to decide whether conducting euro-based business on behalf of PGPIC is worth losing its ability to operate in the US financial market and the broader dollar-based financial system. Norisbank's choice would be easy. PGPIC would soon find itself without a financial institution willing to conduct its euro-denominated business because of the secondary sanctions.

The dollar's global role and the centrality of the US financial system in the world economy greatly enhances American financial power. Washington can choose to exploit global economic dependence on the dollar to achieve its *political* ends. Yet, as this book and others have suggested, doing so may jeopardize the dollar's reputation as an international store of value and medium of exchange. The dollar is the world's currency due to global confidence in its value and the convenience associated with its use as international money. The repeated use of financial sanctions may erode its appeal, at least among actors directly affected by US sanctions. Those targeted by sanctions, or that worry they will be, should recognize the considerable political risk associated with relying on the currency.

The Increasing Use of Financial Sanctions

The US government often employs financial sanctions against individuals or entities linked to non-state groups like terrorist organizations and criminal networks. Washington also uses them to target actors associated with foreign governments. Financial sanctions—sometimes called "smart sanctions"—can precisely target rogue regimes.[39] Whereas trade sanctions, like embargos, result in significant costs for an entire population in a foreign country, financial sanctions can be designed to cause less collateral damage. Yet, while these "smart" sanctions may target individuals or firms, the strategic target is usually the regime to which these entities are linked.

Since the turn of the century, the United States has used its financial sanctions capabilities more frequently, targeting more foreign SDNs—and the governments to which many are tied—than ever before. The use of financial sanctions became especially common during the Obama and Trump administrations. As sanctions expert Daniel Drezner explains, financial sanctions became the "go-to solution for nearly every foreign policy problem."[40] The typical way that Treasury is ordered to enforce a new sanctions program related to a set of SDNs is through an Executive Order issued by the president. The total number of sanctions-related Executive Orders (SREOs) increased by nearly 500 percent, from just twenty-two in the year 2000 to ninety-four by the end of 2020.[41] Figure 2.5 depicts the steady increase in SREOs during this period. While a small number of SREOs were revoked during this period, far more new measures were added.[42] During the twenty years covered in Figure 2.5, the total number of active SREOs decreased only twice, and then only marginally, before rising again.

While some SREOs explicitly target non-state actors with no direct ties to foreign governments, such as the Counter Narcotics Trafficking or the

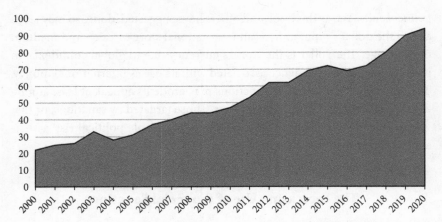

Figure 2.5. Sanctions-Related Executive Orders (SREOs) 2000–2020. The figure presents annual count data on the number of active Executive Orders instructing the US Treasury to enforce a financial sanctions program. Each program targets a suite of specially designated nationals (SDNs).

Counter Terrorism Sanctions programs, most sanctions programs target states.[43] Pressure is applied by blacklisting actors close to the regime or by directly targeting government officials and state institutions. Examples range from family members of a dictator to a country's central bank or sovereign wealth fund. Just as the total number of SREOs has increased steadily since the turn of the last century, so too has the number of states targeted by the US Treasury. In 2000 just four were targeted under an OFAC sanctions program. By 2020, this number had grown to twenty-one—a more than fivefold increase in just two decades. In 2020 alone, more than one in ten countries were targeted by a US financial sanctions program. Figure 2.6 illustrates the growth of state targets. The slope of the increase in countries targeted by OFAC becomes noticeably steeper around 2010, which is consistent with other accounts.[44]

Some governments face pressure from multiple SREOs at once. In 2020, for example, nine of the twenty-one targeted governments faced multiple SREOs. Among these are a few US sanctions "superstars"—Iran, North Korea, Russia, Syria, and Venezuela—which racked up an impressive number of OFAC targets. Figure 2.7 displays the cumulative number of SREOs targeting these states compared to all other state targets over twenty years. For a more detailed discussion of these data, Table B.1 in Appendix B provides a breakdown of each SREO in place during this period.

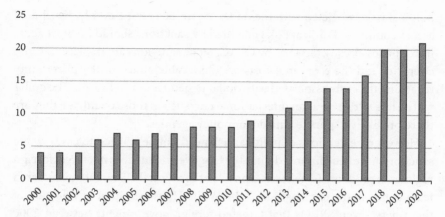

Figure 2.6. Number of States Actively Targeted by SREOs, 2000–2020. Bars represent a count of the number of states, each year, targeted by at least one sanctions-related Executive Order.

What is the effect of increased US reliance on financial sanctions as a foreign policy tool? This book argues that as the United States weaponized the dollar with greater frequency, perceptions of the political risk associated with the currency's international use should have risen. It follows that we should observe efforts to reduce global dependence on the dollar as governments grow wary of their vulnerability to US pressure. Of course, perceptions of

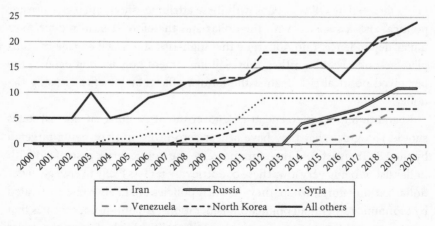

Figure 2.7. SREO Superstar Targets, 2000–2020. Lines represent the total number of unique sanctions-related Executive Orders per year targeting major US sanctions targets.

political risk associated with the dollar are unlikely to be evenly distributed across countries. Political risk generated by sanctions should be most acute in countries already targeted by OFAC. Since sanctions are in place in those countries and the economic costs are observable, much of the uncertainty regarding the costs associated with dollar dependence is removed. The dollar will be less attractive as an international currency in those countries; they are therefore likely to pursue anti-dollar policy agendas.

However, perceptions of political risk need not be isolated to cases where sanctions have been imposed since the US government does not target foreign regimes at random. To generate a profile of the typical US target, my research team conducted a text analysis of the White House's written justification of the ninety-seven SREOs that targeted foreign governments between 2000 and 2020.[45] Each order includes a reason, or set of reasons, explaining why the sanctions were imposed. The "typical" regime target is non-democratic, is a known abuser of human rights, and has foreign policy preferences that conflict with those of the United States. Nearly three-quarters (71 percent, or sixty-nine) of the SREOs justify the measures being taken on US foreign policy or security grounds, 31 percent (thirty total) mention the target's human rights abuses, and 26 percent (twenty-five) cite events or actions that threaten democracy (Figure 2.8). Table B.1 in Appendix B provides this information for each SREO.

As the United States uses sanctions with growing frequency, governments with these characteristics should, all else equal, expect to be at greater risk of being targeted by OFAC. States with these attributes should perceive greater political risk associated with the dollar and therefore seek to reduce their dollar dependence. I do not argue that high-risk states will engage in complete de-dollarization; rather, they will implement policies that balance the perceived political risk against the known efficiency benefits of using the dollar.

In addition to targeted and at-risk governments, a third category of states should recognize that they have a near-zero probability of being targeted by the US Treasury and therefore perceive the political risk associated with dollar use as being very low. These countries are far less likely to engage in de-dollarization efforts; where they do, such policies are likely to be motivated by economic rather than political considerations. An important caveat is that secondary sanctions raise perceptions of the political risk of using the dollar among a broader group of countries due to their impact on entities in third-party countries.

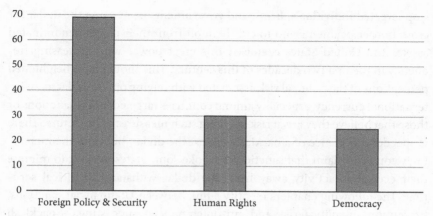

Figure 2.8. Cited Reasons for US SREOs, 2000–2020. The bars represent a count of the three most common reasons cited in each sanctions-related Executive Order (SREO) issued during this period against a foreign government. Sanctions programs aimed at non-state actors, like terrorist organizations or narcotics traffickers, are excluded since they lie outside the scope of this study. SREOs may cite more than one reason, thus the total count is larger than the total number of SREOs.

The Iran example discussed in the book's introduction illustrates the point. While the US sanctions did not directly target European countries, the secondary sanctions targeting Tehran threatened European businesses and banks with severe consequences if they did not cut ties with Iran. This caused European policymakers to criticize the dollar's role in their international economic relationships. Because secondary sanctions function as extraterritorial foreign policy tools, they "often prove to be politically problematic" by provoking strong blowback from affected firms, financial institutions, and governments in third-party countries.[46] Thus, countries not at risk of facing primary sanctions may pursue anti-dollar policies due to the political risk generated by secondary sanctions.

Conclusions

Dollar dominance is the source of the US government's devastating financial sanctions capabilities. The world economy's reliance on the dollar and the centrality of the US financial system in global markets allow Washington to stop targeted individuals, firms, and governments from using the dollar for cross-border payments and to cut them off from their dollar-denominated assets. The United States exercised this great power with increasing frequency in the first two decades of this century. This should have heightened perceptions of the political risk associated with relying on the dollar as an international currency, especially among countries targeted by US sanctions or those that believe they are at risk of facing such measures in the future. There is anecdotal evidence of a backlash against the dollar. But does the increasingly common claim that sanctions provoke some states to work to migrate their economic activity away from the dollar withstand empirical scrutiny? The following chapters identify a link between US financial sanctions, perceptions of political risk, and anti-dollar policies, suggesting the backlash is real.

3

Sanctions, Political Risk, and the Reserve Currency Role

All property and interests in property that are in the United States, that hereafter come within the United States, or that are or hereafter come within the possession or control of any United States person, including any overseas branch, of the Government of Libya, its agencies, instrumentalities, and controlled entities, and the Central Bank of Libya, are blocked and may not be transferred, paid, exported, withdrawn, or otherwise dealt in.

The White House[1]

The Arab Spring reached Libya on February 15, 2011, when thousands of people took to the streets of Benghazi to protest the regime of the country's long-serving autocratic leader, Muammar Gaddafi. The protests quickly erupted into a full-scale, nationwide rebellion. Colonel Gaddafi responded with brute violence against civilians. Within days of the initial public protest, media outlets reported that the Libyan regime ordered snipers to fire on crowds of demonstrators. Gaddafi's thugs used barbaric weapons, including hammers and swords, to attack families in their own homes.[2] Alongside military targets, the Libyan Air Force indiscriminately bombed civilians in what Western reporters on the ground described as a "scorched earth" response to the upheaval. Libya's own deputy ambassador to the United Nations (UN) publicly lamented that Gaddafi's regime had "declared war on its own people."[3] As news of these horrifying events reached Washington, the Obama administration debated a range of policy responses, including a military intervention and the imposition of a no-fly zone. While North Atlantic Treaty Organization (NATO) air and naval forces eventually enforced a UN-sanctioned no-fly zone, this response was initially ruled out due to concerns about vulnerable Americans stuck in Libya. The administration

Bucking the Buck. Daniel McDowell, Oxford University Press. © Oxford University Press 2023.
DOI: 10.1093/oso/9780197679876.003.0004

feared they might be targeted by the regime if the United States responded with force.[4]

Another option was to respond with financial rather than military actions. Experts at the US Treasury, working in the Office of Foreign Assets Control (OFAC), swiftly crafted an Executive Order (EO) that imposed a comprehensive package of sanctions against Gaddafi and his brutal regime. At the heart of the order was a plan to freeze the assets of the Libyan dictator, his close associates, and key state institutions. OFAC estimated that roughly $27 billion in funds linked to the Libyan state—including its central bank, its sovereign wealth fund, and all other state institutions with foreign investments—were held in banks and financial institutions under US jurisdiction and therefore subject to seizure.[5] This was an incredible sum, roughly equivalent to half of the country's $62 billion gross domestic product. Because Gaddafi's hold on power required him to shower loyalists with money from the country's vast oil wealth, OFAC believed that cutting off a large portion of those resources would hasten his fall from power. As one Treasury official put it, "He's in a cash-intensive business. And not having access to the Libyan Investment Authority [sovereign wealth fund] assets, the Central Bank of Libya assets . . . is going to be a problem for him."[6]

Citing "wanton violence against unarmed civilians," President Obama signed EO 13566 on February 25, 2011, setting the Treasury's financial sting operation in motion.[7] Ultimately, more than $37 billion in assets linked to the Libyan regime were frozen—more than the United States had ever seized before under a country program.[8] OFAC not only targeted individuals and firms with close ties to the targeted regime, but it also took aim at the assets of a foreign central bank.[9] The following year, EO 13599 blocked the Central Bank of Iran from accessing any assets under US control.[10] The Trump administration's decision to list the Central Bank of Venezuela as a Specially Designated National (SDN) in April 2019, which blocked it from using any assets in US institutions, was also in line with this trend.[11] In coordination with major allies, Washington froze the US-based assets of the Central Bank of Russia as well as the Kremlin's sovereign wealth fund following Putin's February 2022 military onslaught in Ukraine.[12]

In each case, Treasury's actions demonstrated America's ability to weaponize international reliance on the dollar as a store of value. Governments that had placed their faith in the value of the dollar by holding their national wealth in the currency were now cut off from their foreign exchange reserves. These actions increased the perceived political risk associated with the dollar as a reserve currency in certain capitals. Targeted governments, and those that feared they might be next on the Treasury's blacklist, grew increasingly uneasy about their reliance on the dollar as a reserve currency. Seeking to avoid the same fate as Iran or Venezuela, some cut their dollar-denominated assets and increased their holdings of other currencies. In addition, gold enjoyed a resurgence as a reserve asset partly due to its function as a hedge against political risk. To illustrate these developments, this chapter examines two country cases in which political risk generated by US financial sanctions altered governments' appetite for dollars—Russia and Turkey.

The Dollar's Reserve Currency Dominance

All governments maintain a portfolio of foreign currency assets, more commonly referred to as foreign exchange reserves, which their central banks typically manage. Reserves are a result of engagement in the global economy. When exporters sell their products abroad, they generally receive payment in one of a small number of major currencies—most often the dollar but to a lesser extent the euro, pound, renminbi, and yen. Exporters may exchange foreign currency earnings at their bank of choice for local currency, which they use to pay workers and to transact in their national economy. These banks can then swap the foreign currency for national currency at the country's central bank. Rather than simply holding the foreign currency in a local bank account, central banks invest it in assets that generate interest yet remain safe and liquid, like government bonds (also called "securities"). Importantly, the securities that governments hold in their foreign exchange reserves are not held in physical form in their national vaults. Rather, they are held in foreign accounts, sometimes in accounts at foreign commercial banks and often in accounts in the custody of foreign central banks.

Governments hold foreign exchange reserves for a variety of reasons. For example, reserves can enhance market confidence in a country's own currency, they can be used to influence the national exchange rate, and they help build wealth for intergenerational purposes.[13] They also function as a form of insurance against financial crises or liquidity shocks. Importers rely on foreign currencies to pay for foreign goods, and national firms may have debts denominated in foreign currencies, so a country needs access to foreign exchange to participate in international trade and to ensure that its firms can service their debts. However, economies can get cut off from global liquidity during crises. Foreign exchange reserves function as a sort of "rainy day fund" that allows the central bank to facilitate the processing of international payments or provide foreign exchange credit to firms that need dollars or other hard currency to pay their foreign debts. A typical rule of thumb is that a central bank should hold enough foreign exchange reserves to cover three months of its country's imports or all of its external, short-term debts.[14] Therefore, a government that holds a large cache of financial assets can assure markets that it can pay off its debts and backstop a crisis if one unfolds. Thus, governments value reserves because they increase the economy's appeal as a destination for foreign investment and business activity by enhancing perceptions of creditworthiness and stability. Indeed, possessing a large reserve portfolio may stave off a crisis by preventing a market panic in the first place.

As noted in Chapter 2, most central bank assets are denominated in US dollars. The most popular dollar asset is US government debt, also known as Treasury bills, Treasury bonds, or, more simply, Treasuries. The US dollar—and Treasuries specifically—are very popular among central banks because they help minimize three forms of risk that central bankers consider when deciding how to allocate assets. The first is the risk that a borrower will default on its debt (*credit risk*). Since the US government has never defaulted on its debt, its bonds are widely viewed as the safest store of value in the world.[15] National asset managers are drawn to the dollar in part because of this perceived safety. The second type of risk is that an asset cannot be sold and converted into cash quickly enough to address a financial need (*liquidity risk*). The market for US Treasuries has been aptly described as "the deepest and most liquid government securities market in the world."[16] Governments hold US government debt because they are confident these bonds can be converted into cash at a moment's notice.[17] The third and final type of risk is that the income derived from an investment in one currency will fall relative to potential investments in alternative currencies due to exchange rate movements (*currency risk*). The dollar's value fluctuates like that of any currency with a market-driven, floating exchange rate. Thus, there are times when a country's foreign exchange reserves may have performed better if they were held in another currency.[18] Yet overall, the dollar is widely viewed as having a stable value that is backed by sound economic management.

Of course, one goal of this book is to point out that economic risks are not the only thing that central bankers worry about these days. When the Libyan Central Bank discovered that the US Treasury had frozen nearly $40 billion of its assets, it learned that dollar-denominated assets could become illiquid at the stroke of the US president's pen. As noted in the previous chapter, most central banks hold a significant share of their dollar reserves in accounts with the Federal Reserve Bank of New York; it provides "custody and safe-keeping, and investment services" to nearly all foreign central banks, big or small. Most of the official accounts maintained at the New York Fed are in the form of US Treasury bonds, but it also houses large amounts of foreign monetary gold as a service to foreign governments.[19] All assets held in New York are quite literally at risk of being locked up by an OFAC directive, as are any other assets held in commercial banks with US operations—a group that includes virtually every major global bank.

The more that Washington demonstrates its capacity and willingness to freeze foreign governments' assets, the more likely it is that political risk will be a major concern for governments and central banks with sizable dollar holdings. For some, it may weigh nearly as heavily in their calculus as traditional economic concerns about credit, liquidity, and currency risk. The perceived political risk associated with the dollar is likely to be greatest among national asset managers in countries that have been targeted (or are at risk of being targeted) by US sanctions. In these cases, Washington has demonstrated that it is both willing and able to impose harsh financial penalties on targeted regimes. Even if the central bank is not listed as an SDN, a suite of US measures targeting economic actors with close ties to the regime should raise alarm bells among monetary authorities. Such steps would send a clear signal that their assets are at greater risk of being frozen by Washington than previously thought.

For targets, political concerns should at least somewhat offset the dollar's economic appeal as a reserve currency. As fears about the safety of dollar-denominated assets held in US accounts grow, targeted governments should be more likely to pursue reserve diversification plans. The goal of these efforts is to fundamentally shift the currency composition of the country's foreign exchange reserves by reducing their dollar holdings, shifting a larger share of official investments into alternative currencies or monetary gold. Governments concerned about political risk will also seek to cut the share of reserves held on American soil or under US jurisdiction more broadly.

These concerns should be most pronounced in countries that have already been targeted with sanctions, since the costs of dollar dependence are directly perceptible. If sanctions motivate governments to enact anti-dollar policies, we would be most likely to observe such policy shifts in targeted states such as Russia and Turkey.[20] In these cases, the perceived political risks of holding dollar assets may come to outweigh the economic benefits of dollar reserves. As the Russian and Turkish case studies illustrate, US sanctions appear to have pushed targeted governments to implement anti-dollar policies designed to reduced dependence on the American currency. The evidence of a link between US sanctions and de-dollarization is clear in the Russian case, where the Kremlin determined that dollars were a risky investment due to the increasing pressure of US financial sanctions. Moscow's plan involved selling its dollar assets to buy Chinese renminbi and gold as well as changing the geographic structure of its official reserve holdings. In the Turkish case, the government in Ankara was less vocal in its criticisms of the dollar and refrained from directly linking sanctions to its apparent de-dollarization efforts. Yet, investment data indicate that Turkey reduced the dollar's share in its reserves and increased gold holdings as threats of US financial sanctions loomed and, eventually, were imposed.

Russia Rebalances Its Portfolio

After a decade of détente between the United States and Russia following the dissolution of the Soviet Union, bilateral relations between the countries steadily deteriorated over the next twenty years. Major flashpoints in the downward spiral include clashes between Washington and Moscow over the US invasion of Iraq in 2003, the Russo-Georgian war in 2008, and US air strikes against Syria in 2012. Russian opposition to US foreign policy has previously been linked to de-dollarization policies following marginal diversification away from the US dollar in the early 2000s.[21] At that time, the Kremlin reduced its holdings of US government debt to protest US military and foreign policy operations that conflicted with its interests. However, a far more sweeping and significant process of de-dollarization began in 2014 and picked up considerable steam four years later. These efforts to reduce Russian exposure to the dollar were explicitly linked to US sanctions targeting Moscow. In myriad public statements, Russian policymakers tied dollar dominance to the United States' ability to use the currency as a weapon of foreign policy. In response, the Kremlin implemented a series of measures that reduced its reliance on the dollar as a reserve currency. This swiftly implemented de-dollarization strategy represents an unprecedented, overtly political move away from the US currency.

Background on US Financial Sanctions Targeting Russia

Washington first hit Moscow with sanctions in March 2014 in retaliation for Russia's first invasion of Ukraine, which centered on seizing control of Crimea, a peninsula on the northern coast of the Black Sea. President Barack Obama signed five separate sanctions-related Executive Orders (SREOs) authorizing the US Treasury to designate a list of individuals and entities close to Putin's regime as SDNs. In response, Russian officials quickly lashed out at the United States and its currency. Days before the first SREOs went into effect, a Kremlin official threatened:

> We hold a decent amount of Treasury bonds—more than $200 billion—and if the United States dares to freeze accounts of Russian businesses and citizens, we can no longer view America as a reliable partner. We will encourage everybody to dump US Treasury bonds, get rid of dollars as an unreliable currency.[22]

Meanwhile, sanctions programs targeting Moscow continued to pile up. By the end of 2018, Russian SDNs were targeted under eight separate EOs related to Russian interference in the 2016 US presidential election, other cyber-related crimes, and human rights violations.[23]

On April 6, 2018, the US Treasury unleashed the most severe sanctions to date against Russian interests, listing seven Russian oligarchs, seventeen top government officials, and twelve Russian firms as SDNs.[24] Later that year, Russian president Vladimir Putin directly linked sanctions, political risk, and the dollar's appeal during a speech at a BRICS (Brazil, Russia, India, China, South Africa) leaders' summit. In his remarks, he argued that "political disputes" were damaging the dollar's reserve currency role, calling sanctions a "strategic mistake" that "undermine confidence in the dollar." Putin called on the group to take steps to "minimize risks" related to the dollar and pitched China's currency—the renminbi—as a possible alternative that was "acquiring the qualities" of a reserve currency.[25] Russian Foreign Minister Sergei Lavrov echoed these anti-dollar sentiments later that year, gloating, "I am confident that the grave abuse of the role of the US dollar as a global reserve currency will result over time in . . . [its] weakening and demise." In a reference to de-dollarization, Russian Prime Minister Dmitry Medvedev asserted, "I think . . . [US] sanctions are good . . . because they forced us to do what we should have done 10 years ago."[26]

De-dollarization of Russian Reserves

The Russian government's reaction to US sanctions was not limited to anti-dollar sound bites. It extended to policy decisions that reshaped the composition of Russian foreign exchange reserves. The Kremlin swiftly embarked on an ambitious restructuring of its asset holdings by selling off a substantial share of its US Treasuries and diversifying into Chinese renminbi and, notably, gold. Dismissed as a "barbarous relic" by John Maynard Keynes in the early twentieth century, gold remains a stalwart component of many countries' reserve assets, functioning as an alternative to foreign exchange holdings.[27] Traditionally viewed as a hedge against dollar weakness, the yellow metal operates as a "safe haven" asset for central bankers. Figure 3.1 depicts the Central Bank of Russia's (CBR) gold holdings, reported in metric tons.[28] For the first half of the 2000s, Russia's gold stock remained essentially flat. Following the 2008 global financial crisis, its bullion holdings began to increase and continued to grow steadily.

Russian gold buying following the financial crisis was in line with other emerging market economies that chose to invest more in the precious metal as their confidence in the dollar's value—which hit an all-time low in trade-weighted terms in 2011—fell following the US housing crash.[29] By 2013, Russian gold holdings began to flatten out. This trend quickly changed in

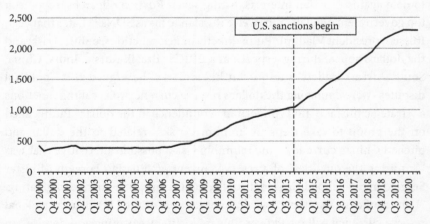

Figure 3.1. Russian Gold Holdings (metric tons), 2000–2020. A clear break in Russian gold purchases can be seen following the first quarter of 2014, after the US Treasury targeted Russia with sanctions following the invasion of Crimea. Data reported are from the World Gold Council.

the first quarter of the following year when the United States slapped its first round of sanctions on Russia for its invasion of Crimea; this event marked a clear change in the pace of CBR's gold investments. Russian gold holdings steeply increased, outpacing anything on record. This trend continued through 2018 as sanctions piled up.[30]

In addition to increasing its gold holdings in response to sanctions, the CBR also made substantial adjustments to its foreign exchange portfolio. Figure 3.2 presents monthly totals of Russia's foreign exchange reserves, including gold, according to International Monetary Fund (IMF) data. Plotted alongside total reserves is Russian residents' total monthly holdings of US government securities (combined long and short term).[31] While these data are not a precise measure of official Russian dollar holdings, they are sensitive to shifts in CBR investment decisions. For instance, if CBR were to make a large purchase (or sale) of US Treasuries, the data would reflect that decision.

The figure shows that Russia's total reserves (all assets) began to decline in 2014 after US sanctions soured market sentiment and the ruble came under increasing pressure. US Treasury holdings also fell during this period. Though the CBR reportedly invested in renminbi for the first time in 2015, these data do not indicate that Moscow was cutting its dollar reserves faster

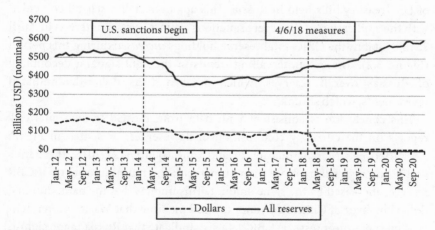

Figure 3.2. Russian Reserves, January 2012–December 2020. Russian reserves and holdings of US Treasuries (dollars) fall together following the 2014 sanctions. In 2018, however, Russian Treasury holdings fall steeply while overall Russian reserves increase, indicating diversification away from the dollar. Reserves data are from the IMF. Data on Russian holdings of US Treasuries are from the US Treasury.

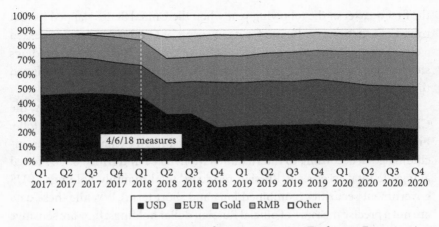

Figure 3.3. Currency Composition of Russian Foreign Exchange Reserves (%), 2017–2020. Following a round of severe financial sanctions against Russian interests in April 2018, Russian dollar (USD) holdings fell significantly while investments in renminbi (RMB) increased. Data are from the CBR.

than its holdings of other foreign currencies.[32] However, that changed between March and May 2018, when there was a visible drop in the total value of US Treasury bills held in Russia. This apparent dollar sell-off coincided with the application of the severe sanctions against Russian interests in April 2018. Notably, the CBR's total reserve holdings *increased* during this period (Figure 3.2). These countervailing trends in the data signal a decoupling of Russia's overall reserves, which grew, and its dollar-denominated investments, which shrank.

This conclusion is consistent with data from the CBR's own quarterly reports on the currency composition of its reserves, presented in Figure 3.3.[33] Between March (quarter 1) and June (quarter 2) 2018, the bank's dollar holdings fell by more than 10 percent; the renminbi's share of CBR reserves increased by the same amount. This implies that the bank dumped dollars in favor of China's currency around the time that Washington ratcheted up sanctions pressure. CBR data also indicate that Russia made significant adjustments to the geographic distribution of its official financial assets. Figure 3.4 illustrates that nearly one-third of Russian reserves were held in the United States at the beginning of 2014. This dipped temporarily following the imposition of the initial round of US sanctions later that year but returned to around 30 percent by 2017.

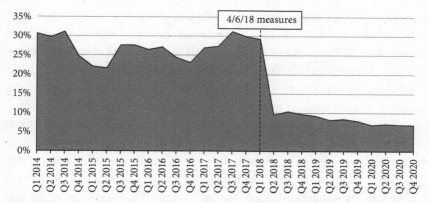

Figure 3.4. Russian Foreign Exchange and Gold Assets Held in the United States (%), 2014–2020. Following the 2014 sanctions, Russia marginally reduced the share of its reserve assets held in the United States. After the April 2018 sanctions, Moscow moved most of its US-domiciled investments to other jurisdictions.

This pattern contrasts with Russia's reaction to the April 2018 sanctions. The CBR's US-based assets dropped to just 10 percent in the two quarters after that round of steep OFAC penalties was levied. Some of this change is attributable to increased holdings of renminbi since those assets were likely held in China. Yet this alone cannot explain the geographic shift. While roughly 30 percent of Russian reserves remained in US dollars by 2020, just 10 percent of its reserves were held in the United States. This disjuncture indicates that Russia took steps to move most of its dwindling, yet still sizable, dollar holdings outside US territory. A portion of these dollar holdings might have been held on Russian soil in physical form. According to one Russian media report, the CBR purchased "cash dollars" in 2018 to limit its vulnerability to US sanctions. Cash, like gold, is a valuable sanctions hedge because it is physical. It can be held in a country's own vaults, beyond the reach of the US Treasury.[34] Other reports indicate that the CBR moved a portion of its dwindling stash of Treasury bills to places like Belgium or offshore tax havens, like the Cayman Islands, to evade Washington's grasp.[35]

Russian Motives

While the CBR did not offer a formal public explanation for its de-dollarization efforts, officials provided clues about the bank's thinking. For example, CBR governor Elvira Nabiullina explained in a 2019 interview, "You see we try to diversify our international reserves composition. Because we estimate all the possible risk, economic and *geopolitical* risks."[36] Sergey Shvetsov, a member of CBR's board of directors, said in April 2019 that Russia needed to "increase forex and gold reserves even more" due to "persisting sanctions risk."[37] Russian media reports have echoed these statements. One outlet likened gold reserves to an "airbag" that protects the country from sanctions.[38] Another report explained that Moscow's gold reserves are safe from foreign confiscation because they are "located on the territory of our country."[39] Similarly, another site noted that the decision to hold more physical dollars is good because "cash, like gold, is good because it lies inside the country."[40] The starkest take argued that "the best defense against sanctions and any external pressure is gold in the vaults of the Bank of Russia and Avangard missiles on combat duty."[41]

Of course, the United States did not sanction the CBR directly until February 2022. So why was the Kremlin cutting its dollar holdings and beefing up its gold and renminbi reserves several years before these measures were in place? The answer is straightforward: past US actions targeting foreign central banks influenced how the Kremlin responded to the initial waves of US sanctions against Russia. A former head of the CBR described the shift out of dollars as a "hedge" by Russia against the threat of reserve confiscation, pointing out that the Kremlin learned from the US seizure of Iranian assets.[42] Pro-Kremlin media echoed this point. One article discussing growing investments in renminbi noted that "there have been several precedents when the US has frozen the assets of central banks." It went on to mention actions taken against Libya and Iran by name.[43] Another article noted that Dmitry Tulin, a member of the CBR's board of governors, publicly hailed gold as an investment that cannot be "arrested or frozen" and explained that there was a precedent for such actions being taken against central banks.[44] An English-language Russian media outlet put it bluntly: "No amount of machinations involving sanctions from the US . . . could take the precious metal away in the event of an asset freeze crisis."[45] The CBR's motives were not lost on financial markets. One analyst at Moody's Investor Services praised the bank's moves away from the dollar for reducing Russia's exposure to additional penalties, describing diversification as "something any responsible policy maker would do" in response to US sanctions.[46]

In sum, Washington's demonstration that it was willing and able to freeze foreign central bank assets as part of its broader foreign policy agenda left an indelible impression on Russian policymakers. The dollar's appeal as a reserve currency quickly declined as US sanctions increased perceptions of the political risk associated with investments in the currency in Moscow. In response, Russia adopted an anti-dollar policy orientation in the composition of its reserve assets, moving more heavily into gold, euros, and renminbi. These moves proved prescient: in 2022, Washington did move to freeze Russian state assets. While those sanctions were extraordinarily costly, Moscow's anticipatory moves limited the damage that the United States could inflict.

Turkey Tiptoes Away from the Dollar

Although a long-standing US ally and NATO member, Turkey's relationship with the United States deteriorated throughout the 2010s. The two sides disagreed over issues including the sanctions on the Iranian regime and the involvement of Kurdish forces in the Syrian Civil War. Tensions further intensified after a 2016 coup attempt failed to topple President Recep Tayyip Erdoğan. The embattled leader signaled a deep mistrust of the United States when he accused Washington of siding with the coup plotters. The deterioration in relations reached a new low in 2017 as the United States threatened Turkey with financial sanctions, culminating in punitive action in the fall of 2018. While the US Treasury did not target any Turkish state institutions, Turkey's response followed the Russian playbook: it increased gold holdings, reduced its stock of Treasuries, and changed the geographic structure of its reserve assets. Though Ankara was less vocal than Moscow about its motives, the timing of these changes—along with select public statements—suggests that the political risk associated with the dollar as a reserve currency helps explain Turkey's moves.

Background on US Financial Sanctions Targeting Turkey

The first indication that the United States might target Turkey with financial sanctions came in late 2017 when a group of Democratic lawmakers publicly floated the idea. They called on the Trump administration to punish Turkey for its purchase of a Russian air defense system that violated the terms of Ankara's NATO membership.[47] In April 2018, a bipartisan group of sixty-six US senators sent a letter to Erdoğan threatening sanctions if detained

American pastor Andrew Brunson was not released from Turkish custody.[48] Ties reached their nadir in August 2018 when OFAC listed two Turkish government officials as SDNs (under an SREO tied to the Global Magnitsky Act) for their alleged role in Brunson's arrest and detention.[49] Though not designed to target a specific government, Magnitsky allows for sanctions against foreign individuals involved in human rights abuses. Many of the individuals targeted with Magnitsky sanctions are closely linked to governments viewed as US adversaries or "rogue regimes."[50]

The measures targeting Turkey were lifted following Brunson's release just three months after their imposition. Yet they left a lasting scar on US-Turkish relations. The move left no doubt in Ankara's mind that Washington was willing to use dollar dominance to punish Turkey when the two countries' interests starkly diverged. Indeed, talk of additional sanctions targeting Turkey picked up almost as soon as the Magnitsky measures were lifted. Once again, renewed threats that the US Treasury might impose new measures centered on Turkey's interest in Russian military hardware.[51]

De-dollarization of Turkish Reserves

Like Russia, Turkey's central bank (Türkiye Cumhuriyet Merkez Bankası, TCMB) increased its gold holdings amid rising US sanctions pressure. After stabilizing at just over 100 metric tons from 2000 through 2016, Turkey became the second-largest sovereign buyer of the precious metal in 2017, behind only Russia. Not only did Turkey increase its total gold holdings; it also rearranged the geographical location of its precious metal cache. In the spring of 2018, amid rising threats of US sanctions, Turkish media reported that the country had repatriated roughly $220 billion in gold that had been held at the New York Fed.[52] The returned gold bars were reportedly placed in various storage facilities on Turkish soil in a move that was described as having a "more political intonation than economic."[53] Figure 3.5 depicts trends in Turkey's gold reserves, along with markers indicating the start of US threats and the imposition of sanctions in 2018. The figure indicates that gold investments increased during the period of worsening ties between the countries. The TCMB's gold holdings started increasing somewhat in 2017, when there was talk of sanctions being imposed on the Erdoğan government. Turkey's gold purchases increased more rapidly following the Treasury's

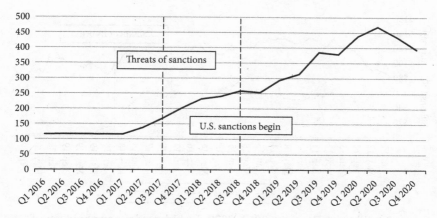

Figure 3.5. Turkish Gold Holdings (metric tons), 2016–2020. Turkey's gold reserves increased amid threats of US sanctions and rose at a faster rate following their imposition. Data are from the World Gold Council.

actions in August 2018. Its gold holdings continued to increase until the COVID-19 pandemic began in 2020.

To the best of my knowledge, Turkey does not publish the currency composition of its reserves. Identifying changes in the TCMB's reserve allocation is thus made difficult. US Treasury data on monthly holdings of US government securities presents some clues, however. As Figure 3.6 shows, Turkey's total reserves closely track US Treasury holdings from 2012 through 2017. As Turkey's total reserves rise, Treasury holdings increase in kind, and vice versa. However, after August 2018 when the Magnitsky sanctions were imposed, these indicators decouple from one another: the TCMB's reserves begin to increase, while Turkish holdings of US Treasuries continue to fall. This disjuncture in the data implies that the bank expedited a process of diversification into non-dollar assets around the time of OFAC's actions. Given that the data are not official Turkish reserves, we should be cautious about drawing a strong conclusion from the observed pattern. However, it is notable that there is no similar divergence between the indicators in the previous six years of data. Moreover, it is encouraging that data from two separate studies on the currency composition of foreign exchange reserves report a fall in Turkey's dollar holdings in 2018 even as TCMB's holdings of non-dollar currencies (in percentage terms) increased.[54] In sum, the pattern in the data and the timing of the decoupling is consistent with an anti-dollar reaction to US sanctions.

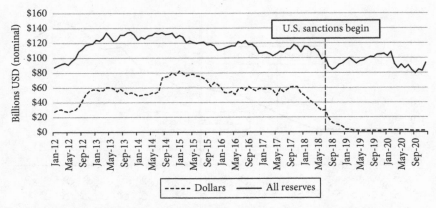

Figure 3.6. Turkish Reserves, 2012–2020. Turkish reserves and holdings of US Treasuries (dollar) move in tandem until September 2018, one month after US sanctions were imposed. While Turkish holdings of US Treasuries continue to fall, its total reserves begin increasing again, pointing to a shift away from the US dollar. Reserves data are from the IMF. Data on Turkish holdings of US Treasuries are from the US Treasury while data on all reserves are from the World Bank Databank.

Turkish Motives

Economic calculations can explain some of Ankara's investment decisions. For example, Turkey's growing interest in gold likely reflected the desperate condition of its economy in late 2017 as the lira came under intense exchange rate pressure. As the TCMB was forced to spend down dollars to support the lira, increasing gold holdings through domestic purchases of mined gold may reflect a desperate move by Ankara to shore up its dwindling financial assets. Yet economic motives alone are an unsatisfying explanation. For example, there is no clear economic explanation for Turkey's decision to physically relocate its gold reserves from New York to its own soil. Indeed, gold repatriation does not make economic sense because moving gold away from key financial centers creates logistical issues that raise the transaction costs for a government if it ever wishes to monetize its bullion.[55] Repatriation suggests a growing political mistrust between Ankara and Washington and increasing concerns within Erdoğan's government that Turkey's bullion may not have been as safe in New York as it once believed. Moreover, evidence that dollar holdings continued to decline even as overall reserves climbed implies that

Turkey was reluctant to shift a greater portion of its assets—including gold—back into dollars.

Unlike Russian officials, who publicly discussed the link between sanctions and the country's anti-dollar efforts, Ankara has been less transparent about its investment behavior. Still, Erdoğan made a few notable, critical remarks about the dollar's dominant global position as US sanctions pressure mounted. For example, amid growing threats of US sanctions in the spring of 2018, the Turkish president called for IMF loans to be repaid in gold rather than dollars. Erdoğan described gold as being "unlike anything else," stressing that with bullion "there is no political allegiance. [Holding] gold makes a lot of countries comfortable."[56] In public remarks days after sanctions were imposed, Erdoğan criticized Washington for launching an "economic war" against Turkey and pledged to replace the dollar with local currencies in trade with China, Russia, Iran, and Ukraine. Erdoğan further characterized the sanctions as a "stab in the back," saying "they may have their dollars, but we have our people, our god."[57] Though the evidence is less clear-cut than in the Russian case, it suggests a link between sanctions and Turkish de-dollarization. A deteriorating political relationship with Washington—fraught with threats of financial sanctions and, ultimately, their imposition—influenced both the currency and geographic composition of Turkey's foreign exchange reserves.

Conclusions

This chapter has presented evidence that US financial sanctions led Russia and Turkey to implement anti-dollar policies designed to de-dollarize their foreign exchange reserves. In the Russian case, the evidence that sanctions-induced political risk concerns were behind those moves is undeniable. US sanctions tarnished the dollar's appeal as a reserve asset in Moscow. Not only did Russia reduce its dollar holdings, moving into euros and renminbi; it also shifted the geographic distribution of its financial assets while significantly increasing its gold purchases. Russian policymakers were not shy about their reasons for the strategy change, consistently citing the US propensity to use the dollar as a weapon of foreign policy. The Turkish case is a bit murkier. Economic and political motives intersected, and corresponded to the timing of changes in the structure of the country's foreign exchange reserves. Ankara was less forthcoming about its motives in its public statements, though political or strategic motives do seem to have played a role.

Of course, two cases alone do not support claims of a broader trend in reserve diversification away from the dollar in response to sanctions. The case studies demonstrate that US sanctions can provoke countries to diversify their reserves away from the dollar due to political risk concerns, but how widespread is this trend? And if there is evidence of a broader trend, what are the implications for the dollar and for the effectiveness of US sanctions? The following chapter examines a broader surge in central bank gold buying between 2008 and 2020, and considers whether rising political risk perceptions surrounding the dollar can help explain this pattern—and what it might mean for the future.

4

The Anti-Dollar Gold Rush

Central Bank Reserves in the Age of Financial Sanctions

> *Oh gold! I still prefer thee unto paper, which makes bank credit like a*
> *bark of vapour.*
>
> Lord Byron[1]

While building a water-powered sawmill for California landowner John
Sutter in 1848, carpenter James Marshall discovered gold flakes in a nearby
stream bed. Marshall and Sutter immediately formed a partnership and
pledged to keep the discovery a secret in hopes of securing their personal
fortunes. Unfortunately for them, their efforts at secrecy failed; Sutter's property was soon besieged by thousands of gold miners also hoping to strike
it rich. Within a few years, more than 300,000 fortune seekers had staked
claims—and risked their futures—to search for the yellow metal. The place
of the California Gold Rush in American folklore is a potent illustration of
gold's enduring allure.

More than a century and a half later, governments in Russia and Turkey also
rushed to buy up tons of gold in response to growing political concerns about
dependence on the US dollar as a store of value. By directly demonstrating its
coercive financial capabilities, Washington had diminished the dollar's appeal in the eyes of officials in Ankara and Moscow; gold, on the other hand,
grew more attractive to them. Both countries' investment decisions were
concurrent with a broader international gold-buying spree that began following the 2008 global financial crisis, reversing nearly two decades of net
gold sales by monetary authorities around the world.

What explains this change in the popularity of monetary gold as a reserve
asset? Part of the renewed interest in gold was generated by the destabilizing
forces of the worldwide financial crisis. Yet economic explanations for its revival as a reserve asset are unsatisfactory on their own. Not all central banks

Bucking the Buck. Daniel McDowell, Oxford University Press. © Oxford University Press 2023.
DOI: 10.1093/oso/9780197679876.003.0005

responded to the crisis by scooping up tons of the physical commodity. Rather, the buying spree was concentrated among a subset of emerging market countries, many of which are engaged in strained political relations with the United States.

This chapter further explores the link between the United States' growing use of financial sanctions and an anti-dollar central bank gold-buying binge. Admittedly, gold is not an ideal substitute for dollars: it is fairly illiquid and nowhere near as convenient. Yet its antiquated properties make it an appealing hedge against US financial sanctions. Short of a military invasion, Washington cannot seize monetary gold held in a foreign government's vaults. Specie can be physically moved around the world, without the involvement of digital financial networks, making it difficult to track. In extreme circumstances, governments can illicitly trade gold for foreign currency on the black market. Embattled regimes that are otherwise blocked from using the dollar-based financial system have come to view gold as a form of insurance against US sanctions. More than any other financial asset, gold can sustain a rogue regime's hold on power when it faces enormous external economic pressure. Thus, by investing more in the yellow metal and less in dollars, targeted and at-risk governments can reduce their exposure to political risk.

This chapter extends the book's analysis by making an empirical connection between US sanctions, perceptions of sanctions' risks, and central bank gold purchases between 2008 and 2020. I demonstrate that both *imposed US sanctions* and the *perceived risk of sanctions* are associated with higher rates of central bank gold purchases. Moreover, additional analysis indicates that US Treasury bond holdings tend to fall in countries targeted by US sanctions.

Trends in World Gold Reserves

For much of modern history, gold was an integral part of the international monetary system. From 1870 to 1914, most major economies participated in the international gold standard. The pre-war monetary regime required each government to set a gold price for their currencies; this meant that foreign exchange values were fixed against each other. Monies issued by governments that were part of the arrangement were backed by gold, which required countries to maintain large gold reserves. The outbreak of war in Europe ended the first international gold standard, but a new monetary regime based on gold was resurrected after the end of the Second World War.

The Bretton Woods monetary system modified the original gold standard system by linking the value of the US dollar to gold and then fixing the value of all other currencies to the lynchpin currency. Under this system, only the United States was required to provide specie on demand in exchange for its money. Still, central banks outside the United States built up their gold reserves in the years following the war, perhaps more out of habit than necessity.[2]

Since 1971, when the United States ended its commitment to a gold-backed currency, the precious metal has not played an official role in the global monetary system. Nonetheless, gold has continued to be a popular central bank asset, valued for its "safe haven" qualities and functioning as a hedge against inflation or devaluation of fiat currencies. As late as 1991, gold comprised nearly one-third of the world's monetary reserves.[3]

In the 1990s gold fell out of favor among central bankers as a reserve asset. The dollar price of gold had been dropping, almost monotonically, since the mid-1980s. With no official reason to maintain a sizable gold stock, central bankers started selling their bullion. The Bank of England sold nearly 60 percent (395 tons) of its gold reserves between 1999 and 2002 due to concerns about volatility in its value.[4] Official gold sales were so common by the end of the 1990s that they pushed the price of gold down to near-historic lows. In 1998, one British financial weekly, referencing gold sales by monetary authorities around the world, declared gold "the asset no-one seems to want."[5] This pressure on the metal's value led to the 1999 Washington Agreement on Gold. The deal, created to prevent the price from collapsing, committed participating monetary authorities to limit collective official gold sales to just 400 tons per year.[6] Gold, by all accounts, was on the outs as a reserve asset.

Official gold holdings continued to fall throughout the 2000s, reaching their lowest point on record in 2008. Then in 2010, central banks were net buyers of gold for the first time in twenty years. By the end of 2016, official gold holdings (measured by weight) had fully recovered the previous decade's decline, reaching levels not seen since before the Bank of England's first gold auction in 1999 (Figure 4.1). What explains gold's post-crisis resurgence among monetary authorities? The following section reviews the economic explanation for rising gold reserves after the 2008 global financial crisis. It then considers why an economic explanation is an inadequate account of

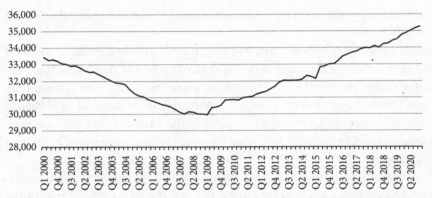

Figure 4.1. Worldwide Monetary Gold Reserves (metric tons), 2000–2020.
Central bank monetary gold reserves fell throughout the 1990s and 2000s.
However, following the global financial crisis in 2008, central banks regained
interest in the precious metal as a financial asset.

gold's revival. What is missing is the role of geopolitical calculations related to
rising political risk in the international currency system due to the increased
use of US sanctions, which also increased during this period. Gold's potential to function as a hedge against sanctions gave it a unique appeal among
targeted and at-risk central banks.

The Economic Motives behind Gold's Resurgence

Unlike debt securities, gold does not accumulate interest. Its value as a medium of exchange is quite limited. For instance, it is not generally used to
settle cross-border trade or other business. Nor is gold especially useful for
"currency manipulation" purposes as it is not convenient for intervention
in foreign exchange markets. In a world where commodity-backed money
is a thing of the past, why do central banks continue to invest in gold reserves? A fundamental attraction to the metal is its tendency to appreciate
during turbulent times, offsetting losses in other asset classes. For example, a
2020 survey of fifty-one central banks conducted by the World Gold Council
found that 79 percent of reserve managers polled cited gold's "performance
in times of crisis" as being somewhat or highly relevant in their decision to
hold the metal.[7] Unlike government debt, including US Treasury bonds, gold
carries no default risk. Unlike fiat currencies, like the dollar, gold cannot be

debased by expansionary monetary policy. Thus, in times of trouble, gold gains appeal among official investors concerned about the potential for government debt defaults or the perceived inflationary effects of ultra-low interest rates and fiscal profligacy.

The global financial crisis unleashed fears about each of these developments. For example, in 2009, Chinese Premier Wen Jiabao publicly fretted about the possibility of an American default on its external debt obligations and what this would mean for Beijing's vast Treasury holdings. This prompted President Barack Obama to pledge that the United States was committed to honoring its debts and would take steps to get its budget deficit under control.[8] The crisis also ushered in an era of unconventional monetary policy among central banks backing the world's key reserve currencies, especially the Federal Reserve and the European Central Bank. The unprecedented crisis response generated concerns in some circles about the long-term impact of these new measures on the value of assets denominated in these currencies.[9] At least one study directly links post-crisis quantitative easing policies to the buildup of gold assets in emerging and developing economy central banks.[10]

Relatedly, the 2008 panic and the subsequent European debt crisis led to an international reevaluation of what assets were considered "safe" for official and private investors. Asset holders had, in relatively short order, absorbed significant losses on AAA-rated mortgage-backed securities and highly rated OECD (Organisation for Economic Co-operation and Development) government debt. Consequently, as the International Monetary Fund's (IMF's) 2012 Global Financial Stability Report noted, investors rushed to safety "at the same time that the universe of what [was] considered safe [was] shrinking."[11] While other formerly safe assets lost their status in the wake of these crises, gold's reputation was left untarnished; if anything, its status was burnished.[12] As one gold industry report explained, "Many markets that reserve managers had assumed to be deep and liquid proved to be the exact opposite. . . . [Conversely] the gold market remained liquid throughout the financial crisis, even at the height of liquidity strains in other markets."[13]

It is not so surprising, then, that gold experienced something of a renaissance as a reserve asset in the decade after the crisis. Official portfolio managers were drawn to gold as a hedge against default and currency debasement alongside a general decline in the availability of safe haven assets. Yet a purely economic explanation focused on the effects of the financial shocks of the early twenty-first century cannot fully explain gold's resurgence.

The financial crisis of 2008 and the subsequent debt crisis in Europe raised concerns about government debt and fiat currencies in every corner of the world. Yet central bank gold purchases since the crisis have not been uniform across countries—far from it, in fact. Some jumped into the gold market with great intensity while others barely dabbled or sat it out entirely (Figure 4.2). Despite the secular trend toward a worldwide increase in gold reserves, thirty-seven countries reported no changes in their bullion holdings between 2008 and 2020; in thirty-four countries, gold reserves fell during that period. The international gold hoarding trend was concentrated among just forty-nine countries that reported increases in their monetary gold stock during these years, including Russia, Turkey, and China. Beijing increased its stock of bullion from just 600 tons in 2008 to nearly 2,000 tons by the end of 2020. The Central Asian states of Kazakhstan and Uzbekistan were also major buyers during this period.

To understand the variation in gold purchases during the post-crisis gold rush, we need a model that accounts for country-specific factors linked to bullion holdings. One such factor that deserves attention is the uneven distribution of political risk in the international currency system, which is directly related to the United States' increasing use of financial sanctions. The next section develops this argument by drawing on the example of Venezuela,

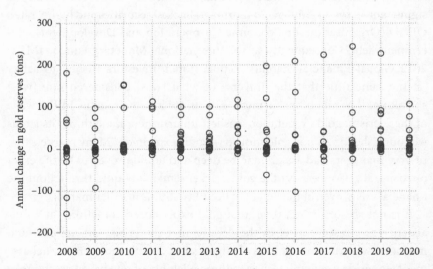

Figure 4.2. Annual Change in Gold Reserves by Country, 2008–2020. Circles reflect yearly changes in gold reserves measured in metric tons as reported by national central banks to the World Gold Council.

which faced severe US financial sanctions beginning in 2015. Caracas found that its gold reserves were an invaluable insurance policy that enhanced the Maduro regime's ability to resist US political pressure and remain in power.

Gold Reserves as Insurance against US Sanctions

Politics has motivated central banks to invest in gold in the past. France's decision to convert dollar reserves into gold in the 1960s was partly a political protest against the "exorbitant privilege" that the United States drew from issuing the world's key currency.[14] Central banks' more recent interest in holding gold also has political roots, though of a different sort. Some monetary authorities during the post-crisis years were drawn to gold as a form of insurance against the political risk linked to reliance on the dollar as a reserve currency. In the same way that gold is valued for its function as a safe haven asset during economic crises, some governments took a shine to the yellow metal because its safe haven properties also apply in times of *political* crisis. While the US Treasury can effectively cut a regime off from the global dollar-based financial system or freeze its dollar-based assets, physical gold can be kept—literally—out of Washington's long reach. Thus, gold reserves can serve as a last layer of defense for regimes targeted by US financial sanctions, such as Venezuela.

The Obama administration first sanctioned Nicolás Maduro's regime in 2015 for human rights violations, freezing the assets of seven government officials. By 2019, five additional sanctions-related Executive Orders (SREOs) had broadened the punitive financial measures against Venezuela. Key targets included the government itself and the central bank. The state-run oil company PDVSA was also listed as a Specially Designated National (SDN); its exports generated a substantial portion of the country's foreign exchange earnings. The cumulative effect of the sanctions, designed to generate "maximum pressure" on the regime, crippled an already weak Venezuelan economy. Yet Maduro managed to hold on to power,[15] in part due to the country's gold reserves.

Banco Central de Venezuela (BCV) had spent most of its foreign exchange reserves in the years after the global financial crisis. Its remaining reserve assets were highly concentrated in gold held on Venezuelan soil after then president Hugo Chavez repatriated 160 tons (85 percent) of the country's gold reserves from Europe in 2011.[16] As US sanctions began to bite in 2015,

Maduro's regime started selling its bullion (see Figure 4.3). As sanctions piled on, the sell-off continued: the BCV dumped more than 73 tons of its gold—valued at roughly $3 billion—between late 2017 and early 2019.

The process of selling gold is labor and time intensive, yet it can be done in relative secret, which is its primary appeal as a hedge against political risk. While the US Treasury carefully monitors digital financial exchanges between banks, tracking the physical movement of gold around the world is virtually impossible for Washington. The Maduro regime transported ingots to buyers in Turkey, Uganda, and the United Arab Emirates on Russian aircraft and accepted payments in cash euros.[17] The funds were then physically transported back to Venezuela and distributed to banks; the euros entered the country's financial system by financing import purchases for the desperate economy. In other cases, the foreign exchange acquired through illicit gold trade was used to service debts to China and Russia, helping Maduro maintain his cozy relations with his regime's two most important supporters.[18] Separately, Venezuela sent about 9 tons of gold to Iran aboard Tehran-based Mahan Airline jets as payment for Iran's assistance in maintaining state-owned oil refineries.[19] In the summer of 2020, Maduro suffered a legal defeat in an effort to repatriate more than $1 billion in gold held at the Bank of England.

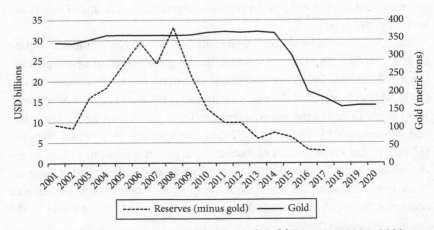

Figure 4.3. Venezuela's Foreign Exchange and Gold Reserves, 2001–2020.
Venezuela's foreign exchange reserves fell quickly following the global financial crisis. Its gold holdings were stable until 2015, when the US sanctioned the regime of Nicolás Maduro, causing the central bank to sell gold on the black market. Reserves data from the World Bank are not available for 2018–2020. Gold reserves data are from the World Gold Council.

The UK High Court sided with the British central bank, which refused to release the gold on the grounds that its ownership was contested between Maduro and Venezuelan opposition leader Juan Guaidó.[20] This episode reinforced the importance of holding bullion in one's own vaults.[21] In summary, the physical possession of monetary gold on Venezuelan territory operated as a lifeline for the Maduro regime—allowing it to service debts, bring in physical cash, and pay its foreign accomplices for critical assistance—when US sanctions blocked its access to the dollar-based financial system.

Venezuela is not the only heavily sanctioned economy to look to gold after being cut off from the dollar. Iran reportedly accepted physical gold as payment for oil sales to Turkey since its oil and banking sectors were unable to use SWIFT messaging or clear payments through correspondent banking accounts (Figure 4.4). Though flat most years, there are two notable spikes in Turkish gold exports to Iran, especially in 2012 following three new SREOs from the US Treasury when reports of the transactions emerged.[22]

Given these examples, it is reasonable to conclude that part of gold's growing appeal after the global financial crisis was its capacity to function as a unique form of insurance against US sanctions.[23] However, all countries should not equally value gold as a hedge against political risk in the international currency system. Governments targeted by US sanctions have observed the direct costs of dollar use; holding gold should have increased appeal in such cases. Put differently, *states targeted by US SREOs should be more likely than other states to increase their monetary gold holdings in the post-crisis*

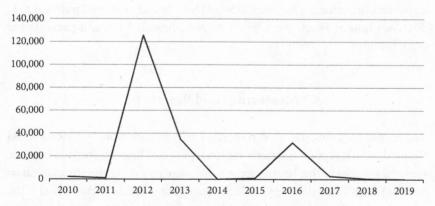

Figure 4.4. Turkish Gold Exports to Iran (kilograms), 2010–2019. Turkey exported physical gold to Iran, reportedly as payment for oil in 2012, to evade US sanctions. Data are from the UN Comtrade Database.

period. It is also possible that *perceptions* of political risk from sanctions influence monetary authorities' gold investment decisions. Governments that do not view themselves as likely targets of US sanctions, all things equal, should have been less attracted to gold as a store of value during this period. They would have had no incentive to hedge if they were convinced they would not be a victim of sanctions in the first place. Conversely, as a government perceives its risk of being sanctioned to be rising, adding more gold to the country's reserves should become more appealing. In other words, *the perceived probability of being sanctioned by the United States should be associated with an increase in monetary gold holdings in the post-crisis period*. After briefly describing how I assess these claims, I present data demonstrating the expected link between US sanctions pressure, perceptions of political risk, and gold investments.

Assessing the Political Risk-Gold Reserves Link

The link between US sanctions and increased gold holdings in Russia and Turkey, discussed in Chapter 3, provides case-level evidence that the political risk generated by US financial sanctions increases the appeal of holding the precious metal among targeted and at-risk central banks. This section builds on the case study evidence by presenting a statistical model of central bank gold investing behavior since 2008, around the time that the latest international gold rush began. It explains how central bank gold holdings are measured, introduces a measure of SREO targets and perceived political risk, discusses how alternative explanations are controlled for, and presents the main findings.

Measuring Gold Reserves

To account for countries' gold reserves, I rely on data from the World Gold Council, which reports quarterly national gold holdings by weight in metric tons.[24] I transform this into an annual measure by taking the mean of quarterly holdings in a calendar year. The dependent variable in the model is the *annual change in a country's gold holdings, measured in metric tons*. I focus on the period 2008 through 2020, as this coincides with both the global uptick in gold holdings and the steady rise in the United States' use of financial sanctions.[25]

I use changes in gold reserves by weight over alternative measures because it is a more reliable measure of a government's gold investing behavior over time. For example, one possible alternative would be the dollar value of a country's gold reserves. This is problematic, however, as the dollar price of gold fluctuated significantly during this period. As gold's dollar price increases, the measure would rise in kind, suggesting an increase in gold holdings even if a government had not purchased more bullion. Thus, movement in a measure based on the dollar price would partially reflect changes in the *value* of the asset rather than a change in actual gold holdings. Another option would be to measure a country's gold holdings as a share of its overall reserves. Yet this measure would also present a distorted picture. For example, if a monetary authority spent down a substantial portion of its dollar reserves but made no changes to its gold holdings, gold as a share of reserves would increase. This change would not reflect increased gold holdings but rather decreased holdings of dollars. By comparison, measuring gold by weight provides a reliable and consistent accounting of a country's gold investing over time, regardless of the dollar value of the asset or a central bank's management of its foreign exchange reserves.

Explanatory Variable 1: Sanctions Related Executive Orders

I use two key explanatory variables to account for the extent of US sanctions pressure on a country. The first is a simple dichotomous variable that indicates whether a country was targeted by a US SREO in a given year ($SREO = 1$) or not ($SREO = 0$). This variable accounts for the tangible direct costs imposed by the US Treasury against targets. In such cases, the political risk of dollar use is not hypothetical; it is observed. If US sanctions generate political risk concerns about dollar dependence and if gold reserves are viewed as a hedge against such risks, central banks in countries targeted by a US SREO should increase their gold holdings more quickly than those that have not been targeted by the US Treasury.

SREOs are an important measure, as they account for the actual implementation of US financial sanctions and, therefore, observed political risk. However, they are also a rare event in the data, occurring in just 70 of nearly

1,500 observations. Given the rising use of US sanctions during this period, some non-targeted states may have *anticipated* that they would one day become targets. To account for this possibility, I employ a second explanatory variable to account for *perceived* political risk.

Explanatory Variable 2: Sanctions Risk

Though governments cannot predict with certainty whether they will be targeted by US financial sanctions, they can make reasoned assessments of the risks they face. Since US sanctions are imposed in public, non-targeted governments can draw reasoned inferences about the *type* of state that Washington is inclined to sanction. The public text of each SREO issued by the president of the United States contains information regarding the motives behind the punitive action. Chapter 1 discussed how analyzing the text of SREOs aimed at state actors helps us develop a "profile" of a likely US sanctions target. Text analysis of all SREOs issued between 2000 and 2020 indicates that three characteristics are most commonly cited to justify the use of financial sanctions: the target government (1) represents a threat to US security or foreign policy interests, mentioned 71 percent of the time, (2) is a known abuser of human rights, mentioned 31 percent of the time, or (3) poses some threat to democracy in that country, mentioned 26 percent of the time.[26] Figure 4.5 illustrates how the justifications for SREOs have fluctuated over time; all three primary motives are well represented. The data indicate that throughout the study period, security and foreign policy concerns are the most cited reasons for action. However, mentions of democracy and human rights issues are also quite common.

I assume that the more a government resembles the "typical" US sanctions target, the more its perceived level of political risk should grow. Other things being equal, a government is more likely to perceive itself as being at risk of US sanctions if its foreign policy preferences or security interests diverge from US preferences and interests, if its human rights record deteriorates, and if its political institutions grow more authoritarian. For governments that fit this description, overdependence on the dollar as a store of value should become increasingly concerning. Washington may seek to freeze the government's assets or lock it and close associates out of the dollar-based financial system, rendering dollar holdings of little use. Conversely, such

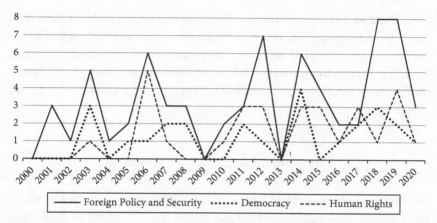

Figure 4.5. Count of Cited Reasons for US Sanctions-related Executive Orders (SREOs), 2000–2020. Data collected and coded based on all SREOs targeting foreign governments during these years. The figure shows that throughout the period, each of these reasons was commonly used to justify a new US financial sanctions program.

states should find it more appealing to hold gold in their reserves, given the commodity's ability to serve as a hedge against sanctions risk.

I use principal component analysis (PCA) to create a single-dimension indicator of governments' level of sanctions-related political risk.[27] The PCA indicator is a composite measure constructed from three variables—each of which proxies for one of the three most commonly stated motives for OFAC sanctions discussed above. To account for US foreign policy and security considerations, I rely on a widely used measure of the distance between a country's foreign policy "ideal point" and the US ideal point[28] based on voting in the United Nations General Assembly; greater distances indicate less overlap in foreign policy preferences.[29] To capture the quality of a state's democratic institutions, I employ Polity IV's commonly used measure of democracy.[30] To measure a state's human rights record, I use the human rights indicator from the Fragile States Index.[31]

Based on these three indicators, I retain a single principal component from the PCA analysis as my primary measure of *sanctions risk*.[32] This measure is designed as a proxy for governments' own perceptions of the likelihood that they will be targeted by the US Treasury based on observable characteristics related to OFAC's public justifications of its sanctions programs. As the value of the indicator rises, states should perceive their risk of being sanctioned as increasing—and should be more likely to increase their gold holdings to hedge against this risk. Though the indicator is designed to reflect the *perceived* level of sanctions risk, rather than the true underlying risk level, it is nonetheless a strong predictor of US financial sanctions. For more on the predictive power of the indicator, see Appendix C where additional analyses are discussed.

Accounting for Alternative Explanations

As discussed above, central banks hold gold for economic reasons unrelated to sanctions risk. Monetary authorities typically strive to hold most of their reserves in so-called safe assets—debt instruments that retain their value even during tumultuous systemic events. The primary supply of such safe assets is a small number of advanced economy governments, the United States chief among them. Consequently, most countries' reserves are highly dependent on dollar-denominated US government debt.[33] Like private investors, governments seek to maintain diverse portfolios that optimize and stabilize their returns over time. Overdependence on any single currency or asset type, like US Treasuries, puts portfolios at risk since fluctuations in the value of a single asset largely determine the value of a government's financial holdings. For example, expansionary US monetary policy following the 2008 global financial crisis resulted in a historically weak US dollar. As a result, central bankers became frustrated about the declining value of their dollar holdings.[34] In a 2019 survey of thirty central banks, nearly half agreed that gold was part of their strategy to "hedge US dollar exposure."[35] Gold purchases may therefore reflect reserve managers' desire to reduce their exposure to fluctuations in the value of the dollar.

The extent to which monetary authorities view gold as an attractive diversifier should be related to the government's existing stock of non-gold reserves. Central banks have strong incentives to hold a substantial portion of their reserves in US dollars or other major currencies. Reserves are not held simply for store of value purposes; they are also used to meet the economy's transactional needs. The market for US Treasuries is the largest, most liquid financial market in the world, meaning the asset can quickly be exchanged for cash if a government needs dollars. Thus, a government with significant US dollar-denominated debt will want to hold a large share of its reserves in dollars to ensure that it can service its debts if financial markets seize up in a crisis. States that rely on the dollar to pay for imports will likewise want to hold dollars to make sure they can cover import payments in times of financial turmoil.

However, monetary authorities' appetite for US Treasuries is not without limit. Once a government has saved enough dollar-denominated assets to cover three months of imports and debt payments (a traditional measure of reserve adequacy), every additional dollar saved is increasingly superfluous for transactional needs. As a monetary authority's cache of total foreign exchange reserves increases relative to its economic size, it should grow more concerned about the risks of overexposure to the dollar (and other hard currencies) in its portfolio and, consequently, look to diversify its holdings into other assets to reduce those risks.[36] Gold makes an especially attractive investment in this regard as its value tends to move inversely to the dollar's; thus it is viewed as an effective hedge against dollar depreciation.[37] If hedging against dollar weakness motivates central bank gold purchases, then as non-gold (currency) reserves increase in relation to the overall size of an economy, we should expect gold purchases to rise. To control for this possibility, I include a measure of a country's currency reserves divided by its gross domestic product (GDP) in my analysis.

A state's current gold holdings may also influence the appeal of gold as a diversifier. The logic is straightforward. If gold already represents a significant share of a country's reserve holdings, then it should become less attractive for diversification purposes. Conversely, if gold makes up only a small part of a country's reserves, it should be viewed as a more appealing investment option. As a share of total reserves, advanced industrial economies have traditionally held far more gold in their reserves (around 20 percent of total assets) than developing and emerging market economies (around 4 percent).[38] This discrepancy, among other reasons, recently led one prominent economist to recommend that emerging economy central banks increase their gold purchases.[39] Moreover, financial media often point out that the central banks buying the most gold tend to hail from "nations with a lower share of reserves in gold" compared to Western countries.[40] Thus, I include gold as a share of total reserves in the models. I also control for GDP and GDP per capita as measures of economic development since some monetary authorities may have responded to public calls to buy gold based on their status as "emerging" or "developing" economies.

Annual gold purchases may also reflect underlying yearly increases in reserves. States that experience large reserve growth, all things equal, will be in a better position to buy more gold—even if they are just maintaining the same allocation of gold in their reserves. The model includes a measure of the yearly change in non-gold reserves to address this possibility.[41] Given the secular trend toward increasing gold reserves during the study period, I also include a linear time trend in all estimations that ranges from zero (2008) to thirteen (2020). To account for unobserved country-specific factors that could influence gold holdings, like domestic gold production, all models include country fixed effects. To address concerns of simultaneity, all explanatory variables are lagged by one period. Finally, I adjust for the possibility of cross-sectional correlation across countries and heteroskedasticity within countries by estimating panel-corrected standard errors.[42]

Results

Given that the outcome of interest, annual changes in gold holdings measured in metric tons, is a continuous variable with both negative and positive values, I fit two ordinary least squares regression models. Figure 4.6 displays

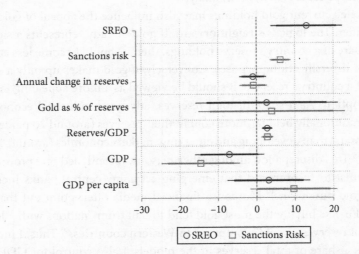

Figure 4.6. Coefficient Estimates, Annual Change in Gold Holdings (tons). Circles/squares represent the coefficient point estimate. Wide lines represent 90 percent confidence intervals, narrow lines reflect 95 percent confidence intervals. SREO = Sanctions-related Executive Order. Country fixed effects and the time trend covariate are excluded from the figure to improve interpretation. Full results are available in Table D1 in Appendix D.

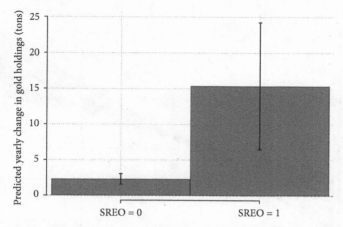

Figure 4.7. Predicted Marginal Effects of SREOs on Gold Holdings. The mean predicted marginal effect of SREO as it varies from 0 (none) to 1 (at least one SREO in place), as indicated by the top of the bars. The vertical lines represent 95 percent confidence intervals around those means. The difference in means between the groups is a 13-ton increase in predicted gold holdings for countries under at least one SREO.

the main coefficient estimates for both models. In each case, the coefficient for the sanctions variable, either *SREO* or *sanctions risk*, is positive and statistically distinguishable from zero, which supports the assertion that US financial sanctions, political risk, and rising gold holdings are linked. Though the analysis does not prove a causal relationship, it is consistent with the book's central argument that US sanctions provoke anti-dollar policy responses. Beyond the main explanatory variables, the results also indicate that gold purchases rise as a country's total reserves (divided by GDP) increase.[43] This is consistent with an economic argument that governments are investing in gold as part of a broader strategy to diversify away from foreign exchange holdings.

To shed further light on the magnitude of the effect of *SREO* and *sanctions risk* on gold purchases, Figures 4.7 and 4.8 display the predicted marginal effects. Beginning with the dichotomous sanctions measure (Figure 4.7), the model estimates that countries not under an SREO increased their gold holdings by an average of 2.3 metric tons a year during the study period. By contrast, countries targeted by an SREO increased their gold holdings by an estimated 15.4 tons annually—a difference of more than 13 tons of

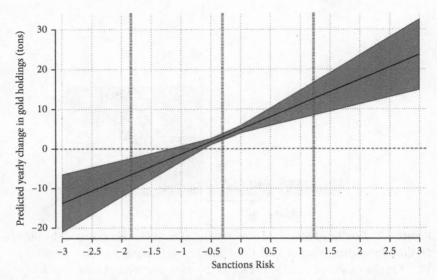

Figure 4.8. Predicted Marginal Effects of Sanctions Risk on Gold Holdings.
The line represents mean predicted marginal effects as the sanctions risk moves
from low to high. The shaded area represents 95 percent confidence intervals
around those means. The three vertical dashed lines identify the sample mean
level of sanctions risk (center), one standard deviation below the mean (left),
and one standard deviation above the mean (right). Moving from the left dashed
vertical line to the right line is associated with an 18-ton yearly increase in
predicted gold holdings.

bullion. For ease of interpretation, we can express the predicted difference in
dollar terms using the average price for an ounce of gold during this period
($1,311),[44] which indicates that an additional 13-ton annual increase in gold
holdings amounts to an additional $601 million in monetary gold added to
central bank coffers per year.

Turning to the continuous measure (Figure 4.8), at one standard deviation below the mean of *sanctions risk* (a value of −1.84, roughly the level of
Japan in 2018), gold reserves are predicted to *decrease*, on average, by a little
over 6 tons per year. Conversely, at one standard deviation above the mean
(a value of 1.23, or about the level of Myanmar in 2016), bullion holdings are
estimated to *rise* by an average of more than 12 tons per year. This equates to a
yearly difference of 18.6 tons in gold holding adjustments, or about $860 mil-
lion in monetary gold.

Sanctions and De-Dollarization of Reserves

The finding that SREOs and the perceived risk of sanctions are associated with central bank gold purchases provides compelling evidence in support of the claim that US sanctions have contributed to the rise of anti-dollar policies in the arena of central bank reserves. Of course, purchasing gold does not necessarily mean that a central bank is also cutting its dollar holdings. Dollars still hold immeasurable value in the world economy, especially in facilitating cross-border investment and trade. Some governments, even those under sanctions or that perceive themselves to be at high risk of sanctions, may have purchased more gold more while continuing to invest more in dollars. In such a case, gold purchases would not necessarily entail de-dollarization. Of course, any investment in gold comes at some opportunity cost to dollar holdings, since every ounce of gold purchased reduces the amount of Treasury bills in which a central bank can invest. So, even if dollar holdings continued to rise alongside gold holdings, additional gold purchases should impact the pace of dollar reserve increases. In other words, gold purchases should have some negative impact on dollar holdings, even if this simply results in a slower increase in dollar reserves year on year. In the final section of this chapter, I consider the link between US sanctions and a more direct measure of de-dollarization: central bank dollar reserves.

Measuring US Dollar Reserves

In an ideal world, we could regress official data on central bank dollar holdings on the two sanctions variables used in the preceding analysis. Unfortunately, most central banks do not publicly release the currency composition of their foreign exchange reserves. Without access to these data, such an analysis is not possible. As a second-best approach, I employ foreign US dollar holdings data from the US Treasury to proxy for central bank dollar reserves.[45] The Treasury data I utilize report all foreign private and public (including central bank) holdings of long-term US Treasury securities for nearly 100 countries. Long-term US Treasuries are the primary instrument in which central bank dollar reserves are held. As monetary authorities change their dollar reserve holdings, the Treasury data reflect such adjustments. However, the measure also includes changes in privately held Treasury bonds. While an imperfect proxy, the data are the best available measure for a large sample of countries. Notably, the US Treasury reports that foreign governments are the dominant investor group within emerging markets holding US securities. Thus, changes in total investor holdings reported in the data typically reflect changes in holdings of the official sector.[46] The main outcome of interest is the yearly percentage change in long-term US Treasury bond holdings.

Other Covariates and Model Specifications

The main explanatory variables used here are the same as above: *SREO* and *sanctions risk*. The main control covariate included is the annual change in total central bank reserves (including all currencies and gold).[47] It is imperative to account for this since the association between SREOs and a decline in dollar holdings may not necessarily reflect intentional de-dollarization of reserves. Rather, it may reflect a broader draw down in reserves as a result of the economic isolation brought on by US sanctions (such as the Venezuela case discussed earlier). By accounting for overall changes in reserves, we can control for the possibility that sanctions are simply causing a drop in total reserves, regardless of the currency in question, rather than intentional de-dollarization. I also include standard macroeconomic controls for GDP and GDP per capita. All estimates include country fixed effects and a linear time trend. Once again, panel-corrected standard errors are used and explanatory variables are lagged by one period. Estimates are limited to the years 2012–2020 because Treasury data begin in 2011.[48]

Results

The main results, reported in Figure 4.9, are mixed. Though the coefficient on *sanctions risk* is negative, it cannot be statistically distinguished from zero. This suggests that perceptions of sanctions risk alone are not associated with cuts to dollar holdings. However, the coefficient on *SREO* is both negative and statistically significant, indicating that countries targeted by at least one US SREO appear to cut their dollar holdings, even after controlling for annual changes in total reserves. The results also suggest, though not conclusively, that as total reserve holdings increase (decrease), dollar holdings also increase (decrease). The variable reaches lower levels of significance

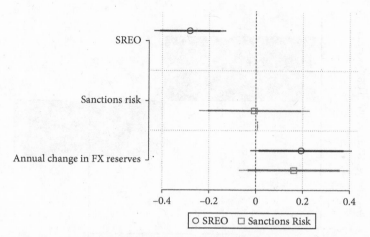

Figure 4.9. Coefficient Estimates, Annual Change in Long-Term US Treasury Holdings. Circles/squares represent the coefficient point estimate. Wide lines represent 90 percent confidence intervals; narrow lines reflect 95 percent confidence intervals. SREO = Sanctions-related Executive Order. Country fixed effects, the time trend covariate, GDP, and GDP per capita are excluded for ease of interpretation. Full results are available in Table D2 in Appendix D.

in the *SREO* model (p = 0.08), though in both cases the coefficient is positively signed. Thus, the broad measure of foreign exchange reserve holdings appears to move in tandem with the data on US Treasury holdings. This correlation is encouraging, since it is consistent with what we would expect if the outcome variable (*US Treasuries data*) is a valid proxy for central bank dollar holdings.

Figure 4.10 displays the predicted marginal effects of *SREO* on US Treasury holdings. The model estimates that US Treasury holdings *increased* by an average of 15 percent each year for countries not under an SREO, but *decreased* by an average of 13 percent annually for those subject to at least one SREO—a predicted difference of nearly 28 percent. Overall, these results suggest that while the perceived risk of US sanctions (*sanctions risk*) does not appear to be linked to the de-dollarization of reserves, the imposition of US financial sanctions (*SREO*) is associated with a reduction in dollar holdings.

Of course, these results should be interpreted with caution given that the measure of central bank reserves used is an imperfect proxy. Because it includes private holders of US Treasuries alongside public holders, including central banks, it is a noisy measure of the outcome we are truly interested in.

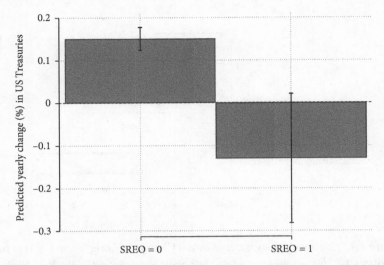

Figure 4.10. Predicted Marginal Effects of SREOs on Long-Term US Treasury Holdings. The mean predicted marginal effect as *SREO* varies from 0 (none) to 1 (at least one SREO in place) is indicated by the top of the bars. The vertical lines represent 95 percent confidence intervals around those means. The difference in means between the groups amounts to a nearly 30 percent difference in predicted changes in holdings of US Treasuries.

Still, it provides some insight into the use of the dollar as a store of value in targeted and non-targeted countries.

Conclusions

Chapter 3 presented evidence from two countries, Russia and Turkey, where the US Treasury's imposition of financial sanctions coincided with anti-dollar policy responses. Both countries significantly increased their gold holdings as part of a general trend toward de-dollarizing their reserves. This chapter expands on the case study evidence by considering whether the relationship between sanctions and gold purchases extends beyond those two cases. Using the case of Venezuela, it illustrates how gold has been used to weather withering US sanctions. Given the asset's unique properties as a hedge against the risk of sanctions, the chapter demonstrates that sanctions have contributed to the increasing popularity of gold as a reserve asset since the global financial crisis. The United States' increasing use of financial sanctions as a tool of foreign policy appears to have provoked targeted states to implement anti-dollar policies and generated more diffuse perceptions of political risk in the international currency system. The results imply that this has affected the reserve allocations of states not yet targeted by OFAC: countries likely assess their risk of being cut off from the dollar by comparing targeted countries' characteristics to their own. As their perception of the risk of sanctions grows, they take precautionary measures such as holding more gold as a hedge against those risks.

Of course, increased gold holdings do not necessarily indicate de-dollarization. Though precise measures of central bank dollar reserves are kept confidential, the chapter employs a second-best option using data on foreign holdings of US Treasuries. Here, the results are mixed. While an increased *risk* of sanctions is not associated with cuts in long-term US Treasury holdings, their *imposition* (measured as the presence of at least one SREO) is linked to de-dollarization. This contrasts with the gold reserves results, where both sanctions measures are robustly correlated with central bank reserve decisions. The difference between the two may suggest that central banks are more willing to preemptively diversify into gold than to formally de-dollarize. They engage in the former when the perceived sanctions risk is elevated, but undertake the latter only if sanctions are imposed.

The illustrations presented here and in Chapter 3 do not imply that sanctions will cause the dollar to lose its reserve currency status in the near term; sanctions are unlikely to trigger widespread diversification out of the dollar. However, the findings do illustrate that anti-dollar policies tend to be concentrated among states targeted by US sanctions and, to a lesser extent, those worried that they are next in line. Most countries, including many of the world's largest economies, are not in this group and thus have no political motive to diversify into non-dollar assets.[49] The dollar still has broad, overwhelming economic appeal whereas political risk concerns are specific to certain countries. To the extent that financial sanctions affect the dollar's global standing, they may be one contributing factor to the long-run, gradual reduction in the dollar's share of global reserves that some observers have highlighted.[50] But this does not imply that sanctions alone threaten dollar pre-eminence.

Yet even if sanctions are unlikely to jeopardize the dollar's reserve currency status, other important (if less seismic) outcomes could follow. As the Venezuelan case demonstrates, gold may be emerging as a form of insurance against US sanctions for pariah regimes. While gold reserves are no replace-ment for US Treasury bonds (especially gold held in a country's own vaults), convenience is not what is drawing certain governments to invest in the yellow metal. Regimes that invest in gold for political reasons do not do so because they view gold as a useful asset in normal times; rather, bullion forms part of a strategy akin to government "doomsday prepping." In the same way that a backyard bunker comes into its own only in the event of a nuclear or biological attack, physical gold held in a nation's own vaults to hedge against political risk realizes its true value only if sanctions are imposed. Once the US Treasury froze Venezuela's dollar-denominated assets, the gold bars on its soil—though inconvenient—became far more useful to the Maduro regime than all of its Treasuries, which a White House directive rendered useless. The same applies to Russian gold when Washington froze billions of dollars of the Kremlin's foreign exchange reserves in 2022.

Gold cannot "sanction proof" an economy. However, the message seems to be spreading that it can place limits on Washington's ability to inflict financial costs on an adversarial regime. The Venezuelan case demonstrates that gold reserves can ease the sting of US sanctions and help keep isolated regimes in power, frustrating Washington's ability to achieve its foreign policy goals. Thus, if the increase in gold reserves among certain central banks is a conse-quence of US financial sanctions, then sanctions may, in time, become less effective by virtue of the responses they provoke.

5

Sanctions, Political Risk, and the Dollar as International Payments Currency

> *We aren't ditching the dollar; the dollar is ditching us. . . . The insta-*
> *bility of dollar payments is creating a desire for many global economies*
> *to find alternative reserve currencies and create settlement systems in-*
> *dependent of the dollar. We're not the only ones doing it. Believe me.*
> Vladimir Putin[1]

The year 2017 was good for Russian businessman and billionaire oligarch Oleg Deripaska. His most important company, Rusal—the second-largest aluminum producer in the world—benefited from some significant economic tailwinds. The price of aluminum rose from roughly $0.80 to over $1.00 per pound that year, making it the best-performing metal on the London Metal Exchange. Prices were surging as analysts projected that the global demand for aluminum would outstrip supply for the foreseeable future. Deripaska approved the construction of a new Rusal aluminum smelting plant in Siberia to exploit these market trends.[2] With the help of some major US investment banks, he also launched a successful fundraising effort in London for EN+ Group, a holding company for Rusal and En+ Power, his hydroelectric power company. It was the biggest Russian initial public offering in the previous five years and the largest in the metals and mining sector that year.[3] Rusal was also attracting media attention for its pioneering development of low-carbon metal production. It used hydroelectric power to produce aluminum with a carbon footprint one-quarter the size of traditional coal-powered operations. International and industry media praised Rusal for "setting the new standard" for environmentally conscious aluminum production.[4] Deripaska was rewarded with a swelling equity valuation. Rusal's stock price nearly tripled between June 2016 and January 2018,

Bucking the Buck. Daniel McDowell, Oxford University Press. © Oxford University Press 2023.
DOI: 10.1093/oso/9780197679876.003.0006

reflecting the market's bullish view of its corporate strategy and expectations of a strong market for aluminum in the near term.

Unfortunately for Deripaska, 2018 was less kind to his corporate empire. As part of an ongoing effort to punish Russia for a range of malign activities, including the invasion of Crimea, human rights violations, interference in the 2016 US presidential election, and other cyber-related crimes, the US Treasury announced an additional round of financial sanctions on Russia on April 6. Among those targeted were seven oligarchs with close ties to Russian president Vladimir Putin and twelve of their companies.[5] Deripaska was at the top of this list, along with Rusal and six more corporations to which he was tied. He found himself in Washington's crosshairs because of a laundry list of alleged activities—operating as an agent of the Russian government abroad, money laundering, extortion, racketeering—some of which were conducted on behalf of Putin personally.

The market reaction to US financial sanctions was swift. By mid-April, Rusal's share price on the Hong Kong Stock Exchange had lost about three-quarters of its value from its January high. But the equity hit was just the start. The firm was unable to accept dollar payments for aluminum exports using US banks as financial intermediaries, which cut into its sales. Even worse, more than half of Rusal's $8.5 billion in debt was in US dollars. Since it was on the Specially Designated Nationals (SDN) list, no bank operating in the US market, including every single crucially important CHIPS correspondent bank, was willing to clear the company's debt payments. Experts warned that it was likely to default on its bonds.[6] Its outstanding debt securities were trading at junk bond status almost overnight. Major credit rating agencies downgraded the outlook on Rusal's bonds and simultaneously withdrew all ratings, while popular debt indexes announced they would no longer carry its debt prices.[7] Any association with Rusal was now toxic. The global financial system turned its back on the now isolated firm.

Deripaska and Moscow scrambled in response. Putin's government pledged to provide Rusal and other targeted Russian companies with the short-term liquidity they needed. Rusal activated a contingency plan requesting that its customers pay for purchases in euros rather than dollars.[8] It also sought the aid of a third-party Russian bank, with no ties to the US market, to facilitate a potential early repayment schedule to its debtors.[9] While none of these alternative solutions were guaranteed to work, Rusal had no choice but to seek the best path forward from a list of bad options. Ultimately, the company was saved when it reached a deal in January 2019 with the US Treasury that resulted in its removal from the SDN list. In exchange for this reprieve, Deripaska was forced to sell off his stake in the company, effectively severing all ties with the firm.

Over the last two decades, thousands of other targets have experienced what happened to Deripaska and Rusal. After being listed as an SDN, individuals, firms, and government institutions quickly realize how dependent they are on the dollar as a cross-border payments currency. They also directly experience the punishing power that the United States exercises over their ability to function in today's global economy by virtue of the dollar's status. Like Rusal, these SDNs learned that while making and receiving cross-border payments in dollars may be convenient and economically efficient, politics can spoil the currency's appeal.

The Dollar's Dominance as International Payments Currency

International payments are financial transactions between at least two parties that involve money moving across national borders. Cross-border payments begin with funds leaving the account of the individual or entity making the payment (the originator) and end when the funds are credited to the account of the individual or entity receiving payment (the beneficiary). Money is moved across borders for a variety of reasons. Commercial transactions, for example, require importers to pay exporters in foreign markets for goods purchased or services rendered. Borrowers repay foreign lenders by making cross-border debt payments. International investors rely on payment operations to complete purchases or sales of securities and equities in foreign markets. In many cases, cross-border payments require that the money being moved around the world—for example, for trade settlement or debt repayment—be converted from the originator's national currency into the currency desired by the beneficiary (typically US dollars).

An example of such transactions is international trade. As discussed in Chapter 2, even though US firms are involved in roughly only one in ten international commercial transactions, the dollar is used in about half of all trade-related transactions. It functions as the most popular third-party, or "vehicle," currency for trade. Understanding the dollar's dominance in trade requires acknowledging the tendency of financial markets to settle on a currency equilibrium that maximizes efficiency while minimizing risks and transaction costs. A significant body of work in economics, both theoretical and empirical, considers why firms choose one currency over others in which to invoice (price) their wares. Though the invoicing role of money is distinct from its medium of exchange role, there is evidence that for an "overwhelming share" of exports, the settlement currency is the same as the invoicing currency.[10] Thus, we can think of the choice of invoicing and settlement currency as one and the same.

Currencies of big economies are most likely to emerge as focal points in the marketplace, partly due to competition among firms. Local firms in larger economies tend to command a significant market share. They are also likely to price their products, and settle trade, in their own currency. Foreign competitors therefore have an incentive to price and settle their own wares in that currency since this eliminates price movements due to fluctuations in their local exchange rate. This logic then develops a sort of entropy: as additional foreign firms begin to price their products in a third-party currency like the dollar, more are expected to follow suit. As expectations converge, a "coalescing effect" develops among exporters' choices of invoicing and settlement currency.[11] Firms wishing to limit changes in the relative price of their products vis-à-vis those of their competitors are compelled to price and settle trade in the currencies of the initial focal point currency.[12]

An additional element is also involved in the market's convergence on the focal point currency. As more firms begin to price and settle trade in that currency, this increases the amount of liquidity in the currency (its "turnover") in foreign exchange markets—which makes it easier and cheaper to obtain and exchange this currency relative to alternative monies.[13] The reduced transaction costs associated with the focal point currency further reinforce its dominance. Finally, once a currency like the dollar establishes itself at the top of the trade invoicing and settlement hierarchy, no individual firm has an incentive to deviate from the norm since doing so would entail greater risks and higher transaction costs, putting it at a disadvantage relative to its competitors.[14] What economists call a "self-enforcing equilibrium" tends to emerge in currency markets. A desire to minimize risk and maximize efficiency, driven by competitive pressures, pushes firms to converge on the use of a small number of monies—the dollar chief among them—for cross-border commerce.

Yet, as this book emphasizes, economic considerations are not the only factor that actors operating in the global marketplace weigh when making currency choices. Politics also matters. Dependence on the dollar for international payments means relying on the US financial system, especially the fifty or so CHIPS correspondent banks that clear nearly all international dollar payments. Thus, maintaining access to these fundamentally important financial services requires staying on good terms with Washington. When Rusal discovered that its placement on the SDN list meant that banks would not clear dollars on its behalf for trade, debt payments, or any other purpose, it learned that politics could instantly—and completely—block the economic efficiency of using the dollar as a payments currency. This has implications for targeted firms and individuals as well as the countries in which they are located. The US government's capacity to bring powerful individuals and strategic industries to their knees by cutting off cross-border dollar payment channels is a formidable weapon that it wields against its adversaries.

As the United States' use of financial sanctions increased in the early twenty-first century, the political risk associated with the dollar as a payments currency should have become a more salient concern in many capitals, provoking anti-dollar policy orientations. We are most likely to observe such reactions in countries where individuals and firms with government ties have been targeted by the Office of Foreign Assets Control (OFAC) at US Treasury—such as Russia, Turkey, and Venezuela.[15] In these cases, the perceived political risks of using the dollar for international transactions should be higher relative to its economic advantages as a payments currency. As concerns about the rising direct costs associated with using the dollar for cross-border payments increase, governments in targeted states should look to implement anti-dollar policies that encourage local firms to use alternative currencies for international business dealings.

As the following discussion shows, US sanctions raised concerns about the political risks associated with the dollar in Ankara, Caracas, and Moscow. The rhetoric swiftly turned against the dollar in each case. Each of the targeted governments responded with a range of anti-dollar policies designed to diminish national dependence on the dollar in trade settlement, including local currency swap agreements between central banks, broader agreements with foreign trade partners to promote trade in local currencies, and launching a national cryptocurrency in the Venezuelan case. Successful de-dollarization varied across cases, however. Russia achieved the most notable progress—especially in its bilateral trade with China, but also broadly in the currency composition of settlement for its exports. Turkey and Venezuela, meanwhile, failed to achieve meaningful de-dollarization.

Russia Reduces Its Reliance on the Dollar

Chapter 3 considered how round after round of financial sanctions levied against Russian interests, beginning in 2014, created political incentives for the Central Bank of Russia (CBR) to cut its dollar holdings and shift more of its reserves into gold and non-dollar currencies like the euro and Chinese renminbi. The link between sanctions, a growing perception of political risk associated with dollar reserves, and anti-dollar reserve policies was unmistakable in that case. Yet Russian efforts to reduce dollar dependence in response to US sanctions pressures were not isolated to its reserves. Some of the most serious direct costs that the Russian economy suffered relate to the use of the dollar as a cross-border payments currency. Blacklisted firms like Rusal and blacklisted individuals like Deripaska found it exceedingly difficult to conduct international business of any sort without access to dollar payments.

Consequently, Moscow took steps to diminish the dollar's role in cross-border transactions alongside its policy of reserve diversification. Anti-dollar efforts in payments achieved some successes but fell short of the CBR's notable achievement in de-dollarizing its reserves. The difference may be due to the number of actors involved in each arena. As unitary actors in control of their own investment portfolios, central banks are capable of quickly implementing diversification strategies. It is more complicated to de-dollarize cross-border payments, which requires altering the behavior of thousands of individuals and firms, including business partners and financial institutions in other countries. Even if Moscow convinces Russian businesses to move cross-border payments out of the dollar, that is only half the battle. If foreign business partners are skeptical of shifting payments out of dollars into euros, for example, de-dollarization efforts will stall. Despite these difficulties, Moscow steadily worked to limit its reliance on the dollar and US financial institutions in the wake of ratcheting sanctions pressure since 2014. It accomplished this by promoting the use of the Chinese renminbi, the euro, and its own currency, the ruble, in cross-border transactions. Though Russia remained dependent on the dollar for cross-border transactions in certain areas, it achieved notable success in de-dollarizing payments in specific sectors of its international business relations by 2020.

Anti-Dollar Policies and De-dollarization in Payments and Trade Settlement

Russia began efforts to reduce dependence on the dollar in cross-border payments when US sanctions were enacted in response to its illegal annexation of Crimea in 2014. Anticipating a response from the US Treasury, Sergei Glazyev, an advisor to Putin and a member of the National Financial Council of the Bank of Russia, signaled how his country would respond: "We will have to move into other currencies, create our own settlement system."[16] Following the announcement of the measures, as Russian companies reportedly began to show an interest in using other currencies for cross-border business, Moscow took steps toward keeping that promise.[17] For instance, in November 2014 it launched the Financial Messaging System of the Bank of Russia (SPFS)[18] to serve as an alternative to SWIFT. The intention was to create a closed communication system that would enable Russian banks to send cross-border payment instructions that the United States would not be able to monitor. Though SPFS launched with only a small number of firms in its user base, it was a visible first step in Russia's efforts to create its own payments infrastructure.

But a messaging system alone could not solve Russia's problems. If foreign partners of Russian businesses still expected payments in dollars, that would require clearing through CHIPS correspondent banks, which would not do business with blacklisted firms. Moscow needed to develop stronger ties between local banks and those in foreign countries to weather US sanctions. This could potentially pave the way to clear payments in currencies other than the dollar. Early on, China emerged as an important partner in the Kremlin's de-dollarization efforts. As early as 2014, there were rumblings that the two governments would jointly pledge to promote payments in their local currencies. The scheme was urgent from the Russian point of view. Yet highly risk-averse Chinese banks responded to US sanctions by curtailing their own foreign exchange operations with Russian banks and cut back on financing trade between Russian and Chinese businesses.[19]

Though a formal agreement remained elusive, in 2015 the state-owned China Development Bank announced a 6 billion renminbi credit line with two major Russian banks, Sberbank and VTB Group, in a ceremony attended by President Vladimir Putin and President Xi Jingping. The new instrument was implicitly aimed at skirting sanctions by financing trade between the two countries in the Chinese currency. Other small steps were taken that year. For instance, VTB and other targeted Russian lenders heralded plans to raise funds in Hong Kong by issuing renminbi-denominated "dim sum" bonds to decrease their dependence on dollar debt. St. Petersburg-based energy giant Gazprom announced it would begin using more renminbi in its trade transactions.[20]

Nearly two years after these efforts were launched, the results remained underwhelming. Russian financial institutions that had borrowed in renminbi decided not to roll those debts over, choosing instead to repay them at maturity—suggesting little interest in maintaining, let alone increasing, the use of China's currency.[21] The head of investment at Sberbank, speaking about the renminbi credit line designed to facilitate trade in the currency, admitted that it was used "sparingly" because the funds were "more expensive than money from alternative sources."[22] The enduring economic efficiency of using the dollar remained a major impediment to making headway in Moscow's de-dollarization efforts. Yet, despite these setbacks, Russia and China managed to cut the dollar's role in trade settlement by more than 20 percent between 2014 and 2018. Efforts started slowly and faced challenges, but progress picked up steam. Press statements from Andrei Denison, the Kremlin's ambassador to China, indicate that these advancements were fueled by the growing number of correspondent accounts between Russian and Chinese banks, which allowed them to cut out US-based "intermediaries."[23]

Moscow also experimented with some more outlandish anti-dollar policies such as a gold-backed cryptocurrency issued by the CBR. However, even the head of the central bank demurred when asked about the idea, adding "in my opinion, it is more important to develop settlements in national currencies."[24] Russia has advocated using local currencies in cross-border commercial relations with other countries as well, including Iran and Turkey, especially after the April 2018 sanctions. Putin publicly trumpeted the growing use of the ruble in trade with members of the Eurasian Economic Union and secured a commitment from fellow BRICS countries to collectively develop an anti-sanctions international payments system.[25] The Kremlin even went as far as to declare its desire to conduct trade with *all* countries in national currencies rather than dollars.[26] To accomplish this, Putin's government enlisted the help of one of Russia's biggest lenders, VTB Group.

The bank was charged with developing a system to transfer trade settlement from the dollar into local currencies. The goal was to help at-risk firms deal with the direct costs of sanctions in the short term and to develop mechanisms to substantially reduce the dollar's role in Russia's international economic relations over the long term.[27] Russian companies targeted by US sanctions sought out partners willing to settle cross-border trade in rubles, euros, or pounds.[28] Others worked to convert their debts from dollars into alternative currencies. Some firms not yet designated by the US Treasury pre-emptively reduced their exposure to the dollar in anticipation that they would be targeted in the future. This included Norilsk Nickel, the world's largest producer of refined nickel, and Alrosa, the world's biggest producer of rough diamonds. Following the 2018 sanctions, both companies indicated that they were testing schemes to settle cross-border payments in rubles with customers in China and India in case they were needed in the future.[29]

Experimentation also took place in Heilongjiang Province, located in the upper northeast corner of China along the Russian border, as US sanctions targeting Russian businesses greatly intensified. Nine commercial banks in the province had established correspondent banking relationships with twenty-three banks in Russia by the end of 2018. These relationships were set up primarily to facilitate trade settlement in renminbi rather than dollars. Yet despite these new ties, the demand for renminbi settlement outpaced the supply of settlement services. The bottleneck was a product of red tape on the Russian side, where the central bank's cumbersome approval procedures for opening correspondent accounts with Chinese banks slowed the development of the budding financial network. A surprisingly analog solution was used to clear the bottleneck: more than 100 million in cash renminbi was transported across the border in five separate transfers.[30] While this was a creative workaround, the physical movement of cash was a nineteenth-century solution to a twenty-first-century problem. If anything, it reinforced the need to redouble the policy effort from both Moscow and Beijing.

The two governments continued to work toward formalizing their joint commitment to sidelining the dollar in trade settlement in a written agreement. Denisov did not hide Russia's motives for such a move, adding, "There has to be a way to have some kind of mechanism . . . to reduce the negative impact of the restrictions imposed by third-party countries."[31] Similarly, Medvedev characterized Russian and Chinese cooperation on cross-border payments as "very useful because . . . no one will be able to block . . . financial traffic."[32] The elusive formal agreement between Moscow and Beijing was finally inked in June 2019 when Xi traveled to Russia to meet with Putin. The deal was viewed in Moscow as an important signal from Beijing. Previously, China had hedged somewhat on its willingness to work with targeted Russian sectors. The deal indicated that Russia's neighbor to the south was now willing to cooperate on de-dollarizing payments for sanctioned and at-risk companies by investing in the infrastructure needed to make this possible.

The deal pledged their joint commitment to using national currencies in cross-border payments and to working together to build messaging platforms as alternatives to SWIFT. The CBR recognized VTB as the officially authorized financial institution at the heart of this new channel. As the only Russian bank with a financial license to operate within Chinese territory, VTB opened correspondent accounts in local currencies with major Chinese banks in China and Hong Kong.[33] In concert with these steps, the two sides also worked to adjust their mutual financial rules to make it easier for Russian businesses to raise funds in China, meaning repayment would be denominated in renminbi, allowing firms to cut out the dollar.[34] By the end of 2020, at least twenty-three Russian banks had joined China's alternative to SWIFT, known as the Cross-Border Interbank Payment System, or CIPS.[35] Major Russian banks were soon facilitating a steady increase in renminbi settlements among clients.[36]

Figure 5.1 presents data from the CBR documenting the success of these bilateral efforts, displaying changes in the currency composition of Russo-Chinese trade settlement between 2013 and 2020. The top panel reports the settlement currency for Russian exports to China (the currencies that Chinese importers used to pay Russian exporters for their goods and services). In 2013, the dollar was used to cover more than 95 percent of these transactions. Following the 2014 sanctions, its position began to decline, albeit modestly, until the US Treasury's April 2018 measures were announced. The dollar's role then fell quickly, settling at less than half of all Chinese payments for Russian goods and services. Russian firms exporting to China quickly shifted from the dollar to the euro as their settlement currency of choice.

This is notable for two reasons. First, the link between this change in the currency composition of trade settlement and US sanctions is undeniable. The harsh penalties imposed in 2018 by the Trump administration provoked a dramatic change in the currency preferences of Russian exporting firms. Second, despite the platitudes from Beijing and Moscow about promoting the use of the ruble and renminbi in bilateral trade, the euro emerged as the dollar's replacement in this case, apparently due to decisions made by large Russian energy firms. Anticipating that they would one day face US financial sanctions, they adjusted their approach to trade settlement. For example,

EXPORTS

IMPORTS

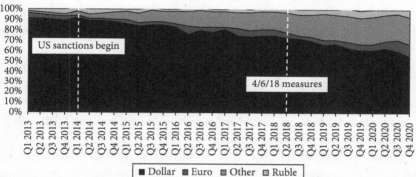

■ Dollar ■ Euro ■ Other ■ Ruble

Figure 5.1. Currency Composition of Russia-China Trade Settlement, 2013–2020. The upper (lower) panel reports the currency composition of payments for Russian exports (imports) to China. Both indicate a clear de-dollarization trend, but it is more notable for Russian export payments, which dropped sharply following the harsh sanctions of April 2018. Those measures, which provoked a rapid de-dollarization of Russian foreign exchange reserves (see Figure 3.3), also led to a significant diminution of the dollar's role in Russian export settlement and an increase in the use of the euro. On the import side, the dollar's role steadily declined following the 2014 US sanctions, yet there is no obvious discontinuity in the trend associated with US Office of Foreign Assets Control (OFAC) actions. For import payments, the "other" category takes the dollar's declining share, indicating that the renminbi was the beneficiary of the de-dollarization of Russian import payments.

oil giant Rosneft began pricing and accepting payments for its exports in euros beginning in 2019.[37] Although top Russian economic officials touted the ruble as "a very good currency" for the energy trade, partners like China appeared to disagree.[38] This may reflect reluctance on the part of Chinese importers to accept pricing and settlement of Russian goods and services in rubles due to its relatively volatile exchange rate compared to a stable currency like the euro.

The bottom panel of Figure 5.1 displays data on Russian payments for Chinese imported goods and services. The general trend away from the dollar holds here as well, but there are notable differences. There is no abrupt change following a specific round of US sanctions. Instead, the use of the dollar appears as a steady, almost linear diminution from 2014 on. In addition, the currency taking the lion's share of the ground ceded by the dollar appears to be the renminbi, not a third-party currency like the euro. Though CBR data do not specifically identify the renminbi's share of settlements in this case, the "other" category—which includes China's currency—expands during this period. By the fourth quarter of 2020, "other" currencies were used to settle nearly a quarter of Russian imports from China; the dollar was used for about half, down from 90 percent in 2013. These data are consistent with case study evidence which imply that Russian businesses' access to China's currency increased over time as correspondent banking relationships developed between the two countries.

Russia achieved mixed success in de-dollarizing its trade settlement with countries other than China (Figures 5.2 and 5.3). The dashed vertical lines indicate when US sanctions begin in 2014 (left) and when the April 2018 sanctions were imposed (right). In two cases, Belarus and Turkey, there is no apparent pattern in the timing of US financial sanctions and changes in the currency composition of trade settlement. The dollar's significant and stable role in Russian–Turkish trade during this period is notable, given that Washington targeted both countries and Putin and Erdoğan have both pledged to push for trade settlement in local currencies. Despite their mutual interest in achieving this outcome, de-dollarization remained elusive. Russian efforts to reduce the dollar's role in trade settlement with the European Union (EU) and India were more successful. In these cases, the observed de-dollarization appears to be related to the timing of US sanctions. Progress was concentrated almost entirely in payments for Russian exports, as the currency structure of Russian import payments was stable in both cases. On the export payment side, however, the use of the dollar declined steadily in each case.

In trade with the EU, the dollar's share fell from around 70 percent in 2013 to just over 40 percent in 2020, as depicted in Figure 5.2. The dollar's declining settlement share in Russian exports to the EU was supplanted by a growing role for the euro. The common currency's position increased by roughly

EXPORTS

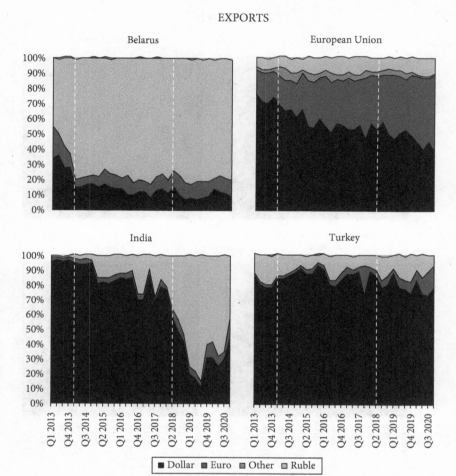

Figure 5.2. Currency Composition of Russian Export Settlement, 2013–2020.
The Central Bank of Russia (CBR) data indicate that the de-dollarization in
export settlement succeeded in some cases but not in others. The link between
de-dollarization and major waves of sanctions (vertical lines) is clear in only
some of the cases. Moreover, where the dollar's role declined, the currency that
absorbed its lost market share varied.

30 percent during this period, becoming the most used currency in Russian
export settlement by 2020. There is a noticeable increase in the euro's role following the 2014 sanctions; the pace picks up again in 2019 following measures the previous year that targeted Russian energy firms like EuroSibEnergo,

IMPORTS

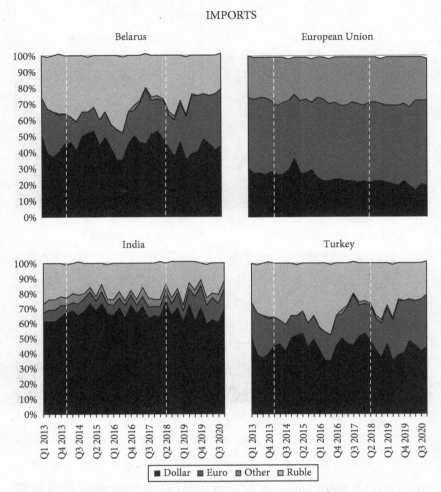

Figure 5.3. **Currency Composition of Russian Import Settlement, 2013–2020.** The Central Bank of Russia (CBR) data reveal that de-dollarization in import settlement was less successful than export settlement. The cases examined here indicate no relationship between the timing of sanctions (vertical lines) and changes in the currency composition of trade settlement.

Renova Group, and Gazprom Burenie. That move not only cut targeted firms off from the dollar payments system; it also sent chills throughout the Russian energy sector as other major firms were forced to recognize their own vulnerability. The EU was Russia's most important trading partner at the time, and energy dominated their bilateral commercial relations. For instance, the EU was the destination for more than three-quarters of Russian oil and gas exports during the study period. Given Russia's dependence on European imports of its oil and gas and the threat posed by US sanctions, it is not surprising that high-ranking Kremlin officials and major Russian energy firms began asking their European partners to shift to euros in trade settlement following the 2018 measures.[39] Putin again called on European importers to use their own currency to pay for Russian energy in 2021 following a new round of US sanctions from the Biden administration.[40] It is worth emphasizing here that just one year prior to Russia's brutal and unprovoked invasion of Ukraine, Europe was bending over backward to help Putin in his de-dollarization efforts. In an extraordinarily rapid foreign policy U-turn, that invasion forced the EU to completely rethink its energy relations with Moscow and target the Kremlin with its own suite of sanctions.

The dollar's settlement share also dropped notably in Russian exports to India during this period, from roughly 95 percent in 2013 to 20 percent in 2019 before rising somewhat the following year. There are two principal differences in this form of de-dollarization compared to trade with Europe. First, in trade settlement with India it was the ruble, not the euro, that took over the dollar's declining role. In this case, Moscow successfully convinced Indian businesses to use its currency in commercial relations. Second, while non-dollar trade settlement was concentrated in the energy sector in the European case, the ruble gained its foothold in Indian purchases of Russian arms. Once again, these moves appear to directly flow from two distinct stages of US financial sanctions.

The first stage was in September 2014 when Washington targeted five major Russian defense firms. This step was taken six months after Treasury's first round of sanctions against Moscow for its invasion of Crimea.[41] Figure 5.2 displays a visible drop in the dollar's role following the third quarter of 2014—slightly to the right of the first dashed line—which coincides with Treasury's move against the Russian defense industry. The next notable, and more sizable, drop in the dollar's use as a trade settlement currency comes just before Treasury's April 2018 sanctions, the second dashed line in the figure. This coincides with the release of a list of thirty-nine Russian "defense or intelligence" firms identified as potential sanction targets by the US State Department in October 2017.[42] In response, India suspended payments to the Russian defense firm Rosoboronexport. This prompted the two sides to develop workarounds. In the summer of 2019, the Kremlin announced a new "confidential" settlement scheme with New Deli, involving Russian state-owned bank Promsvyazbank PJSC, that would enable India to purchase Russian defense products using rubles.[43] However, based on the direction of the CBR data, those systems were functioning prior to any public fanfare surrounding an official deal given the steady decline in the dollar's trade role in the previous year.

There is less compelling evidence, however, that Russia achieved notable de-dollarization in import payments (see Figure 5.3). Besides trade settlement with the EU, where the dollar's already modest role diminished slightly during the period, there are no observable patterns in the other cases. This suggests that Russia's success in de-dollarizing import payments with China may be a unique case. The lack of apparent success on the import side may be less surprising since the dollar's role was already smaller even before US sanctions targeting Russia.

Cross-border payments involve more than just trade settlement. Firms and governments also rely on payment systems to settle debts. As is common around the world, Russian businesses have tended to borrow in dollars in securities markets. Repayment thus requires these firms to maintain access to dollar-based payment channels. Firms that are blacklisted by the US Treasury may not only default on existing debts, but this designation also makes it exceedingly difficult for them to raise additional dollar funds. Numerous anecdotes referenced above suggest that Moscow sought to de-dollarize trade settlement as well as debt repayment. The available data indicate that the Kremlin made modest progress on this front as well.

The top and bottom panels of Figure 5.4 present the currency composition of Russian debt for its banking and non-banking sectors, respectively. Dollar-denominated debts peaked at roughly 70 percent for both sectors in the fourth quarter of 2015, after which the dollar's share begins to fall slowly. By 2020, the dollar's share of Russian corporate debt was about 50 percent, a non-trivial reduction. For the banking sector, the ruble was the main beneficiary of the dollar's declining role. The use of Russia's currency grew from a low of 10 percent in 2014 to more than a quarter of bank debt by the end of 2020. This shift appears to validate Russian officials who, as far back as 2017, indicated that US sanctions made Russian banks prefer to borrow in rubles instead of dollars.[44] For non-banking enterprises in Russia, the euro's share increased from 10 percent to nearly 30 percent by 2020. Though it is only speculation, as Russian energy firms grew flush with euros from accepting more of that currency for export payments, they may have increased their euro-denominated debt

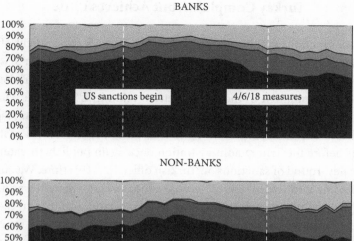

Figure 5.4. Currency Composition of Russian Debt, 2013–2020. Russian corporations cut their use of the dollar in debt issuances during this period to the benefit of the ruble and the euro. Data source: Central Bank of Russia.

issuances in kind. What is less clear in the figure, however, is a noticeable link between the timing of US sanctions and adjustments in the currency structure of Russian debt.

We do not observe any significant increase in the share of "other" currencies (such as renminbi) in Russian business debts among either banks or non-banking firms. This suggests that the joint effort by Beijing and Moscow to boost fundraising in China yielded only tiny gains. This supports anecdotes discussed above indicating that indicate Russian firms had little appetite for renminbi-denominated debts, preferring rubles or euros instead. In sum, Russia managed a 15 to 20 percent shift away from the dollar into non-dollar currencies in its corporate debt structure in a matter of four years. This is a meaningful change that provides additional evidence that sanctions motivated successful Russian anti-dollar policy efforts.

Turkey Complains, but Achieves Little

The 2018 sanctions that blacklisted a group of Turkish government officials with close ties to President Erdoğan, discussed at length in Chapter 3, were in place for less than a year (imposed in April and lifted in November). Yet they marked a key moment in the steady deterioration in US-Turkish relations. Despite the removal of the initial sanctions that were imposed in response to Ankara's imprisonment of an American pastor, it was only a matter of months before the Trump administration once again publicly threatened to enact a new round of sanctions on Turkish officials.[45] This time, Washington was wielding punitive measures because Erdoğan's government was in talks with Moscow about purchasing the Russian-made S-400 surface-to-air missile system, which would violate Turkey's security pact with its NATO allies. Eventually, Washington's threat turned into action. Using the 2017 Countering America's Adversaries through Sanctions Act, the Trump administration hit Turkish undersecretary of defense, Ismail Demir, with a range of travel and economic sanctions, including freezing all his financial assets.

Compared to Russia, Turkey has suffered only limited direct costs from US sanctions. The United States focused its punishment on a relatively small group of Turkish government officials, whereas in Russia it targeted major corporations operating in strategic industries as well as numerous oligarchs, state officials, and state institutions. Yet even if Turkey's economy did not suffer as severely as Russia's, the successive rounds of sanctions demonstrated that the United States was willing to use the dollar as a coercive tool against its NATO ally. Past cases indicate that future rounds of sanctions could be far more severe. Countries like Iran, North Korea, and Russia all initially faced limited sanctions pressure, which increased significantly over time.

Chapter 3 documents Turkey's moves to adjust its foreign exchange reserve holdings amid the pressure of US sanctions, reducing dollars and increasing its exposure to gold and other non-dollar currency assets. Ankara also signaled an interest in de-dollarizing trade settlement, similar in style to rhetoric and policy responses out of Moscow. The threat of sanctions appears to have been at least partly behind that impulse. However, while Russia made notable strides in de-dollarizing its trade relations following US sanctions, the illustrations below demonstrate that Turkey's anti-dollar policies failed to achieve similar levels of success.

Anti-dollar Policies in Payments and Trade Settlement

Turkey's interest in reducing its dependence on the dollar as a trade settlement currency dates back to 2007, when the government began exploring the possibility of settling trade in local currencies with select economic partners.[46] In 2012, Erdoğan's government signed bilateral local currency swap agreements with China and Pakistan to promote cross-border trade and investment in local currencies. Because Ankara's interest in de-dollarizing its cross-border payments began years prior to the US sanctions, these initial steps are not well explained by political risk concerns. Turkish policy at that time was most likely motivated by concerns about stabilizing the exchange rate of the Turkish lira. It considered using local currencies in trade settlement, especially to pay for imports, to reduce pressure that was weakening the lira against the dollar.[47]

The economic motives behind Turkey's initial efforts to de-dollarize cross-border payments complicates this book's effort to discern an independent effect of US sanctions on the government's attitude toward the US currency. Evidence linking sanctions to anti-dollar policies needs to be weighed alongside the broader context in which Turkey has worked to reduce its dollar dependence. A careful review of the timeline of events leading up to and following the US Treasury's targeting of Ankara suggests that Washington's coercive actions intensified the government's interest in de-dollarizing payments due to growing political risk concerns.

Though OFAC did not list Turkish targets as SDNs until the fall of 2018, serious sanctions threats against Turkey became public in September 2017. It was in this context that Erdoğan's rhetoric became increasingly anti-dollar. For example, speaking to business leaders in Kyrgystan, he complained that "international trade dependence on the dollar is becoming a bigger problem.... [D]ependence on dollars should be ended."[48] In an apparent step to make such an outcome possible, the Turkish central bank (TCMB) signed a local currency swap deal with Iran in October 2017.[49] Ankara's interest in de-dollarization had further aligned with that of Tehran, which was also facing the threat of another round of sanctions from a new, hawkish Trump administration. The central banks publicized the deal as a mechanism that would promote bilateral trade settlement in lira and Iran's rial. Though no direct link to sanctions appears in the Turkish media coverage of the deal, it was heralded as part of Turkey's plan to "expand *strategic ties* between the two nations," implying that political motives played a role in the agreement.[50]

Then, the TCMB signed yet another local currency swap agreement with Qatar, just days after OFAC levied Magnitsky sanctions against two Turkish government officials.[51] Shortly afterward, Turkish officials reached a local currency settlement deal with fellow sanctions targets, Russia and Iran. In this deal, the trio publicly pledged to rely less on the dollar and more on their own currencies in the trade of petroleum, natural gas, and other commodities.[52] China, meanwhile, publicly supported Erdoğan's call to use national currencies rather than the dollar in trade.[53]

Erdoğan's public speeches further suggest the link between sanctions and Turkey's post-2017 anti-dollar turn in payments and trade. In the buildup to OFAC's 2018 sanctions, a hardline conservative Turkish newspaper with close ties to Erdoğan's AKP Party described Ankara as having particular "objections to the use of the dollar as a foreign policy instrument." This was followed by a discussion of the government's efforts to reduce dollar dependence in trade settlement, especially with key economic partners like Russia, Iran, and China.[54] Following the announcement of sanctions, Erdoğan railed against Washington's "economic war" against Turkey. He further pledged that his country would move to use local currencies in settling trade: "China, Russia, Iran, Ukraine, countries with which we have the largest trade volume, are preparing to carry out trade in national currencies."[55] When word emerged that Washington might hit Turkey with another round of financial sanctions for its planned purchase of the Russian S-400 air-defense missile system, Ankara and Moscow held "urgent" talks about connecting Turkish banks and firms to Russia's SPFS payment messaging system.[56] In October 2019, the two spurned countries reached a formal agreement laying out plans to use the ruble and lira in cross-border payments and to use the Russian messaging system instead of SWIFT.[57]

Despite Erdoğan's complaints and his government's anti-dollar cooperation with other sanctioned powers in the region, he achieved little. According to Turkey's own national data, the country had no apparent success in reducing the dollar's role in trade. Figure 5.5 displays the currency composition of Turkey's cross-border trade settlement with all partners.[58] The dashed, vertical line indicates when US sanctions threats became public. After that point, OFAC designated Turkish officials on two separate occasions (once in 2018 and once in 2019). There is no indication that the dollar's role in cross-border payments for goods and services was diminished in any way—on either the import or export side.

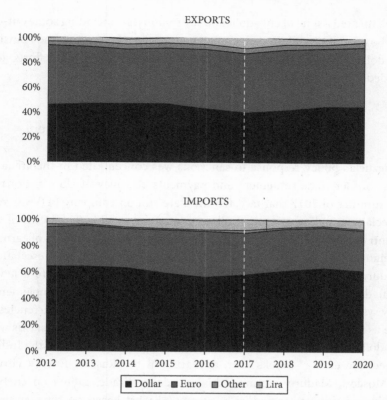

Figure 5.5. Currency Composition of Turkish Trade Settlement, 2012–
2020. Despite public anti-dollar rhetoric and policies following the threat of
US sanctions in 2017 and the imposition of measures in 2018, the data do not
indicate attendant de-dollarization in Turkish trade. Vertical line represents
when US sanctions threats began. Data source: Turkish Statistical Institute.

Venezuela's Crypto Flop

Washington first targeted Venezuela with financial sanctions in 2015. By the
end of 2019, the White House had issued a total of seven sanctions-related
Executive Orders. Despite "maximum" US pressure, the regime of autocrat
Nicolás Maduro held onto power, funding its financially isolated economy
through illicit sales of gold reserves on the international black market. As
access to dollar payments was cut off for central government institutions,
the central bank, and major industries like the state-owned oil sector,
Caracas swiftly recognized the political risk posed by dollar dependence. It

implemented a suite of anti-dollar policy responses—including some out-of-the-box measures—designed to open new avenues for settling trade outside the dollar-based financial system. Despite Venezuela's creative efforts, few yielded meaningful gains.

Anti-dollar Policies in Payments and Trade Settlement

Venezuela's policy response to sanctions was concentrated in the arena of cross-border trade settlement and payments. A volley of US sanctions in the summer of 2017 that targeted the state-run oil company PDVSA were especially crippling given that oil accounted for roughly 95 percent of the country's export earnings. PDVSA was the state's primary means of earning foreign exchange. In response to the Trump administration's escalation, Maduro railed against the dollar. In a marathon address before a newly created sham legislative body, Maduro pledged that he would "implement a new system of international payments" and "create a basket of currencies to free us from the dollar." He then emphatically added, "If they pursue us with the dollar, we'll use the Russian ruble, the yuan [renminbi], yen, the Indian rupee, the euro."[59] Weeks later, appearing at the Russian Energy Forum in Moscow, Maduro continued his anti-dollar tirade, calling on energy-producing states to introduce a currency basket based on the renminbi, ruble, and "other currencies" for oil trading, to extricate the global industry from the dollar's grip.[60]

By telling his country's oil exporters they could no longer accept dollars for payment and that they should begin pricing crude in euros rather than dollars, Maduro implemented the policy equivalent of the expression, "You can't fire me, I quit!"[61] Washington's latest sanctions had made that decision for him, but he took the opportunity to claim credit. To facilitate this transition, the regime encouraged private banks operating in the country to open correspondent accounts with Evrofinance, a Russian bank in which the Venezuelan government had an ownership stake.[62] But funneling all of Venezuela's cross-border payments through one Russian bank was not a workable solution. Plus, Evrofinance ran afoul of the US Treasury and was itself cut off from CHIPS correspondent banks, once again isolating Venezuela.[63]

The Maduro regime responded with a policy that was equal parts ambitious and outlandish: with Putin's assistance, the South American country created its own national cryptocurrency.[64] Unoriginally dubbed the *petro* and issued by the Central Bank of Venezuela (Banco Central de Venezuela, BCV), the monetary unit was, like Bitcoin, based on blockchain technology. What distinguished Venezuela's coin from more commonly known cryptos was its link to the country's vast oil wealth. The initial coin offering amounted to 100 million petros, purportedly valued at $5.9 billion and backed by 5 billion barrels of the country's crude. Upon its launch, banks in Venezuela were ordered to adopt the new money as a unit of account, and industries were encouraged to settle trade in the new coin. Maduro was not coy in explaining the motives behind the currency's creation. The petro, he explained, would help his country "overcome the [US] financial blockade" while "allow[ing] us to move toward new forms of international financing" to challenge the "tyranny of the dollar."[65]

A BCV press release provides further insight into the thinking behind the project. According to the central bank, the petro was designed to facilitate trade settlement, including the "importation of food, medicines and basic necessities."[66] While foreign exporters might refuse to accept the hyperinflated bolivar in exchange for goods, BCV's thinking was that a cryptocurrency tied to Venezuela's natural resource wealth could be more appealing. State-run media also trumpeted the government's desire to sell oil in petros to evade sanctions.[67] A report published on the BCV's website detailed the advantages of cryptocurrencies for economies facing sanctions. It noted that, due to blockchain technology, cryptocurrencies do not require foreign correspondent banks to act as intermediaries between the originator and the beneficiary.

As previously discussed, a key consequence of US sanctions is that SDNs are cut off from CHIPS correspondent banks and thus cannot transact in dollars for cross-border business activities. In a hypothetical cryptocurrency world, both CHIPS correspondent banks and dollars are unnecessary, and US financial sanctions lose their bite. While stopping short of mentioning sanctions as the reason for lost ties with correspondent bank partners, the BCV paper promises that "this mechanism is very attractive for markets that . . . face problems when it comes to obtaining and maintaining their correspondent relationships."[68] This is an obvious allusion to the loss of correspondent accounts due to landing on the OFAC blacklist.

Despite these extravagant claims, the petro failed to gain acceptance as an international medium of exchange. Described by commentators as "worthless," a "shuddering failure," and "a laughingstock," the blockchain did not free Venezuela from the financial isolation caused by US sanctions.[69] Facing the petro's swift failure, in 2019 the Maduro regime explored the possibility of joining the Russian and Chinese payment messaging systems, SPFS and CIPS, respectively. However, neither payment system had listed a single Venezuelan bank as a participant by 2021. In 2019 Venezuela received a lifeline from Beijing, which purchased $700 billion in oil from PDVSA using renminbi. But even this action took months to execute as the two governments struggled to locate banks willing to facilitate the transaction.[70] By the end of 2019, China had reportedly cut off purchases due to fears of angering the United States; however, it eventually restarted purchases the following year.[71]

Conclusions

What do these cases tell us about how US sanctions affect anti-dollar policies and de-dollarization in cross-border payments? In each, US financial sanctions raised political risk concerns in the targeted states. In the wake of US Treasury actions, leaders in all three countries publicly denounced the dollar's dominance in payments and pledged to use other currencies, either local monies or new fantastical crypto coins, to engage in cross-border economic activities. The rhetorical responses demonstrate that targeted states recognized that using their adversary's currency in payments exposed local firms, and at times the state itself, to direct costs associated with dollar use. The responses were not limited to rhetoric, however. In every case, though with some meaningful variation, anti-dollar policies designed to reduce dollar dependence followed from newly realized political risk concerns.

In Russia, Putin's regime launched its own payments messaging system, independent of SWIFT. The Kremlin also enlisted the help of some big Russian financial institutions to develop correspondent banking accounts in key partner countries. This was designed to enable its firms to conduct payments in non-dollar currencies in order to dump the dollar and route around CHIPS banks. Moscow also sought the assistance of foreign governments that shared its interest in de-risking economic relations by diminishing their use of the dollar in cross-border payments. China emerged as the key partner in this endeavor, yet the Europeans and Indians also responded positively to Russian overtures.

In Turkey, a renewed push to settle trade in local currencies began between 2017 and 2018, generating strategic ties with the fellow sanctioned states of

Iran and Russia. Ankara signed new local currency swap agreements with foreign partners, complained about the dollar's dominance, and pronounced a rekindled commitment to settle trade in local currencies. These moves were small in comparison to Russian efforts; however, they are in proportion to the more limited costs the country suffered at the hands of US sanctions. Overall, political risk perceptions and anti-dollar policies in Turkey correlate with the timing of US Treasury actions, which is consistent with a causal story.

Finally, in Venezuela, Maduro's public remarks following US sanctions reveal a clear understanding of the political risk his country faced as a result of dollar centrality. He pledged to move the country's cross-border payments into non-dollar currencies and even sought to route cross-border payments through Russian banks to achieve that end. Overall, Venezuela's anti-dollar policy response was the most experimental, as the insular economy launched its own oil-backed cryptocurrency. Its spectacular, and perhaps predictable, failure made the country appear more helpless than ever and left it no less isolated than it was before.

US sanctions led to a uniform recognition of the political risk associated with dollar use in payments and to an anti-dollar policy response across all cases. However, they did not cause an equally uniform result in terms of de-dollarization. This echoes a point made in Chapter 1: de-dollarization does not necessarily follow from anti-dollar policies. While such policies signal a government's desire to reduce the economy's reliance on the dollar, that goal often remains elusive. Russian efforts to de-link from the dollar in cross-border payments achieved some real successes. For example, there was a steady shift in the currency composition of Russian corporate debts. Firms successfully raised more funds in rubles and euros, cutting dollar dependence and partially insulating themselves from future rounds of US sanctions. There were also notable victories in trade relations with three major partner economies—China, India, and the EU. This was no small feat.

If such changes endure, they may serve as a blueprint for other countries seeking to limit their use of the US currency. At the same time, despite these clear wins for Moscow, the dollar's diminished role in trade was concentrated on the export side. Russian firms still depended on using the dollar to pay for imports at the end of 2020. Coupled with selective cooperation from three key export markets, this pattern suggests that Russian businesses used non-dollar currencies in trade settlement when they had no other choice. De-dollarization was driven mostly by industries that were denied access to the dollar-based financial system or had reason to fear they may soon be blacklisted. In this way, Putin's comments on de-dollarization from June 2021 appear apt:

> Let's assume we are unable to make payments in dollars with our partners in defense cooperation. You see? We have a problem. What should we do? We switch to paying in national currencies or currencies of other countries. Our US partners force us to do this. We are not moving away from the dollar purposefully, we are compelled to do so. When we do this, a system of financial relations with our partners is formed outside dollar transactions.[72]

Russia's cross-border payment messaging system, SPFS, has grown steadily, but slowly, since its launch in 2014. Russian media reports indicated that 400 financial institutions had joined by 2020. Traffic on the network almost doubled that year, making up one-fifth of its domestic traffic. While most participants were Russian banks, twenty-three lenders from six countries—Armenia, Belarus, Germany, Kazakhstan, Kyrgyzstan, and Switzerland—were also identified as users. To put this into perspective, SWIFT boasted more than 11,000 member institutions spanning 200 countries and handled 40 million messages per day that year.[73] Yet for Moscow, the goal was not necessarily to compete with SWIFT but rather to create a functional alternative to limit the damage inflicted by US sanctions. Moreover, the Kremlin and its partners recognized that this project would take time. In the words of Andrei Kostin, head of VTB Group, the Russian bank Putin tapped to lead the development of a new payments system, success "may take ten, maybe 20 years, but the balance will change gradually."[74]

Turkey and Venezuela did not manage to achieve de-dollarization in payments. Turkey's failure may reflect its limited anti-dollar policy response. Had the US targeted strategic sectors of the Turkish economy, as it did in Russia, Ankara may have acted more boldly. However, the structure of Turkey's trade relations make it less able to de-dollarize payments—especially trade settlement. Russia had the most success in de-dollarizing trade settlement on the export side of the ledger. Russia is a prolific natural resource and energy exporter. Its economy also boasted annual trade surpluses between 2000 and 2020. If major Russian firms required non-dollar transactions due to being on a Treasury blacklist, their buyers may have had no choice but to accede to workarounds. By comparison, Turkey's economy was heavily import dependent, consistently running trade deficits during the first two decades of the twenty-first century. De-dollarization in this case would require progress on import payments, which would entail convincing foreign suppliers to accept non-dollar currencies for payment—a more difficult task.

Venezuela's lack of progress toward reducing dollar dependence suggests its efforts may have been symbolic and aspirational. US sanctions so completely isolated the country that even China, a nation that is sympathetic to efforts to weaken the dollar's grip on the global economy, was unwilling to maintain renminbi-denominated purchases of its oil for a time. The case serves as a powerful reminder that launching policy efforts to reduce dollar dependence is the easy part. Achieving de-dollarization is far harder.

6

Payment Politics

Anti-Dollar Responses to Sanctions in Trade Settlement

*Non-American companies that feel restricted in their business activi-
ties by US sanctions . . . have an economic incentive to no longer use the
US dollar in cross-border transactions.*

Jörg Krämer, Chief Economist of Commerzbank[1]

On a cold mid-December day in 1962, President John F. Kennedy spoke to
the Economic Club of New York in the opulent Grand Ballroom of the his-
toric Waldorf Astoria Hotel in midtown Manhattan. Here he laid out his
strategy for sustaining American leadership in the world. The United States'
position would be secured, he declared, by the robustness of its economy. Yet
economic dynamism at home, Kennedy argued, was inextricably linked to
the state of the world economy. "Our strength and growth," he concluded,
"depends on the strength of others, the spread of free world trade." Kennedy
maintained that economic interdependence would allow the United States
to enjoy "continued confidence in our leadership and our currency."[2] At the
time, the United States was still working to rebuild the global trading system
that had been decimated by more than a decade of economic depression and
world war. The General Agreement on Tariffs and Trade (GATT), predecessor to the World Trade Organization (WTO), had just launched its sixth
round of trade negotiations—talks that became known as the "Kennedy
Round" following his assassination.

Ultimately the US-led effort to establish a multilateral, rules-based trading
system was wildly successful. By 2020, the total volume of world trade was
more than forty times greater than it was in 1950—a staggering 4,100 percent
growth rate over a period of seventy years.[3] While the connection may not
seem obvious at first, the post-war explosion in world trade was not unrelated to the dollar's global dominance. The vast majority of world trade, as

Bucking the Buck. Daniel McDowell, Oxford University Press. © Oxford University Press 2023.
DOI: 10.1093/oso/9780197679876.003.0007

this book has described, relies on banks to act as cross-border intermediaries between importing and exporting firms. Trade finance services reassure firms on both sides of an international transaction that the exporter will receive the payment, and the importer will receive the goods.[4] Banks involved in trade provide their services using a small number of currencies. The dollar is far and away the most popular.[5] Exporting firms around the world also tend to prefer pricing (or invoicing) their wares in dollars. Generally, goods are paid for in the same currency in which they are invoiced; thus, about half of all world trade is settled in US dollars. Recent theoretical work in economics links currency dominance in the trade invoicing role to dominance in other financial arenas.[6] That is, once a currency establishes supremacy in trade invoicing and settlement, it is well positioned to gain a leading role as a key international currency in corporate debt issuance, foreign exchange reserves, and so on. This helps explain the tendency for a singular, pre-eminent global currency to emerge. In sum, dollar dominance generally depends a great deal on its supremacy in the trade invoicing and settlement roles.

Of course, the rule of the dollar in cross-border commerce also means that most countries' trade relations are vulnerable to US financial sanctions. For example, US sanctions against state-owned Venezuelan oil company PDVSA in 2019, and related measures the following year, barred all banks with American operations from providing financial services, including trade finance, on behalf of the energy giant or any of its buyers. Venezuelan oil exports, which had been steadily declining since 2015 due to reduced capital investment in the sector, fell farther once the company was cut off from the dollar-based banking system. Washington's financial blockade choked off most of the remaining international market for the country's oil. In January 2019, more than twenty-five active Venezuelan oil rigs were producing over 1 million barrels per day for world markets. By the end of 2020, only one oil rig remained online, and exports had fallen by two-thirds to roughly 340,000 barrels per day.[7]

The Venezuelan case and others like it serve as a warning to US adversaries: Washington can unilaterally disconnect critical export sectors from the dollar-based financial system and, consequently, the world economy. As awareness of these capabilities has grown with Washington's increasing use of financial sanctions, targeted and at-risk governments should be incentivized to explore anti-dollar policy measures in trade. Chapter 5 described how governments in Russia, Turkey, and Venezuela responded to US sanctions with a suite of anti-dollar policies designed to de-dollarize cross-border payments, especially in trade settlement. While many of these efforts were unsuccessful, the Russian case illustrates that cross-border payments can be de-dollarized, especially within certain bilateral trade relationships.

This chapter extends the analysis beyond individual case studies in three meaningful ways. First, if sanctions generate broader political risk concerns associated with the dollar's use in trade, we should observe more widespread evidence linking sanctions to anti-dollar policies—such as local currency swap agreements—in cross-border trade invoicing and settlement. Pairs of central banks sign such agreements to facilitate the settlement of bilateral trade in local currencies rather than dollars. Their popularity has risen alongside the growing use of sanctions. This chapter presents evidence that countries sanctioned by the US Treasury are, on average, more likely to enter such arrangements—strengthening the link between US sanctions and anti-dollar policies in cross-border payments. Yet as this book makes clear, anti-dollar policies do not always result in de-dollarization.

The second part of the chapter extends the analysis by illustrating a link between the risk of US sanctions and dollar dependence in trade. Countries that have been targeted by Washington are less reliant on the dollar in trade settlement than those that have not—a pattern suggestive of de-dollarization. There is also modest, though less consistent, evidence of a relationship between perceptions of the risk of sanctions and de-dollarization in trade. Though the results are far from conclusive, they provide limited evidence of de-dollarization designed to pre-empt US sanctions.

The chapter's third section focuses on the private sector. It explores the effects of US sanctions on how managers of multinational corporations think about the currencies they use in their international trade transactions. Anti-dollar policies in trade will succeed only if firms are willing to take steps to reduce their own dollar dependence in trade. A firm-level survey experiment fielded to over 1,000 multinational firms operating in Vietnam—a country not targeted by the US Treasury—provides limited evidence that sanctions can influence private sector risk calculations: information about sanctions subtly piques managers' interest in learning more about non-dollar trade settlement in currencies other than the dollar.

Collectively, the illustrations in the chapter have meaningful implications for the future of the dollar and the power of US sanctions. In the long term, the partial migration away from the dollar in trade settlement may diminish the dollar's global status, though such changes would likely be minor and

concentrated among a subset of US adversaries. Less seismic, yet meaningful, consequences are also possible. If sanctions *do* provoke governments
to pursue anti-dollar policies, prompt firms to reconsider their currency
choices, and ultimately lead to even modest levels of de-dollarization in trade
settlement in targeted and at-risk states, Washington will be less able to disrupt foreign industries' commercial relationships.

Sanctions and Local Currency Swap Agreements

Prior to and immediately after the United States sanctioned close government
allies of President Erdoğan, the Turkish central bank signed swap agreements
with its counterparts in Iran and Qatar. Such agreements, which facilitate
the direct exchange of national currencies between monetary authorities,[8]
are becoming increasingly popular.[9] In theory, swap deals make it easier for
firms in cooperating countries to access each other's currencies, promoting
the use of local money in cross-border payments, especially trade settlement.
Since the dollar is the most popular currency in trade, these deals are implicitly (or sometimes explicitly) designed to reduce reliance on the dollar for
cross-border settlement of commerce. Indeed, prior studies suggest that local
currency swap agreements can facilitate modest levels of de-dollarization.[10]
Such agreements should therefore serve as an appealing anti-dollar policy
for countries under pressure from US financial sanctions. In principle,
swaps could provide a short-term solution for a country whose exporting
firms have been cut off from dollar-based financial services by increasing its
access to the local currencies of its major trading partners. As banks in the
two countries gain greater access to each other's currencies, they may begin
to conduct trade settlement business directly with one another, cutting out
the dollar and US correspondent banks, including the all-important CHIPS
(Clearing House Interbank Payments System) institutions.

Anecdotal evidence that swaps operate as anti-dollar responses to
sanctions extends beyond the Turkish case. For example, immediately following the initial round of US sanctions targeting Moscow for its 2014 invasion of Crimea, Beijing announced it was willing to increase the size of
an existing currency swap agreement between the People's Bank of China
(PBOC) and the Central Bank of Russia (CBR). Though the size of the swap
line was not increased at that time, the CBR did acquire renminbi through
the arrangement in 2015 and 2016. Russian banks likely used renminbi to

settle commercial deals between the two countries.[11] According to CBR reports, drawings on the PBOC line further increased in 2017, suggesting the growing use of renminbi for Russia's international transactional needs.[12]

Statements from US Treasury officials bolster the idea that local currency swap agreements can be used to dimmish the impact of sanctions. In September 2018 testimony before a congressional oversight panel on US sanctions policy, Marshall Billingslea, US Treasury assistant secretary for terrorist financing, was asked about the growing number of currency swap deals between China and various African nations. Referencing the deals, Representative Chris Smith (R-NJ) declared, "It appears that the US dollar regime on which our sanctions system is built is under threat." To which Billingslea replied:

> On the currency swap issue, I mean, you're very much onto something of great concern to us as well.... [I]t's the maintenance of those correspondent banking ties that is our best line of defense ensure that we maintain not just a degree of transparency and visibility into the transactions occurring in Africa but also for the effective insular sanctions regimes.[13]

The number of bilateral currency swap agreements has increased drastically since the 2008 financial crisis, when the Federal Reserve demonstrated the tool's usefulness amid a global dollar shortage.[14] Figure 6.1 displays the growing number of countries with at least one local currency swap line. Between 2007 and 2020, the number rose from zero to nearly fifty. Swap lines have proliferated alongside the growing use of financial sanctions as a US foreign policy tool. Given their potential to reduce vulnerability to dollar dependence in cross-border payments, one likely reason for the growing popularity of such agreements is the increased weaponization of the US dollar.[15]

All else equal, *governments should be more likely to enter into local currency swap agreements after they have been sanctioned by the US Treasury.* In such cases, the targeted government's experience with the direct costs of dollar dependence should increase the perceived political risk associated with the US currency. Targeted governments should be more inclined to implement anti-dollar policies like local currency swap agreements to reduce their dollar dependence and limit the costs of sanctions. Governments may also pursue swap agreements in anticipation of future US sanctions. Thus, *a government's propensity to sign currency swap agreements will increase as its perception of the risk of sanctions increases, regardless of whether it is currently targeted by*

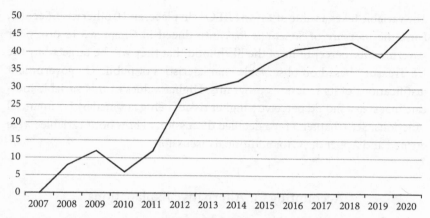

Figure 6.1. Number of Countries with Local Currency Swap Agreements, 2007–2020. Once a rarely used tool in central banking, bilateral currency swap agreements exploded in popularity following the Global Financial Crisis. Their rise in popularity has coincided with the growing use of US financial sanctions. Data collected by the author from various official and media sources.

US sanctions. In this case, the perceived sanctions risk, not just observed sanctions, induces anti-dollar policy responses. To illustrate the potential links between sanctions, perceived political risk, and anti-dollar policies, I model the relationship between US financial sanctions, sanctions risk, and the number of local currency swap agreements a country has signed.

Measuring Local Currency Swap Agreements and US Sanctions Pressure

The main outcome of interest is the total number of local currency swap agreements to which a country is party each year between 2008 and 2020. I collected data from official sources, including central bank websites, as well as media reports about such deals. China had the most swap agreements during this period, peaking at thirty-six in 2018. While the modal number of agreements in the data is 0, by 2020, forty-seven countries had signed at least one such deal. To account for US sanctions pressure, I use the same approach discussed in Chapter 3. First, I use the variable *SREO*, a dichotomous measure that indicates whether one or more sanctions-related Executive Order (SREOs) targeting the country in question was in place in a given year.

The variable takes a value of 1 if an SREO is in place, and 0 otherwise. Second, I use the measure of *Sanctions Risk* introduced in Chapter 3 to proxy for governments' perceptions of the likelihood that they will be targeted by the US Treasury based on observable characteristics of public US government justifications of its sanctions programs. Higher values of this variable indicate that states should perceive a higher risk of being targeted by US financial sanctions. See Chapter 3 for a detailed discussion of how both variables were created and Appendix C for additional discussion.

Accounting for Alternative Explanations

Governments may be motivated to sign currency swap agreements for reasons unrelated to concerns about US sanctions. For example, settling trade in local money can reduce national firms' exposure to the foreign exchange risk associated with using third-party currencies in trade.[16] All else equal, economies that are more dependent on trade should find currency swaps more appealing since promoting local currency trade settlement could reduce the risks faced by local firms. Thus, I include a measure of trade dependence, calculated as total trade (imports + exports) divided by the economy's total output (GDP), in the analysis.[17]

Countries may also find local currency swap deals attractive if they are concerned about future financial and economic crises. Though swaps may be used to promote local currency use in trade settlement, they can also help a country weather periods of economic and financial distress. Swap lines can function as bilateral emergency loans from one country to another; US dollar swap lines were used in this way during the 2008 financial crisis.[18] Anecdotal evidence suggests some countries have used their swap lines with China for such purposes.[19] Drawing on a swap line increases the total foreign exchange reserves held by participating central banks, which can bolster a currency's value in foreign exchange markets or signal to financial markets that the country's economic fundamentals remain sound. When an economy's foreign exchange reserves fall, this increases financial insecurity—and should boost the government's interest in signing currency swap deals as a financial lifeline. Countries that are vulnerable to financial and economic shocks may therefore value swap agreements as an additional form of insurance against potential crises. Consequently, my analysis includes a measure of foreign exchange reserves, including gold, divided by economic output (GDP).[20]

I also account for inflation, measured by the Consumer Price Index. All else equal, a high level of inflation reflects poorly on a central bank's management of the macroeconomy. Countries with above average inflation may be viewed as risky partners for foreign central banks, and find fewer willing swap partners. Measures of economic size (GDP) and economic development (per capita GDP) are also included alongside country fixed effects and a linear time trend. Finally, I exclude China from the analysis since it is an extreme outlier in terms of the number of swap lines it signed during the study period. Since it also scores high on sanctions risk variables, excluding it biases the models against the book's argument, thus providing a harder test. Explanatory and control covariates are each lagged by one period to help address simultaneity concerns.

US Sanctions Generate Enthusiasm for Swap Agreements

I estimate a series of ordinary least squares (OLS) regressions with panel-corrected standard errors to demonstrate that decisions to enter into local currency swap agreements are linked to US sanctions pressure.[21] Figure 6.2 displays the coefficient estimates for the main explanatory variables and key control covariates. Trade dependence is positively associated with swap lines, which is consistent with economic motives for pursuing such deals. However, this result reaches statistical significance in only one model. Inflation is surprisingly positive and statistically significant in both specifications. Turning to our main covariates of interest, the coefficient for *Sanctions Risk* is positive, as expected. However, it falls short of statistical significance, indicating that perceived sanctions risk is not robustly linked to the proliferation of local currency swap agreements. Conversely, the coefficient for *SREO*, the dichotomous indicator of imposed US financial sanctions, is both positive and distinguishable from zero.

Figure 6.3 presents *SREO*'s predicated marginal effects on swap lines. The model estimates that the predicted number of swap lines for countries *not* under an SREO is 0.39, and 0.61 for those that are. These differences are statistically significant from one another.

The results are consistent with the claim that governments targeted by US sanctions are more likely to seek pathways, such as swap agreements, to reduce their dependence on the dollar in cross-border payments. Of course, the results should be interpreted with caution as they do not establish a

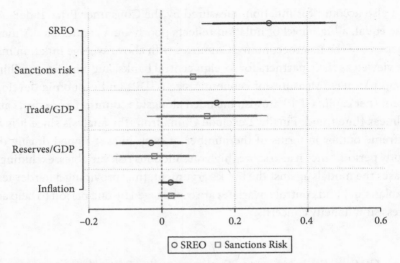

Figure 6.2. Coefficient Estimates, Count of Local Currency Swap Lines.
Circles/squares represent the coefficient point estimates. Wide lines represent
90 percent confidence intervals, and narrow lines reflect 95 percent confidence
intervals. The figure excludes estimates for country fixed effects, GDP, GDP per
capita, and the time trend covariate to improve interpretation. Full results are
available in Table E1 in Appendix E. SREO = Sanctions-related Executive Order.

causal link between sanctions and swap agreements. Moreover, policy
attempts to reduce dollar dependence, like signing local currency swaps,
do not necessarily translate into de-dollarization in practice. Indeed, one
of the key conclusions from the case studies presented in Chapter 5 is that
governments may *wish* to extricate themselves from dollar dominance but be
unable to. Anti-dollar policies may, at times, be more aspirational than transformational. A related question, then, is whether sanctions actually impacted
targeted and at-risk countries' use of the dollar in trade settlement. The following section considers this question and demonstrates such a link.

Sanctions and the Currency Composition
of Trade Settlement

Did Washington's increased use of financial sanctions lead to national-
level reductions in the use of the dollar in cross-border payments? The

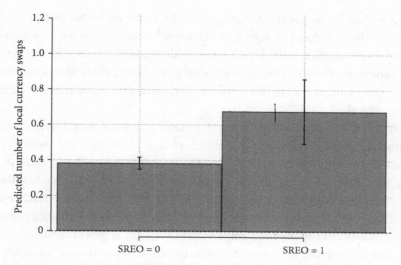

Figure 6.3. Predicted Marginal Effects of SREOs on Local Currency Swap Lines. The top bars indicate the mean predicted marginal effect as SREO ranges from 0 (none) to 1 (at least one SREO in place). The vertical lines represent 95 percent confidence intervals around those means.

case study evidence presented in Chapter 5 was mixed. The data unambiguously show that Moscow reduced its dependence on the dollar in trade—especially payments for exports—following US sanctions pressure. However, the Turkish data demonstrate that Ankara failed to achieve even modest de-dollarization in trade, despite its pledges. In general, the case study evidence implies that while sanctions clearly increase perceptions of political risk, leading to an interest in anti-dollar policies, those policies often fail to achieve their objectives. To explore the impact of the dollar's weaponization on its international use, I next examine the link between sanctions and the dollar's popularity as a settlement currency in cross-border trade.

Measuring the Dollar's Share in Trade Settlement and US Sanctions Pressure

Until recently, SWIFT—the corporation that runs the dominant international financial messaging network—considered researcher requests for access to its cross-national time-series data on the currency composition of cross-border payments. A change in 2019, however, ended that policy.[22] Though this is a blow to research on the subject, some scholars have recently questioned whether SWIFT's data are ideally suited to assess the currency composition of trade settlement anyway, due to difficulties "distinguishing between payment orders that concern trade and those that concern other transactions."[23]

Without access to SWIFT data, I instead rely on a new International Monetary Fund dataset that contains currency invoicing patterns for 102 countries from 1990 to 2019.[24] Though invoicing and settlement are two distinct roles for international currencies, researchers have shown that currency invoicing and trade settlement patterns very closely track one another,[25] which makes invoicing data a reliable proxy for the currency composition of trade settlement. I employ two covariates as outcome variables in my estimations: the yearly dollar share, in percentage terms, of a country's invoicing (settlement) of (1) imports and (2) exports.[26]

To account for US sanctions pressure, I employ the same two covariates used in the book's previous analyses: the dichotomous *SREO* variable and the *Sanctions Risk* measure. All else equal, if US sanctions pressure is associated with a smaller role for the dollar in trade invoicing and settlement, this would lend additional credibility to the claim that sanctions not only promoted anti-dollar policies but also may have contributed to observable patterns of de-dollarization in cross-border payments.

Controlling for Alternative Explanations

Political risk considerations are just one factor that may influence the currency composition of trade settlement. Two other elements of a country's trade relations are likely to be most important. The first is its level of trade with the United States. US firms, whether importing or exporting, should prefer to use the dollar in trade because it reduces their exposure to foreign exchange risk. Unsurprisingly, research shows that the more a country trades with the United States, the larger the dollar's role in trade invoicing and settlement tends to become.[27] To account for this, I control for the share of a country's trade with the United States by dividing the value of each country's exports (imports) to the United States by the value of its total exports to (imports from) to the rest of the world.[28]

Second, because oil is priced in dollars, countries that are major oil importers or exporters should be more likely to use the dollar in trade settlement. Oil-exporting countries are prone to invoice and accept payment for exports in dollars. Likewise, major oil importers should tend to use dollars to pay for imports. As the share of oil in a country's total imports or exports rises, the dollar's role in trade invoicing and settlement should increase. I divide the value of each country's oil exports (imports) by the value of its total exports to (imports from) the rest of the world and employ this as an additional control covariate in the models.[29] Finally, all estimates include standard economic controls for economic size (GDP) and level of development (GDP per capita) as well as country fixed effects and a linear time trend variable.[30] Explanatory and control covariates are each lagged by one period to address simultaneity concerns.

US Sanctions and Reduced Dollar Use in Trade Settlement

Four ordinary least squares (OLS) regression models with panel-corrected standard errors are fitted to appraise whether US sanctions pressure is associated with less reliance on the dollar in trade settlement. Figure 6.4 displays the main coefficient estimates for all four models. The top panel presents the results for export settlement. The coefficients for both sanctions variables are negative. However, the standard errors for *Sanctions Risk* overlap with zero, which indicates that we cannot reject the null hypothesis that this variable has no statistical relationship with dollar use in export invoicing and settlement. *SREO* appears to be robustly related to a reduced role for the dollar in national export settlement. This finding aligns with the claim that—when imposed—sanctions provoke de-dollarization in payments for exports. This tracks with the details presented in Chapter 5 on changes in the currency composition of Russian export settlement. Following US sanctions, the dollar's share in payments for Russian exports fell significantly. Interestingly, neither US export dependence nor oil exports have a statistically significant relationship with the dollar's use in export payments, though the coefficients on these variables are positive, as expected.

The lower panel of Figure 6.4 presents the analogous results for import settlement. *SREO* and *Sanctions Risk* are again negatively associated with the dollar's use in trade settlement. This time, however, those differences are statistically significant, showing that both imposed sanctions and elevated

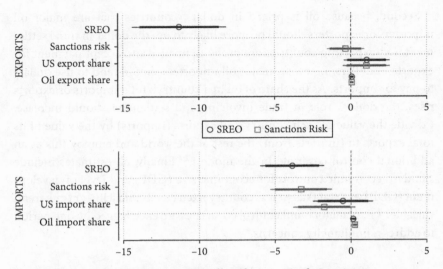

Figure 6.4. Coefficient Estimates, Dollar Share in Trade Invoicing or Settlement. The top (bottom) panel presents coefficient estimates where the dollar's share of export (import) settlement is the outcome of interest. Circles represent the coefficient point estimates. Wide lines represent 90 percent confidence intervals, and narrow lines show 95 percent confidence intervals. SREO = Sanctions-related Executive Orders. The figure excludes country fixed effects, GDP, GDP per capita, and the time trend covariate to improve interpretation. The full results are available in Table E2 in Appendix E.

government perceptions of sanctions risk are linked to a smaller role for the dollar in import settlement. This provides even stronger evidence of a relationship between US sanctions, political risk concerns, and de-dollarization in cross-border payments.

Outside the main variables of interest, the use of the dollar for import payments is, as expected, higher for countries that are highly dependent on oil imports. Surprisingly, US import dependence is negatively correlated with dollar use, though this result is only marginally significant in one model.

Figure 6.5 presents the predicated marginal effects of the two key sanctions variables on the dollar's trade settlement share for three of the four models. Starting with the left panel of the figure, as *Sanctions Risk* varies from one standard deviation below the sample mean to one standard deviation above the mean, the dollar's share in import settlement decreases from 50.7 to 42.6 percent. In the middle panel, the dollar's predicted share in import

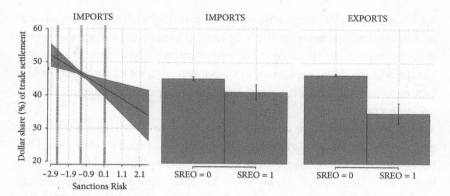

Figure 6.5. Predicted Marginal Effects of SREOs and Sanctions Risk on the Dollar's Share of Trade Settlement. Beginning with the left panel, the solid line represents the mean predicted marginal effect as the sanctions risk varies from its sample low to high. The shaded area represents the 95 percent confidence intervals around those means. Dashed vertical lines represent the sample mean of sanctions risk (center) and one standard deviation above (right) and below (left) that mean. In the center and right panels, the bars represent the predicted marginal effects as SREO varies from 0 (none) to 1 (at least one SREO in place). The vertical lines represent 95 percent confidence intervals around those means.

settlement drops from 45.2 percent for countries not targeted by an SREO to 41.3 percent for targeted states. Though this is a smaller shift in substantive terms, the difference between these groups is highly significant. On the export side of the ledger, shown in the right panel, *SREO*'s predicted marginal effect on dollar use is more sizable. Countries not targeted by US financial sanctions are estimated to invoice and settle 46.4 percent of their exports in dollars, while those targeted by at least one *SREO* invoice settle just 35.1 percent of their exports in US currency—a difference of over 11 percent.

Collectively, these results demonstrate that US financial sanctions may not just provoke anti-dollar policies, such as local currency swap agreements; they may also trigger modest levels of de-dollarization in trade invoicing and settlement among targeted and at-risk countries. Diversification away from the dollar in trade could increase a country's industrial resilience under future US sanctions in the near term. Firms that have carved out trade ties that operate outside the dollar and the US financial system would be better positioned to maintain those ties even if they were blacklisted by the US Treasury. Moreover, firms that have experience in non-dollar settlement might be better able to scale up to higher levels if they are cut off from dollar payments. In the long term, if sanctions provoke even small shifts away from the dollar in trade settlement, we might expect to see similar shifts in the dollar's use in other roles given what we know about the link between a currency's position as a trade invoicing currency and its broader pre-eminence.[31]

Of course, the findings on which these conjectures are based are not conclusive. The statistical correlations do not signify a causal relationship between sanctions and de-dollarization; they merely suggest an association that is consistent with a causal story. Because experimental methods can better establish causal relationships between two variables, the following section extends the chapter's analysis by presenting the results from a firm-level survey experiment that considers how sanctions affect private sector attitudes toward the dollar.

Firm-Level Experiment: US Sanctions and Trade Settlement Preferences

De-dollarization of trade settlement ultimately comes down to decisions made by individual firms. Governments can sign agreements like local currency swap deals that make it easier and more attractive for firms to settle trade in local currencies. Eventually, however, businesses must decide whether to move their cross-border transactions out of the dollar. All else equal, a government that wishes to reduce the role of the dollar in cross-border trade due to political risk concerns will be more likely to succeed if firms in the country are also concerned about dollar dependence. Firm managers who have been awakened to the political risk of relying on the dollar should be more responsive to state-led anti-dollar initiatives than those who have not. The former should be more willing to collaborate with the government and to invest time and resources into changing their payment relationships with foreign partners.

It is thus an important and open question whether firms react to US sanctions with heightened political risk concerns of their own. While US sanctions programs broadly target foreign governments, they often directly target firms. Businesses blacklisted by the US Treasury are cut out of dollar-based payments, causing tremendous harm to their global business relationships. As the United States has increased its use of financial sanctions as a tool of foreign policy, business managers' attitudes toward the dollar may have shifted. Relying on the dollar for cross-border payments may make sense from a purely economic perspective, but the political risks of doing so may make industry executives more willing to consider currency alternatives. If sanctions generate political risk concerns among firms, then priming business managers to think about the growing use of financial sanctions should boost their interest in using non-dollar currencies for trade settlement as well as their support for initiatives that make such an outcome possible.

To explore whether priming firm managers to think about the US government's increasing use of financial sanctions affects attitudes toward dollar alternatives, I fielded an original survey experiment in Vietnam as part of the 2019 Provincial Competitiveness Index (PCI).[32] Multinational corporations (MNCs) from fifty-one countries are represented in the survey of over 1,500 firms operating facilities across fourteen national provinces. Vietnam is a useful case for assessing the impact of US financial sanctions on corporate managers' attitudes toward the dollar. Vietnam has never been the target of US financial sanctions. This is helpful, since firms in countries that have been targeted—like Russia, Venezuela, or Iran—would likely exhibit much higher baseline levels of concern about the dollar. If interest in non-dollar trade settlement is already elevated due to experience with sanctions, this could weaken any potential treatment effect from information about US sanctions. Because Vietnam has no experience with US financial sanctions, it provides a cleaner test of how sanctions impact firm manager attitudes toward dollar payments.

Vietnam is also a useful case because it is currently one of the most important developing economy destinations for investment by MNCs.[33] Between 1980 and 2013, it boasted the highest rate of annual growth of net foreign direct investment inflows in East Asia.[34] In 2019, Vietnam ranked the seventh best performing economy in the region, attracting nearly 6.5 times more new capital investment than its "expected share" based on economic output.[35] Notably, most of these investments were made by firms operating in the manufacturing sector, which tend to be actively involved in international trade. Because cross-border trade settlement typically involves foreign currency transactions and reliance on international banking services, firms involved in trade should be sensitive to the potential for US financial sanctions to disrupt their business. Yet the risk that the US Treasury will target a given individual firm is incredibly low—especially in a country that has not faced US sanctions in the past.

The PCI survey was distributed to top management (CEOs, general managers, general directors, or financial officers) at MNCs operating in Vietnam. Firm managers were randomly assigned control or treatment conditions. Managers in the control group were presented with the following vignette:

> The US dollar is the dominant currency used in international payments and trade settlement. The EU and China are working to create their own cross-border payments and trade settlement systems based on the euro and the [renminbi].[36]

Respondents in the treatment group were provided the same information, but were also primed to think about the United States' increasing use of financial sanctions and how this could potentially disrupt their firm's business operations. The additional information is italicized:

> The US dollar is the dominant currency used in international payments and trade settlement. *The dollar standard is convenient, but dollar dominance also means firms are sometimes constrained by US foreign policy, such as when America imposes financial sanctions on certain countries. America's reliance on financial sanctions is increasing.* The EU and China are working to create their own cross-border payments and trade settlement systems based on the euro and the [renminbi] *which could not be disrupted by US sanctions.*

Subjects were then asked to indicate how strongly they agreed or disagreed with three statements:

(1) The government of Vietnam should work with the EU and China to promote the establishment of euro- and [renminbi]-based payments and trade settlement systems here.
(2) My firm would be interested in learning more about euro- and [renminbi]-based payments and trade settlement systems.
(3) My firm would be willing to make a financial contribution to an organized effort to lobby the government of Vietnam to establish euro- and [renminbi]-based payments and trade settlement systems here.

Responses were measured on a 5-point Likert scale ranging from "strongly disagree" (1) to "strongly agree" (5). Figure F.1 in Appendix F presents the summary statistics for these three main outcome variables.

Information about Sanctions Raises Interest in Non-dollar Trade Settlement

Table 6.1 presents estimates of the average treatment effect for all three outcome questions based on ordinary least squares (OLS) regression models. The results reflect the full sample excluding sixteen US-owned firms.[37] The first row in the table displays estimates of the effect of the sanctions treatment compared to the control group. If information about US sanctions increases firms' interest in renminbi- or euro-based payments, we would expect to see positive coefficient values for each of the three post-treatment questions. Overall, the results are mixed. The sanctions treatment is associated with higher average levels of manager interest in "learning more" and "contributing to a lobbying effort," but lower interest in "government promotion" of a new payment system. Notably, the difference between the treatment and control groups is only statistically significant in one case ("learn more"). This result is statistically significant at the 95 percent level and withstands a stringent correction for multiple outcomes, discussed more in Appendix E.

The average change in the level of interest in "learning more" about non-dollar payment systems between the control and sanctions treatment group is just short of 0.1, an increase of about 2 percent on a 5-point scale. Figure 6.6 depicts the distribution of responses to the "learn more" prompt by treatment group. The overall effect of the sanctions treatment appears to

Table 6.1. Average Treatment Effects, Vietnam Multinational Corporations Experiment

	Learn more	Government promote	Contribute
Sanctions treatment	0.099**	−0.018	0.030
	[0.045]	[0.046]	[0.045]
N	1,150	1,180	1,121

Cell entries present OLS coefficients estimating average treatment effects.
Standard errors are in brackets. ** p < 0.05

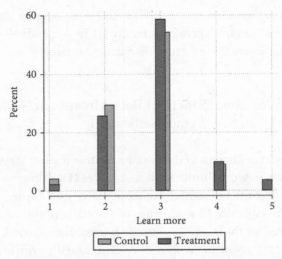

Figure 6.6. Distribution of "Learn More" Responses by Treatment Group.
Bars indicate firm responses by treatment group to the "learn more" question
in percentage terms. The sanctions prime motivated firm managers to be less
disinterested in non-dollar trade settlement systems.

be largely driven by reducing *disinterest* in learning more about non-dollar-
based payments. Managers in the treatment group are more likely to shift
their answer from "somewhat disagree" (2) to "neither agree nor disagree"
(3). The share of MNC managers answering "strongly disagree" also falls in
the treatment group by about half.

The mixed nature of these results does not allow us to draw strong
conclusions regarding whether there is a link between US sanctions and
firm-level attitudes about non-dollar trade settlement. It is possible that the
survey experiment's design may have influenced firm manager responses in
unintended ways. For example, the only outcome in which the treatment had
a statistically significant effect on manager attitudes was the question that
did not mention the Vietnamese government. If businesses in Vietnam are
skeptical of state involvement in the economy, or have questions about the
government's competence, then questions including references to the government may have overshadowed the information about sanctions. That is,
even if information about sanctions changed perceptions of political risk,
a firm manager who is suspicious of the Vietnamese state might still have
reservations about government-led economic policy initiatives.

Nonetheless, the finding that MNC managers are more interested in learning about non-dollar trade settlement does imply that the treatment activated political risk concerns—if only slightly. The sanctions treatment provided very broad and basic information about US sanctions use and how it may impact trade. It did not, for instance, suggest that firms in Vietnam were at a higher risk of facing sanctions than those elsewhere. Given the incredibly low likelihood that any given firm would be directly impacted by US sanctions, the substantively small effect size of the treatment is understandable. If such a subtle treatment can induce interest in exploring de-dollarization among firm managers operating in Vietnam, the actual demonstration of US financial sanctions capabilities should have a much stronger effect on manager attitudes, especially in targeted countries. Finally, these results suggest that governments concerned about future sanctions could engender firm-level cooperation toward diversifying cross-border payment practices if the political risks facing industry are clearly communicated.

Conclusions

As President Kennedy understood, world trade and dollar dominance go hand in hand. The US currency is the most popular cross-border medium of exchange in global commerce. That popularity gives the United States the capacity to cut foreign industries out of the global trading system by shutting off their access to dollar-based banking services. It also underpins global dollar supremacy, as the currency's trade role promotes its role in other arenas. Yet as the United States has increasingly relied on financial sanctions, Washington has demonstrated to foreign governments and firms alike that relying on the dollar can be politically risky. As awareness of those risks rises, governments—and even firms themselves—are likely to reconsider their relationship with the world's leading trade settlement currency. This chapter presented three separate studies linking US financial sanctions to perceptions of political risk and anti-dollar policies in cross-border payments. The first shows that governments targeted by US sanctions were more likely to sign local currency swap agreements, which operate as anti-dollar policy tools capable of aiding a transition away from the dollar in trade settlement. The second study takes this a step further by demonstrating that sanctions pressure is associated with a smaller role for the dollar in countries' cross-border trade settlement. This suggests that sanctions provoke modest levels of de-dollarization. Finally, firm-level experimental data reveal that priming firms with information about the growing use of US sanctions increases interest in learning about non-dollar trade settlement, indicating the potential for governments to cultivate private sector interest in their anti-dollar policy agendas.

Collectively, the illustrations in this chapter imply that US financial sanctions have generated an appetite for non-dollar trade settlement options, especially among targeted states. While incremental diversification into non-dollar currencies would weaken the effectiveness of US sanctions capabilities over time, US sanctions policy is unlikely to seriously jeopardize dollar pre-eminence in trade. Governments and firms that wish to extricate their cross-border economic relations from the dollar's grip inevitably struggle to find a replacement. Reducing the dollar's role by using local currencies in a handful of bilateral trade relationships is different from a wholesale migration away from the US currency. Targeted and at-risk governments may wish for—or even demand—a suitable dollar alternative, but most are incapable of creating a world with more choices on the currency menu. Invoicing and transacting in dollars is likely to remain more convenient, and thus more popular, than all other options for the foreseeable future. One of the dollar's current great strengths is thus the lack of a proper alternative or a true rival. However, the United States' increased use of financial sanctions just might provoke a change in the competitive landscape of the international currency system, which is where this book turns next.

7

Financial Sanctions and the Dollar's Rivals

*It has been proved time and again that sanctions are a boomerang and
a double-edged sword. To politicize the global economy and turn it
into one's tool or weapon, and willfully impose sanctions by using one's
primary position in the international financial and monetary systems
will only end up hurting one's own interests.*

Xi Jinping, President of China[1]

*The main reason that I see for [calls for the euro to assume a stronger
international role] relates to the growing perception of a shift in global
governance, from leadership built on trust and common identities . . . to
leadership based on . . . hard power where policies and doctrines are
imposed on others.*

Benoît Cœuré, Executive Board member at
the European Central Bank[2]

Financial experts and analysts have been forecasting the dollar's decline, or
even demise, for decades. They attribute the approaching end of the dollar's
halcyon days perched atop the global currency hierarchy to a variety of
factors. Dollar decline is often characterized as an unavoidable result of the
broader (relative) US economic decline, or as a consequence of American
financial mismanagement evidenced by the ever-ballooning national debt.

In the late 1970s and early 1980s, amid a general mood of pessimism about
the future prospects of the US economy, observers characterized the world
economy—including the international currency system—as growing ever
more "polycentric."[3] Potential rivals to the dollar then included the Japanese
yen and the German deutschemark. As one scholar put it at the time, "the
idea of moving away from the dollar as the sole pillar of the [international
monetary] system is broadly accepted."[4] Influential economist Charles
P. Kindleberger declared, "The dollar will end up on history's ash heap, along

Bucking the Buck. Daniel McDowell, Oxford University Press. © Oxford University Press 2023.
DOI: 10.1093/oso/9780197679876.003.0008

with sterling, the guilder, florin, ducat, and if you choose to go way back, the Levantine bezant."[5] Of course, such predictions ended up being wrong: the dollar's grip on global finance increased in subsequent decades.

After the global financial crisis of 2008, scholars started arguing again that the dollar's dominant position was weakening relative to potential currency rivals. Barry Eichengreen suggested that a global economy characterized by unchallenged dollar dominance was giving way to one in which "several international currencies coexist."[6] Similarly, Jonathan Kirshner anticipated a "multipolar currency order."[7] Some predicted that the euro or renminbi might supplant the dollar as the world's primary currency.[8] Yet once again, such predictions were out of step with reality: a decade after the crisis, little had changed in the global currency hierarchy. Indeed, by some measures, the dollar's dominance had increased.[9]

The most recent wave of such predictions emerged during the COVID-19 pandemic. Political economist Benjamin J. Cohen suggested that the United States' lack of global leadership under President Donald Trump's "America First" foreign policy amid the global health crisis did not "augur well for the US dollar."[10] Several high-profile, ultra-rich American investors added to the chorus, predicting that the Federal Reserve's expansionary monetary policy and the federal government's massive COVID-induced fiscal stimulus would hasten the dollar's inevitable downfall.[11] Even investment bank Goldman Sachs piled on, questioning the post-COVID longevity of dollar dominance.[12] It remains to be seen whether the latest round of dollar pessimism finally got the timing right or whether, once again, the US currency will prove more resilient than its skeptics imagined.

This book ostensibly has something to say about the dollar's future. If US financial sanctions generate political risk concerns associated with its use, which provoke anti-dollar policy orientations among targeted and at-risk countries, the dollar's international role may diminish over time. Sanctions thus represent another potential pathway to dollar decline. However, past predictions of the dollar's downfall failed to deliver partly because they wrongly assumed that suitable alternatives to the dollar would emerge to take its place. Whether an attractive alternative to the dollar will rise in this decade, or even the next, remains an open question. One recent study suggests that the dollar could be felled by the emergence of a group of small to middling challengers that collectively chip away at its pre-eminence.[13] Regardless, if the dollar loses its foothold in the global currency system in the coming decades, sanctions and political risk concerns will likely play a part.

The top two current challengers to the dollar's grip on global finance are the euro and the renminbi; in time, either could emerge as its primary competitor or together help create a multipolar currency system. The euro's bona fides as an international currency have already been established. As the clear "number two" in the global currency hierarchy for more than twenty years, the euro boasts a sizable position in government foreign exchange reserves and is widely used in cross-border payments and debt markets. Yet its use remains "confined mostly to a limited number of economies with close ... links to the European Union."[14] The euro may be an international currency, but the dollar is still the only truly *global* currency. As for the renminbi, financial observers became transfixed (and perhaps even obsessed) with its potential as a threat to the dollar following the 2008 financial crisis. Despite what appears on paper to be a strong case for an emerging dollar-renminbi rivalry, China's currency has consistently failed to live up to the hype.

The unrealized potential of both monies is based on a range of institutional, economic, and political shortcomings in China and the European Union (EU).[15] Not least among these is a lack of political will in Beijing and Brussels. Internal politics and concerns about the costs of issuing a truly global currency have caused policymakers in both capitals to balk at taking the necessary steps to allow their currencies to assume larger international roles. However, that may be changing. US financial sanctions have provoked a notable shift in attitudes among the financial elite in Beijing as well as in European capitals.

In Europe, US secondary sanctions have stung businesses and generated concerns among policymakers about a lack of financial autonomy. Promoting the euro's role as an international currency became a focal point for frustrated Europeans looking to preserve their economic independence and send a shot across Washington's bow. In China, policymakers and other elites recognized the opportunity that US sanctions presented for the renminbi. With a little help, they argued, the Chinese currency could make significant inroads among the growing number of economies dissatisfied with the dollar. Additional concerns that Washington might one day use sanctions against China further fueled interest in renminbi internationalization. While this shift in attitudes is unlikely to bring about seismic policy changes that greatly diminish the dollar's international status, public debate around the international role of the euro and renminbi undeniably changed in serious and significant ways as a result of Washington's reliance on sanctions. These observed shifts in attitudes would be a necessary first step toward emergence of the euro or renminbi as a more serious challenger to the dollar.

The European Response

Europe has long had a troubled relationship with the dollar. In the 1960s as the United States was running persistent yearly balance-of-payments deficits, France frequently raised questions about the long-term stability of the currency's exchange rate, then fixed at $35 to an ounce of gold. A high-profile French economist who had the ear of President Charles de Gaulle published a series of open letters to the chief executive of Le Monde blaming the United States for inflation in France. The letters called on de Gaulle to use emergency powers to force a devaluation of the dollar in order to end its role as an international reserve currency.[16] De Gaulle eventually lambasted dollar dominance and called on the world to dump America's money in favor of a return to a system like the nineteenth-century gold standard.[17]

This rocky history may explain why some in Europe were so excited by the creation of the euro in 1999. Some European economists claimed the newly minted money would become the "second global currency."[18] Former European Commission president Jacques Delors proudly proclaimed, "The little euro will become big."[19] In one sense, these predictions were right: the euro *has* become a widely used international currency. However, it remains a distant second in most respects to the dollar. Political economist and international money expert Benjamin J. Cohen has attributed the euro's limited rise to a range of factors. Central among these is "the absence of any proactive policy by European authorities to promote a major role for the euro."[20] Randall Germain and Herman Schwartz likewise assert that "the EU lacks the will, the ideas and the capacity to promote the euro into the status of a top international currency."[21] Perhaps this should come as no surprise given that the European Central Bank openly declared in 1999 that internationalizing the euro was "not a policy objective" and would "be neither fostered nor hindered by the Eurosystem."[22]

Yet the discussion below illustrates that the EU's neutral position regarding the international use of the euro has moved toward a pro-internationalization stance as a direct result of US sanctions policy—particularly the use of secondary measures. As described in Chapter 2, secondary sanctions force actors in third-party countries (e.g., those not directly targeted by the US

Treasury) to choose between doing business with the United States or with the target state. Given the United States' economic size and financial centrality, the choice tends to be an easy one. European policymakers criticized secondary sanctions as illegal, "extraterritorial" measures, expressing their resentment that the United States can force its financial institutions and businesses to toe the US foreign policy line.

This was an issue even prior to the Trump administration's decision to pull out of the Iran nuclear deal. Between 2008 and 2020, the US Treasury imposed $29 billion in penalties on foreign banks for violating US financial sanctions; $22 billion of that was levied against European banks. In 2014, when the multinational French lender BNP Paribas was forced to pay nearly $9 billion in penalties to the United States, the governor of the Bank of France pitched the idea that Europeans should start conducting trade in currencies other than the dollar. "Trade between China and Europe," he opined, "do it in euros, do it in renminbi, stop doing it in dollars."[23] However, prior to 2018, these sorts of statements were mostly one-offs. Any anti-dollar momentum lost steam as the penalties were paid and the issue receded into the background. That changed when Washington reimposed a suite of harsh sanctions, including secondary measures, on Iran when it exited the Joint Comprehensive Plan of Action (JCPOA).

This move showed that Europe's economic dependence on the dollar, and the euro's international limitations, exposed the European economy to significant political risk. This heightened awareness of financial vulnerabilities caused many European political elites to advocate measures that would enhance the continent's financial autonomy. Europe's response followed two tracks. The first track involved developing a short-term response to keep business ties open between Europe and Iran, even in the face of renewed US sanctions. The second, and more meaningful, track centered on crafting a long-term strategy designed to promote the euro's international role as a settlement and investment currency.

Europe's Short-Term "Fix"

Just three months after the United States unilaterally withdrew from the JCPOA, the EU's top foreign policy official, Federica Mogherini, announced that the bloc was working on a new payment mechanism that would enable businesses on the continent to evade US sanctions while transacting with

Iran. The move was a first draft response to calls from German foreign minister Heiko Maas and French finance minister Bruno Le Marie for an "independent" or "autonomous" payments architecture.[24] The press characterized the "special purpose vehicle," as it was first called, as a "blatant show of defiance" directed at Washington's financial overreach.[25] This joint project, led by Germany, France, and the United Kingdom, was troubled from the start. Its launch was delayed because none of the founding member countries were willing to host the mechanism for fear it could expose them to additional US sanctions.[26] France eventually agreed to host the new system. Officially launched in January 2019 and dubbed the Instrument in Support of Trade Exchanges, or INSTEX, it was set up to facilitate trade with Iran without involving the dollar, US correspondent banks, or SWIFT. It was effectively designed as a barter system so that money would never move between Europe and Iran. Moreover, INSTEX was set up primarily as a channel to facilitate trade in humanitarian goods; oil exports were excluded.

Here is how it was designed to work: a European company agrees to sell N95 masks to an Iranian buyer. At the same time, another European firm agrees to buy figs from Iran. The two European companies notify INSTEX and its equivalent system in Iran. The European company importing figs from Iran then pays the European firm exporting masks, using euros. The Iranian buyer importing the masks from Europe simultaneously pays the Iranian fig producer the equivalent amount in Iranian rial. While the goods cross international borders, the rials and euros stay within Iran and Europe, respectively. By avoiding the key components of the dollar-based international payment system, INSTEX was designed to deny Washington the capacity to identify or punish parties involved in transactions. Initially, INSTEX captured some attention as a notable anti-dollar move by the Europeans. The Russians expressed interest in coordinating with the Europeans to make the most of the new system. There were also reports that Brussels was looking to extend the barter system to include Cuba, another economy long isolated by US sanctions.[27]

INSTEX turned out to be more symbolic than functional as an anti-dollar tool, dismally failing to facilitate de-dollarization. Due to its barter system design, trade between European countries and Iran had to be in balance for it to work. For a deal to occur, buyers and sellers had to be found on each side with equal-sized transactions, which was not easy to arrange. Problems with the system also extended beyond mere mathematical inconvenience. Despite the promise that Washington would not detect these exchanges, European companies and banks still worried that involvement in an INSTEX transaction would somehow land them in hot water with the Office of Foreign Assets Control at US Treasury.[28] Indeed, just months after its creation Washington had threatened that participating in the special purpose vehicle might result in a "loss of access to the US financial system."[29] Even two years after its introduction, INSTEX had been used on only one occasion, which was to facilitate the export of medical products to Iran during the COVID-19 pandemic.[30] As one German newspaper put it, "Almost all EU companies have ended their business with Iran, the risk of getting into trouble with Washington was too great for them."[31]

Europe's Long-Term Strategy for Financial Autonomy

INSTEX was never a serious anti-dollar policy tool. Political elites in the EU recognized that its value was almost entirely symbolic.[32] The system was developed to send a message to the United States that Europe would not stand idly by as Washington blew up the Iran deal and employed harsh extraterritorial measures against its allies. It also signaled to Tehran that Europe was still "in" the nuclear deal, inviting Iran to remain in compliance with the JCPOA.

As a cross-border payments mechanism, however, it was doomed to fail. For Europe, the surest route to financial autonomy was through a globally ascendant euro capable of challenging the dollar for dominance in cross-border payments and investment. European leaders understood this; as they were developing the INSTEX scheme, they were simultaneously crafting a new grand strategy to encourage broader international use of the euro.

Following the Trump administration's fateful decision on Iran, European Commission president Jean-Claude Junker made the internationalization of the euro a centerpiece of his 2018 State of the Union Address.[33] That speech foreshadowed a detailed commission report, released a few months later, entitled "Towards a Stronger International Role of the Euro." The report explained that the common currency had not lived up to its full potential and had even lost some ground as an international currency following the 2008 financial crisis. It further highlighted how the dollar's dominance in trade invoicing and settlement was especially high in strategic sectors like energy, raw materials, food, and aircraft. The assessment expressed in the report was that dependence on the dollar exposed the European economy "to currency and political risks, such as international sanctions that directly affect dollar denominated transactions."[34]

The study generated a series of recommendations to the commission, such as increasing the amount of euro-denominated bonds issued in Europe, using diplomacy to promote the use of the euro as a reserve and payments currency, providing technical support to developing countries to increase their access to euro payment systems, and encouraging the wider use of the euro in the energy sector.[35] In 2021, the commission followed up the initial report with additional plans to "foster [the euro's] status as an international currency."[36] Each of the policy recommendations aimed to boost the appeal of using the common currency for trade and investment. The stated motive behind the plans remained the "extraterritorial application of sanctions by third countries"—a not-so-veiled swipe at Washington.[37]

Influential European think tanks with connections to the policy world also turned their attention to the issue of euro internationalization. They called for the unification and deepening of "separate European financial markets" and for "cooperation with commodities markets to set reference prices in euros" because the "extraterritorial reach of US rules and decisions, granted by the very extensive international role of the dollar, would be reduced if the euro was used more widely."[38] Others considered how introducing a "digital euro" could help increase Europe's financial autonomy, "enhancing the resilience of European trade relations to sanctions." However, since the development of a functional, widely used central bank digital currency would take years to get off the ground, European analysts concluded that establishing an independent European payment system should be the priority.[39]

The Chinese Response

China's historical relationship with the dollar has been less contentious than Europe's. Between 1992 and 2007, when its economy enjoyed sustained, rapid economic growth, China was viewed as the key cog in a global financial system that sustained dollar dominance. In what was dubbed the "revived" Bretton Woods system or "Bretton Woods II," East Asian export-dependent economies—the most important of which was China—were portrayed as major supporters of the dollar's reserve currency status. This support was part of an informal quid pro quo between the two sides. As part of this system, Chinese leaders implicitly agreed that in exchange for US willingness to accept large and persistent bilateral trade deficits, Beijing would "under-write future [US budget] deficits." This was accomplished by continuing to purchase mounds of US debt. The effect was that China's ever-growing stock of dollar assets held in its foreign exchange reserves further entrenched the dollar's international pre-eminence.[40]

The global financial crisis provoked a meaningful change in tone from the Chinese government, leading to greater awareness of the economic risks of dollar dependence. Beijing's apprehensions stemmed from at least two factors. First, there were concerns that unprecedented monetary stimulus employed by the Federal Reserve might, in time, debase the dollar and re-duce the value of China's vast US Treasury holdings. Second, volatility in the currency's exchange rate and the lack of dollar-based trade financing during the crisis threatened Chinese export industries because Chinese businesses relied heavily on the dollar for trade invoicing and settlement.[41] Amid these shocks, Chinese Premier Wen Jiabao publicly fretted about the long-term value of his country's dollar-denominated investments in 2009.[42] In the same year, Zhou Xiaochuan, then China's central bank governor, published an attention-grabbing essay that highlighted the risks of the dollar's global dominance and advocated reducing the country's dependence on the cur-rency.[43] In the context of this shifting public rhetoric on the dollar, China also began more actively promoting the international use of its own cur-rency, the renminbi.

After what appeared to be some early progress in the wake of the global financial crisis, Beijing's renminbi internationalization efforts were incon-sistent over the course of the 2010s. As external conditions shifted, internal policy disagreements between pro- and anti-internationalization factions within the Chinese state stunted the currency's global ascendance.[44] The most critical moment was in 2015 when significant capital outflows from the mainland put downward pressure on the value of the renminbi. As the exchange rate's stability was in jeopardy, Chinese authorities reacted by fur-ther clamping down on cross-border capital flows. This draconian policy re-sponse demonstrated that Beijing's commitment to economic and financial stability trumped its interest in renminbi internationalization.[45]

Without strong central government backing for internationalization efforts, the renminbi's use outside China as a store of value and medium of exchange remained limited. For instance, at the end of 2020, the renminbi accounted for just 2.26 percent of global foreign exchange reserves, placing it a distant fifth place from the US dollar and just above the Canadian dollar. As a payments currency, the renminbi again ranked a very distant fifth in 2020, accounting for just 1.8 percent of cross-border payments.[46] For the currency to live up to its oft-vaunted potential, Beijing would need to pursue a suite of policy reforms. In the decade following the global financial crisis, Chinese authorities' unwillingness to make such moves diminished the renminbi's international appeal. The central government's policy would only change if it came to view the benefits of a global renminbi as outweighing the costs.

The United States' increased use of financial sanctions impacted the cost–benefit analysis surrounding renminbi internationalization in China. While Beijing was officially tight-lipped about the topic, elites in China openly acknowledged the risks and opportunities that the United States' weaponization of the dollar created. As the US Treasury more actively used sanctions, as it did against China directly in 2020, public remarks fretting about the dollar from former top Chinese policymakers and members of the country's financial and academic elite became common. The consensus among these groups signaled an awareness that dollar dependence resulted in political, not just economic, risks for China's economy. National security concerns abounded as fears of US exploitation moved from remote to prominent. Renminbi internationalization, specifically as a payments currency, was increasingly championed as integral to maintaining China's economic sovereignty. In addition, the pro-internationalization camp within China seized on the notion that global mistrust of the dollar and desire for an alternative presented the ideal conditions for renminbi internationalization. In sum, the tenor of policy debates on renminbi internationalization noticeably shifted in response to US financial sanctions.

The View from Beijing: Risks and Opportunity

US sanctions targeting Russia following its invasion of Crimea were eye opening from Beijing's vantage point. While Washington had been steadily increasing its use of sanctions since the global financial crisis, it typically targeted small states with small economies. Prior to 2014, the largest economy the US Treasury had directly sanctioned was Iran, which was not a surprise given the long-standing tension between the two countries.[47] The United States' harsh financial response to Russia's invasion of Crimea was the first time Washington had used the dollar as a weapon to directly target a major power. Beijing took note as the ruble crashed and Russian equity markets tanked following the Obama administration's punitive actions.

Chinese state media characterized the initial round of Russia sanctions as creating a new kind of "closeness" between China and Russia. This moment, they suggested, presented an opportunity for the renminbi's global ambitions as Russian firms were looking to conduct business in currencies other than the dollar.[48] Elsewhere, reducing dollar dependence was depicted as a "more urgent task" that was in line with China's plan to enhance the global status of the renminbi.[49] An academic at Xiamen University mused in a Tencent blog post that China should capitalize on this opportunity by introducing its own payment system to the Russians to encourage cross-border settlement in renminbi.[50] Such commentary was not confined to media and academic circles, either.

In a speech a few months after the Crimea sanctions, the president of the Bank of China (one of the four big state-owned Chinese financial institutions) called on his country to strengthen bilateral cooperation with Russia on using local currencies in business dealings. He said that reducing reliance on the dollar was in the "strategic interests of both sides."[51] In 2017, as an additional wave of US sanctions against Russia was being prepared, the state-run *Global Times* suggested that China was willing and ready to enhance financial cooperation between the two countries. This could include increasing the size of the renminbi-ruble currency swap agreement between their respective central banks.[52] That same year, a Chinese official meeting with the head of Iran's central bank complained about the United States' control over global payments and floated local currency swaps as a useful anti-dollar policy tool for aggrieved countries.[53]

Like the Europeans, China's attitude toward the dollar turned sharply negative following the US decision to pull out of the Iran nuclear deal. Beijing objected to the use of secondary sanctions that would force Chinese firms and banks to cut ties with Iran, resulting in lost business opportunities. US sanctions also meant that energy-hungry China would have a more difficult time importing oil from Iran. There was also a growing unease in Beijing that the United States might one day use the dollar as a weapon against China. Some in China viewed this development as an opportunity for renminbi internationalization. Public expression of such sentiments became surprisingly mainstream among the Chinese financial elite, including former high-ranking policymakers and high-profile academics.

Many such remarks were made at various events held by the influential Beijing-based *China Finance 40 Forum*, a Chinese think tank that analyzes economic and financial policy issues. US sanctions were a frequent topic of discussion at these events. In the immediate aftermath of the Trump administration's Iran decision, experts focused on the unique opportunity that the apparent backlash against the dollar provided for China and its currency. The vice mayor of Beijing speculated that the renminbi's global status would rise because the United States had "abused the privilege of having an internationally dominant currency."[54] Xiaolian Hu, deputy governor of the People's Bank of China (PBOC), pointed out that US sanctions had pushed some international financial activity away from the dollar and challenged her country to "seize this opportunity and take advantage of it."[55] Former PBOC chair Zhou Xiaochuan spoke about the renminbi's progress as an international currency and observed that Washington's use of sanctions would have some negative impacts on the dollar's use as a reserve and payments currency.[56] Yu Yongding, an influential Chinese economist with deep connections to the policy community, traditionally known for his circumspect views about the pace of renminbi internationalization, pulled no punches:

> Although frustrated, we should not give up the ultimate goal of renminbi internationalization. . . . [N]ew possibilities have presented themselves. For example, Trump wielding the stick of sanctions against Russia and Iran provides us with an opportunity to promote renminbi internationalization. . . . We suggest Iran use renminbi as the pricing and settlement currency through the alternative payment system newly established by China.[57]

In the spring of 2019, as Beijing began cracking down on democratic activists in Hong Kong, Chinese media outlets and elites began to worry that the United States would sanction China as it had Russia and Iran. Such concerns were prescient. In the months leading up to the August 2020 measures targeting Hong Kong chief executive Carrie Lam and ten other government officials, the political risks of dollar dependence became the prominent theme discussed among China's financial elite. The *Global Times* bluntly noted that the country could face Iran's fate and, thus, "China should be prepared for the worst-case scenario."[58] A plethora of financial elites called for a redoubling of renminbi internationalization efforts as the antidote to US pressure. Experts in China were sounding alarm bells: "The chances are not low" that Washington would soon target China. This required action from Beijing to "disentangle" itself from the dollar to defend against such risks.[59] A Bank of China report urged Chinese financial institutions to start using China's cross-border messaging and payments system, known as CIPS, to avoid US sanctions. The report also advised that holdings of dollar assets in the United States should be cut and moved to "relatively safe countries and regions" since they were vulnerable to being frozen by the US Treasury.[60] In a prominent Chinese financial periodical, the former vice president of a major state-owned bank argued that Beijing should convert US dollar reserves into gold and "move it back to China."[61]

Experts in China focused on the plumbing of the cross-border payments system. They considered CHIPS and SWIFT instruments through which the United States "exercises global hegemony" and maintained that continuing to rely on the dollar payments infrastructure left the country highly vulnerable to the long reach of the US Treasury.[62] Once again, Chinese financial elites and policymakers emphasized the importance of renminbi internationalization as a remedy for these risks. Pointing to the use of sanctions against Russia, Iran, and Venezuela, former PBOC chair Zhou explained "we must pay close attention to the internationalization of the renminbi," since this was the only way China could "effectively resist" US sanctions pressure.[63] Referencing the sanctions threat, another Chinese banker and former PBOC economist put it this way: "Yuan [renminbi] internationalization was a good-to-have. It's now becoming a must-have."[64] In public remarks at a financial policy summit, the vice chairman of the China Securities Regulatory Commission rhetorically asked whether China's current cross-border payment channels were safe. Then, using Chinese proverbs, he suggested that state policy surrounding renminbi internationalization should shift from "水到渠成" (let the water build the canal) to one of proactive planning, "未雨绸缪" (preparing an umbrella before the rain).[65]

Conclusions

The US dollar remains the king of currencies. It has held this position for nearly a century, making all who prognosticated its demise look foolish in hindsight. A key reason for the dollar's durability is the lack of attractive, viable alternatives. Despite early hopes that accompanied the euro's launch in

1999, the monetary union did not endeavor to boost the currency's global rise. It became a key player, but never seriously challenged the dollar. And, for a long time, European policymakers were fine with that. China, for its part, helped sustain (and even increase) the dollar's grip on the world economy during its rapid economic growth in the 1990s and early 2000s. Policies to promote renminbi internationalization following the 2008 financial crisis quickly fizzled out.

Financial and policymaking elites in both Europe and China began reevaluating the risks associated with dollar dependence as Washington came to rely more and more on sanctions as a tool of coercion. For Europe, a slow simmer of objections became a rolling boil following the United States' move to blow up the Iran nuclear deal. In response, the Europeans failed to create a functional short-term fix in INSTEX but began crafting a longer-term strategy to increase their financial autonomy by articulating a muscular euro internationalization strategy. For the first time since the euro's creation, the Europeans abandoned their neutral position on the currency's international role in a direct response to US sanctions. It is too soon to tell whether Europe will succeed, but there were early signs of progress in 2020 as the share of natural gas contracts signed in euros increased to 64 percent from just 38 percent in 2018.[66]

In China, it was Washington's decision to use sanctions in 2014 to punish Russia for seizing Crimea that first raised eyebrows. Subsequent measures by the US Treasury led many Chinese elites to see an opportunity to promote the renminbi as an option for the growing number of burned, blacklisted countries. Hong Kong sanctions poured gasoline on these discussions. Renminbi internationalization was no longer something to be desired for reasons of economic efficiency; it became a matter of Chinese sovereignty and economic survival. Of course, awakening to the political risks associated with dollar dependence does not mean that Europe and China will follow through on their renewed interest in promoting their currencies. It is easier to talk of such things than it is to accomplish them. But for the sake of protecting the United States' awesome power to sanction, it may have been better had the anti-dollar conversations never started.

8

China's Play for Payments Power

The strategic significance of China's establishment of a renminbi cross-border payment system is not only that it [gives us] alternatives under extreme pressure, but also has a far-reaching significance in promoting the internationalization of the renminbi.

Desheng Gao, Vice President, Bank of China
Johannesburg Branch[1]

The June 2011 announcement read: "We'd like to bring the nuance and richness of real-life sharing to software. We want to make Google better by including you, your relationships, and your interests. And so begins the Google+ project."[2] Between 2004 and 2011, Facebook had amassed 800,000 users around the globe. Google, though a multi-billion-dollar company, lacked a foothold in the growing online social media space. Google+ was to be its grand entrance. At the time, the threat to Facebook appeared real. Its founder and CEO, Mark Zuckerberg, reportedly put his company into "lockdown" in preparation for a war designed to "crush" its new rival.[3] In the end, Google+ turned out to be a catastrophic failure; the site was shuttered by April 2018. The expected dynamic user growth never arrived. Without enough people on the platform, there was little reason for others to join. A Reddit poster succinctly summed up the problem in a 2015 online discussion board about the soon-to-be-defunct site: "I think it's just that facebook [*sic*] is so huge at this point. . . . Everyone is on facebook [*sic*] so leaving it to go somewhere else doesn't make much sense."[4]

This lesson about the power of network effects applies to any country hoping to challenge the dollar's global dominance. From an end user's perspective, the choice between Facebook and Google+ boiled down to one question: who else is on the social network? Even though Google+ had a

Bucking the Buck. Daniel McDowell, Oxford University Press. © Oxford University Press 2023.
DOI: 10.1093/oso/9780197679876.003.0009

more aesthetically pleasing interface than Facebook as well as new and innovative features that allowed friends to connect online—not to mention better privacy and security protections—it simply did not have a big enough user base. Facebook was more attractive to the average social media user because it was more attractive to most other social media users. The circularity in that statement is the point: network dominance is self-sustaining. Once achieved, this equilibrium is difficult to upset. Though network dominance is an imperfect metaphor for the global currency system, there are similarities. A small number of national monies have become international currencies largely due to network effects (see Chapter 2). The more that market actors make or accept payments in a given currency, the more useful and efficient it is for others to do the same. The dollar remains the most attractive international currency for the average individual market actor because it is the most attractive international currency for most other market actors. These two truths reinforce each other through iterative market interactions.

As the United States has wielded its sanctions capabilities more frequently, financial and policy elites in China have awakened to the political risks of depending on the dollar network. As the vice chairman of the China Securities Regulatory Commission explained, "If we can make greater progress in the internationalization of the [renminbi], our ability to financially decouple [from the dollar] will be greatly enhanced."[5] As Chapter 7 established, Beijing senses both a need and an opportunity to further internationalize the renminbi to protect its economy from future US sanctions and weaken Washington's coercive capabilities in the process. Yet for China, creating an alternative, renminbi-based payment network is akin to Google+ trying to challenge Facebook. To paraphrase the Reddit post quoted earlier, just about everyone is using the dollar at this point, so using the renminbi makes little sense. But Beijing is pressing ahead. Its motives cannot be entirely reduced to concerns about US sanctions, of course; there are economic considerations as well. But sanctions are a significant factor propelling Beijing forward. Perhaps even more notable is evidence that sanctions have played a role in the rising number of foreign banks that have joined the upstart Chinese financial platform. If that trend continues, it could give Beijing the user base it needs to grow the payment network sufficiently to loosen the dollar's grip on cross-border transactions and diminish US sanctions capabilities.

Closing the Loop

US sanctions have been an important driving force behind Beijing's motivation to develop its own anti-dollar payment system based on its currency. The more that Chinese businesses use the renminbi for cross-border trade and investment, the more difficult it will be for Washington to weaponize the dollar to disrupt China's economic relations. If US sanctions are less effective against China, the United States will lose economic leverage in future conflicts, including a potential struggle over Taiwanese independence. China's effort to internationalize its currency, beginning around 2006, has proceeded in fits and starts with a mixture of successes and setbacks. However, the renminbi has steadily emerged as an important currency for the country's cross-border settlement of trade and investment. A survey of Chinese firms involved in the international economy conducted in 2020 by a major state-owned Chinese bank found that three out of four businesses polled had used the renminbi to settle trade, while one in three had used renminbi-denominated cross-border investment services. Both figures topped responses to the same questions on all previous surveys.[6]

Yet Beijing must do more than internationalize its currency to effectively insulate itself and its economic partners from US sanctions. As described in Chapter 2, the dollar-based payment system consists of three key components: a medium of exchange (dollars), a communication platform (SWIFT), and a network of correspondent banking hubs (CHIPS). China therefore needs to create a "closed loop" financial system that is disconnected not just from the US currency but also from CHIPS and SWIFT.[7]

For example, major Chinese financial institutions could develop their own renminbi-clearing correspondent accounts with smaller banks around the world, effectively displacing CHIPS. Yet if payment instructions continue to depend on SWIFT, the US Treasury will have access to details about the transactions—including the identities of the originator (the entity making the payment) and the beneficiary (the entity receiving the payment). US access to SWIFT's messaging data,[8] pursuant to a 2001 agreement and enhanced by the fact that the messaging corporation maintains a critical data center in Virginia, could enable Washington to curtail cross-border renminbi payments by pressuring SWIFT to cut off targeted entities. This is precisely what occurred in 2018 when the Trump administration pulled the United States out of the Iran nuclear deal and then quickly compelled SWIFT to cut off operations with Iranian banks.[9] This move left financial institutions in Iran unable to send or receive payment messages on the all-important platform. Similarly, following Russia's invasion of Ukraine in 2022, the United States and its European allies instated SWIFT sanctions against a group of major Russian banks, including VTB, the country's second-largest lender.[10]

Cross-border renminbi payments that rely on SWIFT messaging remain vulnerable to US sanctions for another reason as well. Imagine the following scenario: Washington blacklists a foreign business owned by a Russian oligarch with close ties to Vladimir Putin, and a Chinese bank is settling cross-border trade in renminbi on behalf of Chinese firms doing business with this oligarch's company. Even though no US banks are involved in these transactions, payment messages are sent via SWIFT, giving the United States the capacity to identify and punish the parties involved. The US Treasury instructs all banks with US operations to cut ties with the Chinese bank or else face severe financial penalties. This bank, now cut off from correspondent banking relationships with most major global financial institutions, is forced to reconsider its renminbi-based business with the targeted oligarch's firm. If the United States enforces secondary sanctions against China,[11] this would push banks operating outside US legal jurisdiction to cut ties with the Chinese bank as well, intensifying its isolation and further raising the costs of its business relationship with the Russian target. This hypothetical case demonstrates that even if cross-border renminbi payments cleared through Chinese financial institutions expand greatly, the actors involved remain vulnerable to US financial pressure as long as they rely on SWIFT.

For China to develop a renminbi-based payment system that is far less vulnerable to US pressure, it must craft a closed loop network that disconnects from all three components of the dollar-based system: the dollar, SWIFT, and CHIPS. To accomplish this, China must build an independent payments messaging network. It would also need to enlist major Chinese financial institutions to establish a CHIPS rival—a network of renminbi-based correspondent accounts with foreign banks, especially those not operating in the US market. Building such a network would deprive the United States of both the panopticon and chokepoint effects, described by Farrell and Newman and discussed in Chapter 2.[12] Payments in the network would take place in renminbi. Instructions, including the identities of the originator and beneficiary of a transaction, would be sent confidentially, away from Washington's watchful eye. Similarly, the clearing of payments would route around CHIPS banks to avoid US legal jurisdiction.

The Renminbi's Rough Road Ahead

China would face at least two important challenges in any attempt to create such a system. The first is the *Field of Dreams* effect. In this 1989 film, Iowa corn farmer Ray Kinsella (played by Kevin Costner) hears a disembodied voice telling him, "If you build it, he will come"; the "it" is a baseball field, while the "he" is Kinsella's deceased, baseball fan father. Though the subject is quite different, a similar premise holds in the world of international payments. Foreign interest in cross-border renminbi payments will remain stunted until China can create an efficient and convenient payment network. If China builds such a network, then foreign interest might very well come next.

Yet even an attractive payment network could still fall short of its ambitions, which relates to the second challenge facing China: the government must transition the renminbi into a fully convertible currency while raising its profile as an investment currency. If foreign partners do not have confidence that there is an ample supply of safe, liquid, freely tradable renminbi-based assets in which to invest their renminbi receipts, there will be limited appetite to use the currency in payments, regardless of how well built the system is.[13] After setbacks in the mid-2010s, China has made progress in opening its financial markets to foreign investment. Beijing has cut red tape and reduced the transaction costs associated with foreign inflows. Major global investment indexes now include Chinese equities and bonds in their portfolios, a move that has directed significant investment inflows into China.[14] Yet Chinese financial markets remain more closed to foreigners than the fully liberalized, larger, and more liquid US financial market. Moreover, Xi Jinping's less-than-transparent leadership and Machiavellian efforts to consolidate state power in his own hands have jeopardized international trust in the stability of China's economic policies. It remains an open question whether foreign investors in China can fully trust Beijing's commitment to the free movement of capital across borders, which may limit their appetite for renminbi-denominated assets on the mainland.[15] Taken together, China has much work to do if it intends to contest the dollar's supremacy in payments as a means of diminishing Washington's sanctions capabilities.

The narrow use of the renminbi as an international payments currency demonstrates how much work remains to be done before other countries consider it a realistic alternative to the dollar. According to SWIFT data, by 2020 the renminbi had established itself as the fifth-most used currency

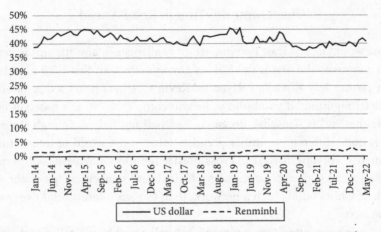

Figure 8.1. Currency Share of Cross-Border Payments, 2014–2022. The renminbi, which never tops 3 percent of cross-border payments, lags far behind the dollar for the entire period. Data source: Society for Worldwide Interbank Financial Telecommunication (SWIFT).

for cross-border payments.[16] Figure 8.1 compares the share of international payments made in dollars versus renminbi since 2014. While the dollar share fluctuated between 40 and 45 percent and usually holds the top spot, the renminbi never cracked 3 percent. Nor did its popularity noticeably increase during this period.

Yet the SWIFT data belie some progress that China has made on this front, which the remainder of this chapter will explore. In time, and if it implements the right policies, China may be able to transform its currency from a bit player into an attractive dollar alternative—at least among some states. US financial sanctions may contribute to this transformation if their use both accelerates Beijing's renminbi internationalization efforts and pushes targeted and at-risk states into China's arms.

The Challenge from the Cross-Border Interbank Payment System (CIPS)

Since 2012, China's central bank, the People's Bank of China (PBOC), has been building its own renminbi-based international payments network, known as CIPS. Officially launched in 2015, CIPS represents an effort to combine SWIFT's international messaging functionality with the clearing system of CHIPS into a single system based on the renminbi. Financial institutions can either participate directly or indirectly in CIPS. Direct participants are analogous to the roughly fifty elite CHIPS banks that operate as dollar clearing hubs between all other banks involved in cross-border dollar payments. At the end of 2021, there were seventy-six direct participants, up from just nine at the end of 2016 (see Appendix Table G.1 for a list). Though not all direct participants are located on the mainland, the PBOC requires them to be legally established in China to ensure they are subject to Chinese law[17]—similar to the requirement that all CHIPS banks must be incorporated in the United States. Direct participants can send payment instructions using either the system's dedicated messaging lines or via SWIFT, with which CIPS partnered in 2016 to help speed up the network's development.

Many more indirect participating banks, both on the Chinese mainland and in foreign countries, connect to the renminbi-clearing system via their accounts with direct participants. Indirect participants are unable to use the CIPS messaging lines and instead rely on SWIFT. Given that Washington is privy to SWIFT data, this is an obvious limitation of the system's capacity to blunt US financial sanctions. At the end of 2021, nearly 1,200 banks on every major continent were part of the system according to CIPS' own accounting. Figure 8.2 displays the rapid growth in the number of direct and indirect network participants (both foreign and Chinese banks), and Figure 8.3 depicts the regional distribution of foreign indirect participants. Unsurprisingly, given China's regional economic links, CIPS is most popular in Asia and the Middle East. However, the system has also gained a foothold in Europe and increasingly in Africa as well.

While SWIFT's cross-border renminbi payments data suggest little growth during the second half of the 2010s (see Figure 8.1), PBOC data on CIPS traffic suggest otherwise. According to the central bank's numbers, in January 2016 roughly 2,000 daily transactions occurred via CIPS. By the end of 2020, this had grown to 12,000. Similarly, the average daily volume of renminbi cleared on the platform, displayed in Figure 8.4, grew from about 10 billion ($150 million) to nearly 240 billion ($35.6 billion) in the same period. While the reason for the discrepancy between the SWIFT and PBOC data is not clear, one possibility is that the growth in CIPS transactions occurred largely among direct participants using the platform's own messaging system, which would not show up in SWIFT's records.

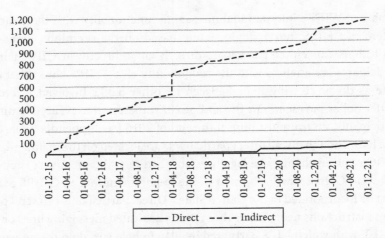

Figure 8.2. Number of Direct and Indirect CIPS Participants, 2015–2021. The total number of direct and indirect participants includes banks on the Chinese mainland. Data are based on CIPS' own membership data. The significant spike in indirect participants in April 2018 coincides with CIPS' shift from Phase 1 to Phase 2, during which a range of technical improvements were implemented. It is possible that this increase is also due to a change in reporting by CIPS.

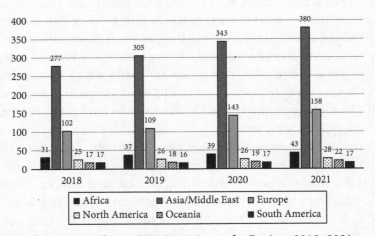

Figure 8.3. Foreign Indirect CIPS Participants by Region, 2018–2021. Mainland Chinese banks are omitted from the "Asia/Middle East" category. Data source: CIPS.

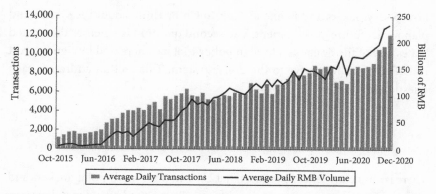

Figure 8.4. Monthly Payments Traffic and Volume, 2015–2020. Use of the CIPS system, both in terms of the number of transactions and the volume of payments, has steadily increased since its launch in 2015. Data and figure adapted by author from PBOC report.

The Chinese statistics tell two competing stories. The first is that renminbi payments via CIPS rose steadily in the five years after the network's 2015 launch. The second is that despite this growth, CIPS and the renminbi remain far, far behind the dollar-based payment system. SWIFT processes more than 40 million payment requests worth a total of roughly $5 trillion every day.[18] This dwarfs CIPS, which in early 2022 handled the renminbi equivalent of $46 billion per day.[19] CIPS is the Google+ to the dollar system's Facebook. Calling the renminbi a "competitor" to the dollar would devalue the very concept of competition. But then Rome was not built in a day, and neither is a new global payments network. More important for the purposes of this book, the question is not whether the renminbi will emerge as a peer competitor of the dollar in the near or medium term. Rather, it is how China's currency, relying on the upstart CIPS, might carve out a niche for itself in the world economy and gain a foothold by attracting users looking to protect themselves from US financial coercion.

Running from the Dollar

Two key questions should be considered in assessing whether US financial sanctions have influenced the development of CIPS and the renminbi's popularity as a payment currency. The first is whether sanctions have changed how policymakers and financial elites in China think about the system and plan for its future development. The second question is whether the United States' use of the dollar as a foreign policy tool has increased foreign interest in CIPS as an alternative to the dollar system. This section addresses each question in turn.

From Sanctions to CIPS: The View from Inside China

There is ample evidence to suggest that US sanctions made policymakers and elites in China more aware of the vulnerabilities posed by a dependence on dollar payments and made CIPS a more attractive solution. CIPS became a popular topic of discussion around the time of the Trump administration's 2020 decision to sanction a group of Communist Party officials in Hong Kong; the sanctions were in opposition to the officials' role in quashing democratic protests against Beijing's encroachment on the special administrative region's political autonomy. Chinese experts homed in on a major limitation of CIPS: its reliance on SWIFT messaging. Wang Yongli, a former vice president of a large Chinese state-owned commercial bank, expressed skepticism on social media that China could successfully challenge the dollar's network dominance, pointing out that "the actual effect [of CIPS] will be very limited" if it continues to rely on SWIFT messaging.[20] This sentiment was echoed in a major Chinese investment bank report released at the time (aptly titled "If the US imposes financial sanctions on Chinese banks, how should we respond?"). The bank recommended that Beijing "promote the use of CIPS dedicated line messages (or the development of a new message system) for cross-border receipts and payments . . . to reduce the exposure of international payment information to the United States."[21] At a forum involving policymakers and banking elites, the head of a Shanghai-based research institute asserted that CIPS was key to protecting China from US financial sanctions, but only "as long as [messages] can be transmitted internally" and if "no out-of-line systems such as SWIFT are used."[22] These examples demonstrate how US sanctions have reshaped Chinese thinking about how best to develop a renminbi-based international payment system.

Yet Beijing faces a trade-off: on one hand, it would like to rapidly scale up the renminbi's role as an international payment currency, and partnering with SWIFT is a good way to accomplish this. On the other hand, it also has an interest in creating a fully independent, closed-loop international payment network—with no connections to the dollar system, since this would best insulate it from US sanctions. Unfortunately for Beijing, these two goals are at odds with one another. Because SWIFT is the unquestioned payment messaging standard, renminbi payments via CIPS are more appealing to the average foreign financial institution when transaction requests can be sent over the communication channels they are already using. Indeed, a desire to broaden CIPS' appeal is why the PBOC partnered with the dominant messaging network in the first place. However, the SWIFT partnership also prevents CIPS from closing the loop, which gravely limits the system's ability to help evade sanctions—and greatly weakens its value to foreign states seeking a haven from US sanctions.

There are, in short, two discrete markets for CIPS that push Beijing in opposing directions. The first (larger) market includes financial institutions that rely daily on SWIFT and operate in the dollar payment system with few or no concerns about US sanctions. For this group, participating in China's new platform is less attractive if it relies on its own, dedicated messaging system. The second (smaller) market consists of financial institutions in sanctioned and at-risk states that are deeply aware of the political risk inherent in the dollar system. Some of these institutions are themselves cut off from CHIPS and SWIFT because the US Treasury has blacklisted them. For this group, which is primarily interested in conducting cross-border payments beyond Washington's reach, any Chinese payment platform that lacks its own messaging system represents little improvement over the status quo. Which market Beijing decides to target will play an important role in how the payment network evolves and whether the renminbi becomes the focal currency for sanctions evasion or remains just another option on the SWIFT currency menu.

From Sanctions to CIPS: The View from Outside China

It is difficult to determine the extent to which US sanctions have increased foreign interest in renminbi-based payments via CIPS. While the PBOC has released information about all *direct* participants in the CIPS system, including their locations, it has largely kept confidential similar details about *indirect* participants. Confidently illustrating a broad-based link between US sanctions and foreign participation in CIPS would require a complete and accurate accounting of the number of indirect participants at the country level. If the average number of CIPS participants is higher in countries under US sanctions or those at a higher risk of facing sanctions, it would suggest that CIPS is gaining interest due to political risk concerns. Yet absent good data on the geographic distribution of indirect participants, there are limited options for addressing this question and there is much greater uncertainty about any conclusions reached. Still, given the stakes involved, an imperfect effort to address this question is better than no effort at all.

While access to information is highly constrained, I use three sources to stitch together a partial picture of the emerging payment network. First, while the PBOC did not release comprehensive details on indirect participants, CIPS' periodic press releases from its launch in 2015 until early 2019 included selective information on more than 100 new indirect participants, including bank names and locations. Second, various media and industry reports contain additional information about where the platform's participants are located. Finally, requests to central banks for information about national

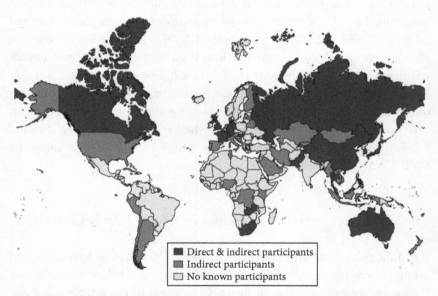

Figure 8.5. CIPS Participation by Country, 2022. Countries shaded dark gray have at least one financial institution that is an indirect participant and at least one that is a direct participant. Those shaded light gray have at least one indirect participant, but no direct participants. CIPS participation in unshaded countries is unknown.

bank participation in CIPS yielded some supplementary details. Figure 8.5 maps CIPS country-level participation.

The figure does not report the total number of participants in each country, as this information is not reliably available. However, it does distinguish between countries that are known to have both direct and indirect participants, those that just have one or more direct participants, and those that are not known to have any participants. The data identify a total of fifty-six countries as hosting financial institutions that are participants in the CIPS network as of April 2022. At that time, CIPS reported that its system had participants in 104 countries; these data therefore capture just over half of the full picture, assuming Chinese reporting was accurate.[23]

I estimate a logistic regression where the outcome is *CIPS Membership*, which equals 1 if a country is known to have at least one direct or indirect participant, and 0 otherwise. If US sanctions have increased participation in CIPS, we would expect to see a positive association between sanctions variables and involvement in the Chinese payment network. As in previous analyses, I employ *SREO* and *Sanctions Risk* as my key explanatory variables; Chapter 4 describes both in detail. Given that larger, more developed economies should have more banks involved in cross-border payments, and therefore more opportunities to participate in the system, I control for GDP and GDP per capita. Since time-series data on CIPS participation is lacking, the sample includes one observation per country, based on the data displayed in Figure 8.5. China is excluded from the analysis.

Figure 8.6 displays the results. Both sanctions variables are positively associated with CIPS participation, which indicates that countries facing US sanctions and those at a higher risk of sanctions are more likely to have financial institutions involved in the Chinese platform. The coefficients for these covariates are displayed in the left panel of the figure. Both are statistically significant, though *Sanctions Risk* falls short of higher levels of statistical confidence. The right panel shows the predicted probability of country-level participation in CIPS contingent on whether the state has been targeted by US sanctions, holding other covariates at their means. According to the model, there is a roughly one in four chance (0.24) that an unsanctioned country (*SREO* = 0) has at least one bank participating in CIPS. For sanctioned states (*SREO* = 1), the probability of having at least one bank participating in CIPS more than doubles to better than a one out of two chance (0.64). The differences between these estimates are both substantively and statistically significant (at the $p < 0.01$ level).

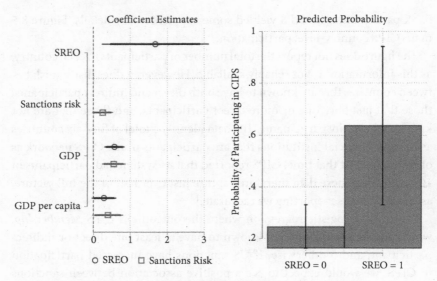

Figure 8.6. Coefficient and Predicted Probability Estimates, CIPS Participation. The left panel presents logistic coefficient estimates of CIPS participation based on the described model. Circles/squares represent the coefficient point estimates. Wide (narrow) lines represent 90 (95) percent confidence intervals. Both sanctions variables are positive and statistically distinct from zero, though statistical confidence in SREOs is higher. Table G2 in Appendix G reports the full results. The right panel displays estimates of the predicted probability of CIPS participation as SREO varies from 0 to 1.

In sum, the results are consistent with a scenario in which US financial sanctions raised political risk concerns about dependence on the dollar payment system and pushed financial institutions in targeted states to participate in CIPS. However, it is possible that the full data on CIPS participation would yield a different conclusion. The most that can be said is that the available data illustrate a picture that is not *inconsistent* with a story linking sanctions to participation in China's anti-dollar payment system.

To complement this analysis, we can also explore anecdotes about the timing of banks' decisions to join CIPS. If, for example, US financial sanctions targeting a government are followed shortly by banks in that country joining China's anti-dollar payment network, it would further imply a link between sanctions and CIPS. Once again, while details about most participants were never released, some examples paint a suggestive picture. For example, according to CIPS' own reporting, four Turkish banks joined the network as indirect participants between October and November 2018.[24] This closely followed US financial sanctions that targeted a group of Turkish government officials linked to the country's detention of an American pastor. Prior to this, only one Turkish bank had been identified as a CIPS participant, joining in April 2017. Similarly, media reports first noted Iranian banks' participation in CIPS in 2019, the year after the Trump administration pulled out of the Joint Comprehensive Plan of Action, though the precise date of their membership is unclear.[25] In each case, the timing of bank participation in CIPS implies that sanctions may have played a role in those decisions.

Sanctions also apparently triggered interest in CIPS in April 2022 following the Russian invasion of Ukraine and a subsequent barrage of US sanctions targeting Moscow. At that time, Belarus—a close Russian ally as well as a target of sanctions—announced it was completing the process of acceding to CIPS. The Belarussian finance minister acknowledged his country was planning to use CIPS to settle trade with China in renminbi. He explained that the system could help Belarus route financial transactions around US sanctions, noting that "for various reasons, mainly sanctions-related, not all [our foreign liabilities payments] go through."[26] Elsewhere, a 2019 investigative report identified Russia as having twenty-three banks participating in CIPS—including VTB, the country's second-largest lender—more than any country besides Japan at the time.[27] In July 2014, VTB got its first taste of US sanctions. In March 2016, it was one of the first 100 banks to join CIPS, barely three months after the network's launch.[28]

Of course, none of these anecdotes provides decisive proof of a sanctions–CIPS link. But collectively, and in combination with the cross-national evidence presented in this chapter, it is not unreasonable to conclude that foreign interest in CIPS is partly driven by political risk concerns stemming from Washington's use of the dollar payment system as a weapon of foreign policy.

Conclusions

Though privately Mark Zuckerberg took seriously the challenge posed by Google+ in 2011, he remained confident in public. At a Facebook product launch days after his company's new rival was introduced, he said of the competition: "We're years ahead."[29] The United States might say the same thing about the dollar's head start in cross-border payments compared to the upstart renminbi-based rival. The distance between the two platforms is cavernous, and the challenge facing China's currency is about as daunting as it gets. Yet CIPS' user base grows year after year, leading to an expansion in the volume of daily cross-border transactions. At least some of that growth may be attributable to rising political risk concerns stemming from US sanctions. Washington's coercive economic policies appear to have redirected the attention of at least some financial institutions in targeted states toward CIPS. Its mere existence functions as a beacon of hope for banks that are already on the US Treasury's blacklist and those that worry they will be next.

While China's interest in internationalizing the renminbi pre-dates significant concerns in Beijing about US sanctions pressure, the importance of developing a system that is resilient to such pressure has risen alongside Washington's increasing reliance on financial coercion.

US sanctions have also awakened Beijing to the risks of depending on dollar payments and the limitations of its own budding payment network, especially its continued reliance on SWIFT messaging. The challenge for China is how to close the loop without diminishing the network's potential for broad appeal. If the risk of sanctions becomes the driving force behind the development of CIPS, then Beijing may have to settle for a less ambitious, if more politically secure, system. This is just the sort of system that would be most appealing to foreign governments and businesses facing (or fearing) US sanctions. How China proceeds, and whether it succeeds, will have important consequences for the unfolding US–China rivalry and Washington's ability to use the dollar dependence as a pressure point in any future dispute between the powers.

Conclusion

A foundational concept taught in all International Relations 101 courses is deterrence: the act of using threats to prevent an opponent from undertaking an undesired course of action. For deterrence to work, the state making the threat must convince its adversary that it has (1) the capacity to hurt something the opponent values and (2) the "resolve" to carry out the threat if the opponent defies its demands. Yet deterrence can still fail even if the threatening state credibly communicates that it possesses both qualities. If the opponent calculates that the benefits of acting outweigh the associated costs, it will proceed undeterred. For example, the United States failed to deter Russia's February 2022 war in Ukraine. The previous month, US President Joe Biden made the unusual move of revealing intelligence that Russia was planning to invade and warned Russian President Putin "that if he were to move into Ukraine, that there would be severe consequences, including significant economic sanctions."[1] US National Security Adviser Jake Sullivan candidly explained that the administration was "trying to, first of all, deter and prevent a potentially massive Russian invasion."[2] Putin, of course, dismissed these threats and proceeded with his brutal war.

In the days and weeks that followed, the United States unleashed a barrage of wide-ranging punitive commercial and financial measures targeting Russian oligarchs, businesses, the Central Bank of Russia (CBR), and even Putin himself. While it will take historians years to untangle the full details of Putin's calculations, it is logical to conclude that deterrence failed *not* because the United States did not effectively signal its capacity to hurt Russian economic interests or because it was unable to convince the Kremlin that it had the resolve to follow through with such penalties. After all, the United States had repeatedly demonstrated its sanctions capacity and resolve over the previous eight years. By 2022, Russia had been targeted by thirteen separate US sanctions-related Executive Orders in response to various offenses, including its 2014 invasion of Crimea, election meddling, human rights violations, and cyber-attacks. Rather, deterrence most likely failed because the United States did not get the costs right. Putin calculated that the benefits of undertaking

Bucking the Buck. Daniel McDowell, Oxford University Press. © Oxford University Press 2023.
DOI: 10.1093/oso/9780197679876.003.0010

a war in Ukraine would exceed any economic costs that Washington and its allies could inflict. The failure to deter Russian aggression was the result of a policy problem, not a messaging problem.

It may be that no amount of threatened economic costs could have convinced Putin to rethink his malicious aims. After all, economic sanctions have their limits. However, it is also possible—perhaps even likely—that Putin dismissed sanctions threats because Moscow had taken steps to minimize its exposure to such penalties after previous rounds of US sanctions. For nearly a decade, Russian officials had been "doomsday prepping" for this very moment. Did Putin's calculus change because the CBR had drastically cut its dollar holdings, shifted 20 percent of the nation's financial assets into physical gold, and put another 10 percent into renminbi? Did the rise in non-dollar trade settlement in Russia's bilateral commercial relations increase his confidence that the damage from US sanctions would be seriously diminished? It is not unreasonable to conclude that Russia's anti-dollar policy efforts at least partially influenced Putin's thinking in the run-up to the war. The Kremlin's pre-emptive steps to reduce its exposure to the dollar may have weakened Biden's hand by diluting the potency of US economic threats.

Yet no country can fully "sanction proof" its economy. I have demonstrated in this book that the dollar is still king of all currencies and is likely to remain so for decades to come. Reducing dependence on the dollar is not the same as fully decoupling from the currency. Even modestly successful de-dollarizers like Russia remain quite vulnerable to US financial pressure. Still, as this book has shown, the more that the United States has flexed the awesome financial power of the dollar, the more that brutal autocrats like Putin have felt compelled to innovate to address the rising political risk concerns. Just as baseball hitters adjust to a pitcher over the course of nine innings and improve their chances of getting on base as the game progresses, Washington's adversaries are adapting to its financial coercion tools. The analyses presented in this book illustrate that US sanctions have generated political risk concerns that have provoked certain states to pursue anti-dollar policies. While these have not always succeeded, good evidence suggests that those efforts have yielded de-dollarization in many cases. Targeted and at-risk governments are learning from their own experiences as well as those of other sanctioned countries. They are increasingly sharing information and collaborating, just as hitters in the dugout share tips about how to spot the opposing pitcher's curveball.

If the United States wishes to preserve the potency of its financial coercion tools and protect the dollar's pre-eminent position in the world economy, its sanctions policy should become more discerning. Financial sanctions are an appealing foreign policy instrument because they can be swiftly enacted in response to a foreign threat or wrongdoing. This can reassure a concerned public, and even government officials, that "something" is being done. Yet this book has demonstrated the potential costs of using the dollar in this way. Future US sanctions policy should be guided by four broad considerations to preserve the dollar's coercive power.

First, Washington should use sanctions only if its core interests, or those of its allies, are threatened. For the last twenty years, the United States has used financial sanctions to inflict costs on state targets to redress human rights violations, punish democratic backsliding, and respond to security threats. While it is appropriate for the United States to craft policy responses to each type of incident, financial sanctions are not always the best tool. There are ways to inflict costs on individuals, firms, and government institutions that do not "politicize" the dollar system. Employing financial sanctions to punish foreign governments for cyber-attacks against American corporations—as both the Biden and Trump administrations have done—is a misguided use of dollar supremacy that could weaken the tool's effectiveness when circumstances demand its use, such as Russian efforts to redraw borders in Europe.

Second, policymakers must carefully reflect on the target's capacity to adapt in response to sanctions pressure. Small countries with economies positioned on the periphery of the globalized financial and trading systems, like Sudan or Myanmar, are constrained in how they can respond to US sanctions. They are unlikely to find economic partners interested in using their national currencies for cross-border transactions. Nor can such countries create scalable alternative payment messaging platforms. Any adjustments they might make to the currency composition of their foreign exchange reserves will have little or no impact on the dollar's status at the macro level. Sanctions that target small states present far less of a threat to the dollar or the long-term effectiveness of financial sanctions.[3] It is riskier to target larger, more developed economies that are situated closer to the core of the world economy—such as China—because they may have the capacity to act as "suppliers" of alternative currencies and financial networks. Similarly, secondary sanctions that adversely impact European interests pose high potential costs to the dollar. In short, targeting major US economic rivals that have the capacity to successfully implement anti-dollar policies, and the economic size and centrality necessary to attract new users to an emerging anti-dollar system, motivated each one to take action. While the success of any initiative designed to weaken the dollar's grip on global finance is far from certain, Washington would be wise to avoid provoking such efforts in the first place. The case of middle powers is somewhat murky. Russia, for example, is neither helpless nor capable of independently crafting an effective anti-dollar system that will attract a critical mass of new adherents. In such cases, the decision to employ financial sanctions should hinge on additional context, including the specific goals of the sanctions program.

This relates to the third factor Washington should consider before proceeding with sanctions: whether its foreign policy goals align with what it can reasonably hope to accomplish by weaponizing the dollar. The precise goals of sanctions vary by case, and sometimes over time within a single case. For instance, sanctions may be threatened with the hope of deterring a foreign government from undertaking a specific action. However, if deterrence fails, they may be imposed in an attempt to compel that government to change its behavior and return—in part or in full—to the *status quo ante*. Alternatively, sanctions may be employed to degrade an adversary's capabilities over time, limiting its capability to complete or sustain the action it has undertaken. Finally, US policymakers may introduce sanctions simply to send a message, to both the target and the US public, that certain behaviors will result in economic punishment. Some of these goals, including deterrence, are harder to achieve because they are contingent on the target's response. However, other goals—such as degrading the target state's capabilities through imposing economic costs or sending a message to the target and a domestic audience— are easier to achieve because they do not depend on the target's response. Yet these lesser goals may not always be worth the risk of diminishing sanctions' effectiveness in the future. The dollar should not be vainly weaponized in the pursuit of a highly unlikely foreign policy goal or for a small foreign policy achievement.

The Trump administration's decision in 2020 to impose financial sanctions on a handful of officials in Hong Kong for their role in the Beijing-backed crackdowns on pro-democracy protests fits into this category. Those measures were far too limited to compel China to relinquish its increasingly authoritarian grip on the semi-autonomous region or to degrade Beijing's capacity to control Hong Kong. They only served to signal to Beijing that the United States was willing to use financial sanctions against Chinese state officials, and that China needed to devise a response to the blunt the future use of the dollar as a coercive tool against its national interests. In the future, the United States may have real cause to impose sweeping financial sanctions against Beijing—for instance, in response to an assault on Taiwan. Such sweeping measures will be more effective if the United States stops weaponizing the dollar when its goals are small or unlikely to be achieved.

Finally, Washington should coordinate financial sanctions with its major allies in Europe and Asia wherever possible. If coordination cannot be achieved, US policymakers should carefully weigh the potential costs of going it alone before acting. In many cases, acting without allies' support may pose few risks, such as targeting entities and individuals associated with governments in small, peripheral states. However, in other cases, going it alone can be quite risky, such as Trump's decision to pull out of the Iran nuclear deal in 2018. Because the Europeans did not support this move, the Trump administration resorted to secondary sanctions, which compelled Europe to comply with Washington's revived Iranian sanctions regime and prevented Tehran from diverting its cross-border financial activities into euros. While these secondary sanctions worked, they drove a deep wedge between the United States and Europe on sanctions policy and the role of the dollar. This division not only propelled Europe to begin crafting a vision of a more autonomous financial system and a more muscular stance on euro internationalization; it also created opportunities for US adversaries to capitalize on the newfound division. This was perhaps best illustrated by Russia's success in convincing Europe to pay for more of its oil and gas in euros rather than dollars. Conversely, multilateral sanctions programs can build trust between allies, as demonstrated by the Biden administration's efforts to work with European allies and Japan in response to Russia's invasion of Ukraine in 2022. Rather than generating concerns in Europe about the downsides of dollar dominance and provoking anti-dollar rhetoric and policy responses, the coordinated approach allowed US allies to operate as willing partners—stakeholders, even—in the flexing of American financial power. Moreover, multilateral responses do not require coercive, extraterritorial measures like secondary sanctions to withhold alternative currency "exit" options from targets. With Japanese and European cooperation, Putin was denied the option of moving his country's international economic activity or financial assets into yen or euros.

Dollar dominance is a critical and unrivaled power resource for the United States that is worth protecting. Washington has grown too comfortable, lazy even, in the use of that power. Introducing financial sanctions is easy. It satisfies the urge to "do something" in response to objectionable or threatening events. Yet this book illustrates that employing them too often could jeopardize the future effectiveness of US sanctions capabilities. By using the dollar as a weapon of foreign policy, Washington diminishes the currency's appeal and raises political risk concerns in capitals around the world. US policymakers should thus consider the long view when crafting sanctions policy. There may come a day when an American president will need to call upon the full legal authority of the US Treasury to inflict severe financial costs on an adversary that poses an existential threat to the United States and its allies. In the meantime, Washington would be wise to limit its use of financial sanctions for the sake of preserving the tool for such a moment.

Appendixes

Appendix A

Chapter 1 notes that the book's theory does not provide an explanation regarding why some anti-dollar policies succeed at producing de-dollarization while others fail. There are at least three factors that might influence the effectiveness of various anti-dollar policies. The first is the arena in which anti-dollar policies are being pursued. For instance, all else equal, the de-dollarization of reserves may be easier to achieve than the de-dollarization of trade settlement because the former relies only on the investment decisions of the country's central bank. Reserve managers can, in relatively short order, independently change the currency and asset composition of their investments. Yet to de-dollarize trade settlement, hundreds or even thousands of independent firms operating in the country must willingly change the currency in which they (and foreign businesses) conduct international business; success should thus be more difficult to achieve, at least in the short term. Second, the extent to which an anti-dollar policy is "experimental" also influences the likelihood of success. A government that launches a cryptocurrency in an effort to reduce dollar dependence in cross-border payments may be less likely to achieve its aims than one that works to shift contracts into an alternative state-backed currency such as the euro. Third, the scope and severity of the sanctions imposed on a country may affect the potential for success. Governments facing severe, sweeping sanctions are likely to have more limited response capabilities. For example, severe sanctions may deplete foreign exchange reserves, which would complicate any effort to diversify reserves away from the dollar. A country facing multilateral sanctions, where US financial measures are imposed alongside similar measures from other major currency issuers, will have very few alternative currency "exit" options, which reduces its chances of success.

Appendix B

Table B.1 displays sanctions-related Executive Orders (SREOs) in effect for some or all of the period between 2001 and 2020. Orders that revoke existing SREOs are not listed as new rows; rather, they are listed next to the SREO that they revoke. Orders that partially revoke SREOs are not listed since they do not add new sanctions measures and do not fully revoke an existing measure. Included in the table is the title of the sanctions program given by the US Treasury under which each SREO is classified, the official EO number, the year the order was issued, and the year the order was revoked (blank entries indicate the order was not revoked by the end of 2019). The table also includes the actors targeted under the SREO. Where country names are listed, this indicates that the order targets and is designed to put pressure on a specific government. This does not necessarily mean that state institutions or government officials are directly

Table B.1. Active Sanctions-related Executive Orders (SREOs) 2001–2020

Program Title	Year Issued	Year Revoked	Executive Order#	Target(s)	Justification
Balkans-Related Sanctions	2001		13219	Non-state	FPS
Balkans-Related Sanctions	2001		13304	Non-state; Bosnia and Herzegovina in 2017	FPS
Belarus Sanctions	2006		13405	Belarus	FPS, D, HR
Burma	2003	2016 (EO 13742)	13310	Burma	D
Burma	2007	2016 (EO 13742)	13448	Burma	FPS, D, HR
Burma	2008	2016 (EO 13742)	13464	Burma	D
Burma	2012	2016 (EO 13742)	13619	Burma	FPS, D
Burundi Sanctions	2015		13712	Burundi	FPS, HR
Central African Republic	2014		13667	Non-state	FPS, HR
Chinese Military Companies	2020		13959	China	FPS
Cote d'Ivoire	2006	2016 (EO 13739)	13396	Non-state	FPS, HR
Counter Narcotics Trafficking Sanctions	1995		12978	Non-state	FPS
Countering America's Adversaries Through Sanctions	2018		13849	Iran, Russia, North Korea	FPS
Counter Terrorism Sanctions (CTS)	1995		12947	Non-state	FPS
CTS	1998		13099	Non-state	FPS
Counter Terrorism Sanctions	2001		13224	Non-state	FPS
Counter Terrorism Sanctions	2002		13268	Non-state	FPS
Counter Terrorism Sanctions	2005		13372	Non-state	FPS

Counter Terrorism Sanctions	2019		13886	Non-state	FPS
Cuba	1993		12854	Cuba	D, HR
Cyber-Related Sanctions	2015		13694	Russia	FPS
Cyber-Related Sanctions	2016		13757	Russia	FPS
Democratic Republic of the Congo-Related Sanctions	2006		13413	Non-state	FPS, HR
Democratic Republic of the Congo-Related Sanctions	2014		13671	Non-state; DRC in 2016	HR
Former Liberian Regime of Charles Taylor	2003	2015 (EO 13710)	13348	Non-state	FPS, D
Foreign Interference in a US Election	2018		13848	Ambiguous state, non-state	FPS
Global Magnitsky Sanctions	2017 2018 2020		13818	Burma (Myanmar), Russia, South Sudan in 2017; Cambodia, Turkey, Saudi Arabia in 2018; Yemen, China in 2020	FPS, D, HR
Hong Kong Related	2020		13936	China	HR, D
Iran	1979		12170	Iran	FPS
Iran	1980		12211	Iran	FPS
Iran	1981		12284	Iran	FPS

(continued)

Table B.1. Continued

Program Title	Year Issued	Year Revoked	Executive Order#	Target(s)	Justification
Iran	1981		12294	Iran	FPS
Iran	1981		12276	Iran	FPS
Iran	1981		12277	Iran	FPS
Iran	1981		12278	Iran	FPS
Iran	1981		12279	Iran	FPS
Iran	1981		12280	Iran	FPS
Iran	1981		12283	Iran	FPS
Iran	1981		12281	Iran	FPS
Iran	1987	1997 (EO 13059)	12613	Iran	FPS
Iran	1995	1997 (EO 13059)	12959	Iran	FPS
Iran	1995	1997 (EO 13059)	12957	Iran	FPS
Iran	1997		13059	Iran	FPS
Iran	2010		13553	Iran	HR
Iran	2012		13608	Iran	FPS
Iran	2012		13606	Iran	HR
Iran	2012		13599	Iran	FPS
Iran	2018		13846	Iran	FPS
Iran	2019		13876	Iran	FPS
Iran	2019		13871	Iran	FPS
Iran	2020		13902	Iran	FPS

Iran	2020		13949	Iran	FPS
Iraq-Related	1990	2004 (EO 13350)	12722	Iraq	FPS
Iraq-Related	1990	2004 (EO 13350)	12724	Iraq	FPS
Iraq-Related	1992	2004 (EO 13350)	12817	Iraq	FPS
Iraq-Related	2003	2004 (EO 13350)	13290	Iraq	FPS
Iraq-Related	2003	2014 (EO 13688)	13303	Iraq	FPS
Iraq-Related	2003	2004 (EO 13350)	13315	Iraq	FPS
Iraq-Related	2007		13438	Non-state	FPS
Lebanon	2007		13441	Non-state	FPS, D
Libya	2011		13556	Libya	FPS, HR
Libya	2016		13726	Non-state	FPS, D, HR
Mali	2019		13882	Non-state	FPS, HR
Nicaragua	2018		13851	Nicaragua	FPS, D, HR
Non-proliferation	1994		12938	Non-state	FPS
Non-proliferation	1998		13094	Non-state	FPS
Non-proliferation	2005		13382	Non-state	FPS
Non-proliferation	2012		13608	Iran, Syria	FPS
Non-proliferation	2019		13883	Russia	FPS
North Korea	2008		13466	North Korea	FPS
North Korea	2010		13551	North Korea	FPS

(continued)

Table B.1. Continued

Program Title	Year Issued	Year Revoked	Executive Order#	Target(s)	Justification
North Korea	2011		13570	North Korea	FPS
North Korea	2015		13687	North Korea	FPS, HR
North Korea	2016		13722	North Korea	FPS
North Korea	2017		13810	North Korea	FPS, HR
Rough Diamond Trade Controls	2003		13312	Non-state	HR
Somalia	2010		13536	Non-state	FPS
Somalia	2012		13620	Non-state	FPS, HR
South Sudan	2014		13664	South Sudan	FPS, D, HR
Sudan and Darfur	1997		13067	Sudan	FPS, HR
Sudan and Darfur	2006		13412	Sudan	FPS, HR
Sudan and Darfur	2006		13400	Sudan	FPS, HR
Syria	2004		13338	Syria	FPS
Syria	2006		13399	Syria	FPS
Syria	2008		13460	Syria	FPS
Syria	2011		13582	Syria	HR
Syria	2011		13573	Syria	D
Syria	2011		13572	Syria	HR
Syria	2012		13608	Syria, Iran	FPS
Syria	2012		13606	Syria	HR
Syria-Related	2019		13894	Turkey	FPS

Transnational Criminal Organizations	2011	13581	FPS, D
Transnational Criminal Organizations	2019	13863	FPS, HR
Ukraine/Russia-Related	2014	13685	FPS
Ukraine/Russia-Related	2014	13662	FPS, D
Ukraine/Russia Related	2014	13661	FPS, D
Ukraine/Russia-Related	2014	13660	FPS, D
Ukraine/Russia-Related	2018	13849	FPS
Ukraine/Russia-Related	2019	13883	FPS
Venezuela-Related	2015	13692	FPS, HR
Venezuela-Related	2017	13808	D, HR
Venezuela-Related	2018	13850	FPS, D
Venezuela-Related	2018	13835	FPS, D
Venezuela-Related	2018	13827	FPS
Venezuela-Related	2019	13884	D, HR
Venezuela-Related	2019	13857	D, HR
Yemen-Related	2012	13611	FPS
Zimbabwe	2003	13288	FPS, D
Zimbabwe	2005	13391	D
Zimbabwe	2008	13469	FPS, D

Note: FPS = foreign policy and security; D = democracy; HR = human rights

targeted (though, typically it does). In some cases, it may mean that individuals with close ties to high-ranking government officials were targeted as a way of indirectly pressuring state actors. Entries marked "non-state" indicate that the order targets actors that are neither members of a foreign government nor closely associated with a government. In these cases, targets could include members of terrorist organizations, organized crime, or businesses involved in illicit economic activity that threatens US interest but is not taking place in coordination with a foreign government. My research team hand coded information regarding the targets by reading through the text of each SREO, press releases from the Treasury and the State Department, and in some cases, media reports. Finally, the table also includes the justification given for the SREO, per the text of the order itself. As presented in Chapter 2, this information was hand coded using three categories: foreign policy and security (FPS), democracy (D), and human rights (HR). Figures 2.5, 2.6, 2.7, 2.8, and 4.5 in Chapters 2 and 4 present data drawn from Table B.1.

Appendix C

I employed principal component analysis (PCA) to create a single dimension indicator of perceived sanctions risk based on three widely used variables designed to proxy for the most common public justification for US SREOs: a country's distance from the US ideal point in US General Assembly voting (higher values indicate greater dissimilarity in foreign policy preferences), a country's human rights record (higher values indicate a poorer human rights record), and the level of democracy (where higher values indicate that a country is more democratic). A total of three principal components were generated by the PCA. I retained only the first of those components as the *sanctions risk* measure in my analysis. This decision was made according to Kaiser's criterion that dictates that all components with Eigenvalues under 1.0 should be dropped. Eigenvalues are displayed as a Scree plot in Figure C.1. As the figure shows, there is a significant drop-off between the first and second component produced by the PCA.

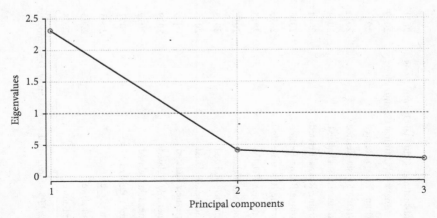

Figure C.1. Scree Plot of Eigenvalues after Principal Component Analysis

Table C.1. Correlation between Principal Components (PC) and Composite Covariates

	PC1	PC2	PC3
UN ideal point distance	0.8663	0.4364	−0.2432
Human Rights	0.9072	0.0303	0.4196
Democracy (Polity)	−0.8591	0.4721	0.1979

In addition to the Eigenvalue comparison, the first component is strongly correlated with all three of the individual measures in the expected direction (positively correlated with UN ideal point distance and human rights measures, negatively correlated with the level of democracy). By comparison, the second and third components are only weakly correlated with the original variables used to create the composite indicator and, in each case, the correlation is incorrectly signed vis-à-vis one of the original measures. These correlations are reported in Table C.1. Unsurprisingly given these correlations, the first component explains 77 percent of the variation in the original three covariates while the second explains 13.8 percent and the third 9.1 percent.

I used the first principal component to account for a government's perceived level of *sanctions risk* in the analysis first presented in Chapter 4, and again in subsequent chapters. Higher values correspond to higher levels of perceived sanctions risk based on the component covariates (e.g., countries that have foreign policy preferences that conflict with US preferences, have poor human rights records, and are non-democratic would score high on this measure). Based on the sample of cases in the analysis of gold reserves presented in Chapter 4, the variable ranges from a minimum of −3.167 to a maximum of 2.787 with a mean of −0.29 and a standard deviation of 1.53. Figure C.2 presents the distribution of *sanctions risk* based on this sample. Dotted vertical lines reflect the variable mean (middle) and one standard deviation above and below that mean (right, left).

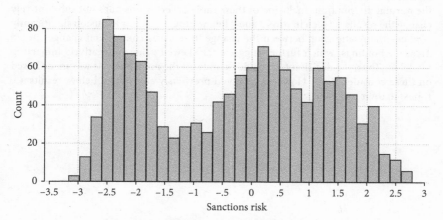

Figure C.2. Sample Distribution of Sanctions Risk Variable

While the *sanctions risk* indicator is designed to reflect the *perceived* level of sanctions risk, as opposed to a perfect measure of the true underlying level of sanctions risk, I assessed whether the measure is a good predictor of US financial sanctions. I estimated a logistic regression model with *sanctions risk* as the explanatory variable and where the outcome of interest explained was a binary (0,1) variable indicating whether OFAC sanctions were in place targeting a country or not in a given year between 2008 and 2020. The coefficient for sanctions risk was positive (2.04) and highly significant (>0.001). Moreover, I conducted additional tests to judge the variable's accuracy at predicting positive and negative cases of OFAC sanctions. First, I set the cutoff/threshold to 0.5. This means when *sanctions risk* predicts the probability of OFAC sanctions to be above 0.5, it is classified as a predicted positive case. When the predicted probability is 0.5 or below, it is classified as a negative case. Based on these parameters, *sanctions risk* correctly predicts 78.3 percent of positive observations (OFAC sanctions = 1) and 94.8 percent of negative observations (OFAC sanctions = 0).

Appendix D

Table D.1 displays OLS results that correspond to Figure 4.6 in Chapter 4. The dependent variable is yearly changes in monetary gold reserves.

The first two rows of Table D.2 display OLS results that correspond to Figure 4.9 in Chapter 4. The dependent variable is yearly changes in public and private long-term holdings of US Treasuries. The estimates presented in Chapter 4, and in rows 1 and 2 below exclude three outliers from the analysis: Samoa (2019), Seychelles (2017), and Suriname (2012). In each case, the annual percentage change in US Treasury holdings was larger than a tenfold increase. In the case of Seychelles (2017) it was a twentyfold increase. These observations for these small economies lie far outside the normal distribution of the data (more than 8 standard deviations above the sample mean). Careful review of the US Treasury TIC data indicate that these large values reflect the fact that US Treasury holdings are moving from levels near zero to slightly higher, though still low, levels. However, the percentage change is sizable and outside the normal distribution. Inclusion of these three observations does not substantively change the results, as seen in rows 3 and 4 below. However, their inclusion significantly weakens the relationship between the change in reserves control and changes in US Treasury holdings, which further suggests the skewed value is negatively impacting model fit. Thus, the decision to exclude them from the main analysis was made based on these considerations. However, as noted previously and shown below, results are robust to their inclusion.

Table D.1 Gold Reserves and US Financial Sanctions

	Sanctions-related Executive Orders (SREOs)	Sanctions Risk
SREO	13.06***	
	(0.006)	
Sanctions risk		6.243***
		(0.000)
Annual change in reserves (log)	−0.942	−0.781
	(0.592)	(0.667)
Gold as % of reserves (log)	2.644	3.969
	(0.780)	(0.683)
Reserves/GDP (log)	2.766***	2.813***
	(0.000)	(0.000)
GDP (log)	−7.085	−14.54***
	(0.121)	(0.005)
GDP per capita (log)	3.145	9.646*
	(0.565)	(0.094)
Time Trend	0.263**	0.506***
	(0.129)	(0.143)
Country Fixed Effects	YES	YES
N	1497	1435
Countries	120	116
R-sq	0.635	0.633

Note: Cell entries are OLS coefficient estimates with p-values based on panel corrected standard errors in parentheses. Row 1 displays the model estimates when using SREO as the sanctions indicator whereas row 2 displays results when using the sanctions risk indicator. * $p < 0.1$, ** $p < 0.05$, *** $p < 0.01$

Table D.2 Long-Term US Treasury Holdings and US Financial Sanctions

	(1) SREO	(2) Sanctions Risk	(3) SREO (all observations)	(4) Sanctions Risk (all observations)
SREO	−0.282***		−0.237**	
	(0.000)		(0.027)	
Sanctions Risk		−0.00638		0.0986
		(0.958)		(0.474)
% Change in Reserves	0.193*	0.162	0.187	0.156
	(0.079)	(0.173)	(0.425)	(0.501)
Time Trend	−0.00890	−0.0118	−0.0115	−0.0225
	(0.543)	(0.444)	(0.537)	(0.110)
Country Fixed Effects	YES	YES	YES	YES
N	792	733	796	735
Countries	94	87	94	87
R-sq	0.187	0.182	0.188	0.179

Note: Cell entries are OLS coefficient estimates with p-values based on panel corrected standard errors in parentheses. Row 1 displays the model estimates when using SREO as the sanctions indicator whereas row 2 displays results when using the sanctions risk indicator. Rows 3 and 4 replicate these models but include three previously excluded outliers. * $p < 0.1$, ** $p < 0.05$, *** $p < 0.01$.

SREO = Sanctions-related Executive Order.

Appendix E

Full regression results from Chapter 6 are presented below in Tables E.1 and E.2. In addition, because the data take on the form of count data, I include results from a Poisson regression with the same covariates. The results are substantively unchanged. Descriptions and additional details are provided below each table.

Table E.1 Local Currency Swap Agreement Regression Results

	SREO (OLS)	Sanctions Risk (OLS)	SREO (Poisson)	Sanctions Risk (Poisson)
SREO (Sanctions-related Executive Order)	0.295***		0.446**	
	(0.002)		(0.048)	
Sanctions Risk		0.0865		0.122
		(0.221)		(0.376)
Trade/GDP (log)	0.151**	0.124	0.350	0.486
	(0.044)	(0.137)	(0.378)	(0.232)
Reserves/GDP (log)	−0.0285	−0.0198	−0.370***	−0.367**
	(0.564)	(0.730)	(0.002)	(0.003)
Inflation (log)	0.0243	0.0258	0.0387*	0.0309
	(0.144)	(0.159)	(0.073)	(0.153)
GDP (log)	0.129	−0.138	3.864***	4.926**
	(0.423)	(0.485)	(0.003)	(0.002)
GDP per capita (log)	0.0120	0.271	−3.000**	−4.085**
	(0.946)	(0.190)	(0.020)	(0.008)
Time Trend	0.0551***	0.0647***	0.105***	0.101***
	(0.000)	(0.000)	(0.000)	(0.000)
Country Fixed Effects	YES	YES	YES	YES
N	1648	1494	1648	1494
Countries	150	137	150	137
R-sq	0.680	0.679		
Pseudo R-sq			0.659	0.656

Note: Cell entries in rows 1 and 2 are OLS coefficient estimates with p-values based on panel corrected standard errors in parentheses. Cell entries in rows 3 and 4 display coefficient estimates using a Poisson regression with robust standard errors. * p < 0.1, ** p < 0.05, *** p < 0.01.

Table E.2 Dollar Share of Trade Settlement Regression Results

	Imports	Imports	Exports	Exports
Sanctions-related Executive Order (SREO)	−3.870***		−11.29***	
	(0.000)		(0.000)	
Sanctions Risk		−3.292***		−0.344
		(0.001)		(0.579)
US export share (log)			1.054	1.032
			(0.170)	(0.192)
Oil export share (log)			0.0727	0.0639
			(0.229)	(0.317)
US import share (log)	−0.535	−1.769*		
	(0.594)	(0.089)		
Oil import share (log)	0.142*	0.253***		
	(0.076)	(0.000)		
GDP (log)	25.48***	29.77***	10.96**	17.30***
	(0.000)	(0.000)	(0.035)	(0.000)
GDP per capita (log)	−26.20***	−30.49***	−10.85**	−16.28***
	(0.000)	(0.000)	(0.036)	(0.000)
Time Trend	−0.363**	−0.389***	−0.166***	−0.253***
	(0.001)	(0.000)	(0.000)	(0.000)
Country Fixed Effects	YES	YES	YES	YES
N	639	609	512	511
Countries	80	77	75	72
R-sq	0.982	0.985	0.992	0.992

Note: Cell entries are OLS coefficient estimates with p-values based on panel corrected standard errors in parentheses. Rows 1 and 2 display model estimates when the dollar's share of import settlement and invoicing is the outcome of interest. Rows 3 and 4 present estimates when the dollar's share of export settlement and invoicing are the dependent variable. * $p < 0.1$, ** $p < 0.05$, *** $p < 0.01$.

Appendix F

Outcome Variables Summary Statistics

Figure F.1 presents summary statistics of the three main outcome questions for the full PCI sample. For all three questions, the most common response was "neither agree nor disagree" (3) suggesting relatively low interest in non-dollar-related payments. In terms of the outcome questions, firms showed the highest average level of interest in contributing to a lobbying effort aimed at the government of Vietnam with a mean of 3.2 compared to means of 2.8 for the other two outcome questions ("learn more" and "government promote"). Yet the difference between these means falls short of statistical significance.

Multiple Outcomes Test

Because the Provincial Competitiveness Index (PCI) experiment presented in Chapter 6 assesses the impact of a single treatment on responses to three distinct outcomes prompts ("learn more," "contribute," "government promote"), there is an increased possibility of landing on a statistically significant result for one of these outcomes increases due to random chance alone. Consequently, I may have incorrectly rejected the null hypothesis that the sanctions treatment had no effect on multinational corporations (MNC) managers' interest in "learning more" about non-dollar-based payment systems. When an experiment tests more than one outcome, it is appropriate to adjust the results to correct for the problem of multiple comparisons. The Bonferroni method is one commonly used approach and is quite easy to implement. It is also quite stringent in that it heavily penalizes the use of multiple outcomes. Thus, results that withstand the Bonferroni correction can be viewed as especially strong. The method requires that investigators adjust the target significance level at which they reject the null hypothesis. This is done by dividing the accepted target p-value for a single outcome (here, $p < 0.1$, or 90 percent level) by the number of outcomes in the experiment (in this case, 3). Thus, the Bonferroni

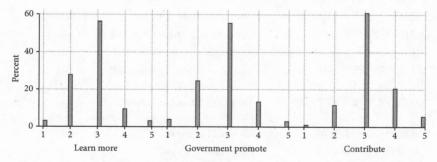

Figure F.1. Multinational Corporations' (MNC) Interest in Euro and Renminbi-based Payment Systems. Bars indicate firm responses to three main outcome questions in percentage terms. Lower (higher) values indicate lower (higher) levels of agreement with the statements.

correction adjusts the target significance level from 0.1 to 0.034. Any result with a p-value larger than 0.034, then, means we cannot reject the null that the sanctions treatment has no effect on firm manager attitudes toward the dollar. Because the p-value of the "learn more" results is 0.030, the correction does not alter the conclusion that the treatment did in fact influence MNC managers' attitudes and the result is not due to random chance.

Appendix G

Table G.1 List of Direct Participants in Cross-border Interbank Payment System (CIPS), December 2021

Bank Name (Chinese)	Bank Name (English)	Region
中国工商银行股份有限公司	Industrial and Commercial Bank of China	Asia
中国农业银行股份有限公司	Agricultural Bank of China	Asia
中国银行股份有限公司	Bank of China	Asia
中国建设银行股份有限公司	China Construction Bank	Asia
交通银行股份有限公司	Bank of Communications	Asia
招商银行股份有限公司	China Merchants Bank	Asia
上海浦东发展银行股份有限公司	Shanghai Pudong Development Bank	Asia
中国民生银行股份有限公司	China Minsheng Bank	Asia
兴业银行股份有限公司	Industrial Bank	Asia
平安银行股份有限公司	Ping An Bank	Asia
华夏银行股份有限公司	Huaxia Bank	Asia
汇丰银行（中国）有限公司	HSBC Bank (China)	Asia
花旗银行（中国）有限公司	Citibank (China)	Asia
渣打银行（中国）有限公司	Standard Chartered Bank (China)	Asia
星展银行（中国）有限公司	DBS Bank (China) Limited	Asia
德意志银行（中国）有限公司	Deutsche Bank (China) Co., Ltd.	Asia
法国巴黎银行（中国）有限公司	BNP Paribas (China)	Asia
澳大利亚和新西兰银行（中国）有限公司	Australia and New Zealand Bank (China) Company Limited	Asia
东亚银行（中国）有限公司	The Bank of East Asia (China), Limited	Asia
中信银行股份有限公司	China CITIC Bank	Asia
广发银行股份有限公司	China Guangfa Bank	Asia
上海银行股份有限公司	Bank of Shanghai	Asia
江苏银行股份有限公司	Bank of Jiangsu	Asia
三菱日联银行（中国）有限公司	MUFG Bank (China), Ltd.	Asia
瑞穗银行（中国）有限公司	Mizuho Bank (China), Ltd.	Asia

Table G.1 Continued

Bank Name (Chinese)	Bank Name (English)	Region
恒生银行（中国）有限公司	Hang Seng Bank (China) Co., Ltd.	Asia
中国银行（香港）有限公司—人民币清算行	Bank of China (Hong Kong)—RMB Clearing	Asia
中国光大银行股份有限公司	China Everbright Bank	Asia
银行间市场清算所股份有限公司	Shanghai Clearing House	Asia
中央结算公司	Hong Kong Securities Clearing	Asia
摩根大通银行（中国）有限公司	JPMorgan Chase Bank (China) Co., Ltd.	Asia
网联清算有限公司	NetsUnion Clearing Corporation	Asia
城银清算服务有限责任公司	City Commercial Banks Clearing	Asia
三井住友银行（中国）有限公司	Sumitomo Mitsui Banking Corporation (China) Limited	Asia
农信银资金清算中心有限责任公司	Rural Credit Banks Funds Clearing Center	Asia
国家开发银行	China Development Bank	Asia
中国工商银行新加坡分行	Industrial and Commercial Bank of China (Singapore)	Asia
中国工商银行（亚洲）有限公司	Industrial and Commercial Bank of China (Asia)	Asia
中国银行股份有限公司澳门分行—人民币清算行	Bank of China Macau Branch—RMB Clearing	Asia
交通银行首尔人民币清算行	Bank of Communications (Seoul)—RMB Clearing	Asia
中国邮政储蓄银行股份有限公司	Postal Savings Bank of China	Asia
中国银联股份有限公司	UnionPay	Asia
中国建设银行股份有限公司纳闽分行	China Construction Bank (Labuan Branch)	Asia
中国建设银行（亚洲）股份有限公司	China Construction Bank (Asia)	Asia
中国银行股份有限公司新加坡分行	Bank of China (Singapore)	Asia
中国农业银行股份有限公司香港分行	Agricultural Bank of China (Hong Kong)	Asia
中国农业银行迪拜分行	Agricultural Bank of China (Dubai)	Asia
哈尔滨银行股份有限公司	Harbin Bank	Asia
香港金融管理局CMU	Hong Kong Monetary Authority (Central Moneymarket Unit)	Asia
交通银行股份有限公司香港分行	Bank of Communications (Hong Kong Branch)	Asia

(continued)

Table G.1 Continued

Bank Name (Chinese)	Bank Name (English)	Region
交通银行（香港）有限公司	Bank of Communications (Hong Kong) Ltd.	Asia
中国工商银行股份有限公司卡拉奇分行	Industrial and Commercial Bank of China (Karachi)	Asia
中国工商银行（澳门）股份有限公司	Industrial and Commercial Bank of China (Macao), Ltd.	Asia
中国工商银行（泰国）股份有限公司	Industrial and Commercial Bank of China (Thailand), Ltd.	Asia
中国工商银行股份有限公司多哈分行	Industrial and Commercial Bank of China (Doha)	Asia
中国建设银行股份有限公司东京分行	China Construction Bank (Tokyo)	Asia
中国银行首尔分行	Bank of China (Seoul)	Asia
中国银行马尼拉分行人民币清算中心	Bank of China Manila RMB Clearing Center	Asia
中国银行（马来西亚）有限公司	Bank of China (Malaysia)	Asia
中国工商银行万象分行	Industrial and Commercial Bank of China (Vientiane Branch)	Asia
中国进出口银行	Exim Bank of China	Asia
中国农业发展银行	Agricultural Development Bank of China	Asia
中国银行台北分行	Bank of China (Taipei)	Asia
中国银行东京人民币清算中心	Bank of China Tokyo RMB Clearing Center	Asia
中国工商银行（加拿大）	Industrial and Commercial Bank of China (Canada)	North America
中国建设银行苏黎世分行	China Construction Bank (Zurich）	Europe
中国建设银行股份有限公司伦敦分行	China Construction Bank (London)	Europe
中国银行法兰克福分行	Bank of China (Frankfurt)	Europe
中国银行匈牙利分行	Bank of China (Hungary)	Europe
中国银行巴黎分行	Bank of China (Paris)	Europe
中国银行伦敦分行	Bank of China (London)	Europe
中国银行法兰克福分行人民币清算行	Bank of China (Frankfurt)—RMB Clearing Center	Europe
中国工商银行俄罗斯人民币清算行	Industrial and Commercial Bank of China (Russia)—RMB Clearing Center	Europe
赞比亚中国银行	Bank of China (Zambia)	Africa
中国银行约翰内斯堡分行	Bank of China (Johannesburg Branch)	Africa
中国银行股份有限公司悉尼分行	Bank of China (Sydney)	Oceania

Table G.2 Cross-border Interbank Payment System (CIPS) Participation Regression Results

	Sanctions-related Executive Orders (SREO)	Sanctions Risk
SREO	1.678**	
	(0.023)	
Sanctions Risk		0.254*
		(0.074)
GDP (log)	0.572***	0.552***
	(0.000)	(0.001)
GDP per capita (log)	0.288*	0.392*
	(0.086)	(0.066)
N	165	148

Note: Cell entries display logistic regression estimates with p-values based on robust standard errors in parentheses. * $p < 0.1$, ** $p < 0.05$, *** $p < 0.01$.

Notes

Introduction

1. Pengelly 2018.
2. @zeitonline 2018.
3. Donahue 2018.
4. Associated Press 2018.
5. Mogherini et al. 2018.
6. Maas 2018.
7. Schaer 2018.
8. Mehreen and Brunsden 2018.
9. Junker 2018.
10. Obama 2015.
11. Warren Strobel 2015.
12. Cramer 2015.
13. Investor's Business Daily 2015.
14. Strobel 2015.
15. Lew 2016.
16. Bolton 2020, 364.
17. Wheatley and Smith 2022.
18. Alloway and Weisenthal 2022; Grice 2022.
19. Wolf 2022.
20. Wang 2022.
21. Strange 1971a.
22. E.g., Helleiner 2008; Norrlof 2010; Zimmermann 2002.
23. One exception to this is the work of Juliet Johnson on US foreign policy and Russia's dollar policy. More recently, several prominent scholars have raised concerns that Trump administration policies undermined foreign support for the dollar. Though not related to financial sanctions, these studies represent an important turn in the literature that examines the possibility that US policy hurts, rather than helps, the dollar's status. See Johnson 2008; Eichengreen 2016; Cohen 2016; Helleiner 2017.
24. Drezner 2015; See also Farrell and Newman 2020; Rosenberg et al. 2016, 13.
25. For a history of European complaints about the dollar, see Gavin 2004.
26. The concept of political risk is most widely used in research on foreign direct investment. From this perspective, firms must consider political risk when weighing the costs and benefits of entering a foreign market. If we distill the concept to its most

basic elements, however, political risk simply refers to the way that political events affect economic value and, in turn, how rational actors' anticipation of these effects influences their economic decisions. Thinking about political risk in this simplified way allows us to consider how the concept might apply more broadly, for example to the international currency system.

27. Roche 2022.
28. Lew 2016.
29. China's currency is also referred to as the yuan. I use renminbi unless quoting a source that uses yuan.

Chapter 1

1. Strange 1971b, 305.
2. Gilsinan 2019.
3. E.g., Pape 1997; Elliott 1998; Francis and Jakes 2016; Mulder 2022, 295–296.
4. Drezner 2003.
5. E.g., Ashford 2016; Drezner 2011.
6. E.g., Ordoñez, Charles, and Daugherty 2019.
7. Heavey and Layne 2019.
8. Lew 2016.
9. Cohen 2015, 9.
10. Eric Helleiner adeptly summarizes the nuances of the scholarship on the economic determinants of international currency status, highlighting three key characteristics: (1) sound economic management by the issuing state that engenders international confidence in the stability of the currency's value over time; (2) large, liquid, and open financial markets in the issuing state that enhance the currency's attractiveness as an investment and transactional unit; and (3) a large international transactional network on the part of the issuing state leading to the currency's broad acceptability worldwide. See Helleiner 2008; see also Cohen 2011, 12–13.
11. Helleiner and Kirshner 2009, 15.
12. Oatley 2015, 85–86.
13. Kirshner 2008, 427.
14. Murphy 2006, 43; Posen 2008, 78; Spiro 1999, 148.
15. Helleiner 2008, 363–364; Helleiner and Kirshner 2009, 12; Strange 1971a, 17–18.
16. Norrlof 2014, 1059; Norrlof et al. 2020, 132–37; Wong 2016.
17. Zimmermann 2002, 126–137; Gavin 2004, 110–113.
18. E.g., Strange 1971a; Liao and McDowell 2016; Pacheco Pardo, Knoerich, and Li 2019.
19. Johnson 2008, 379.
20. Norrlof et al. 2020, 114.
21. The hypotheses presented in Figure 1.1 reflect directional, not point, predictions.

Chapter 2

1. De Palma, *Scarface*, 1983.
2. Daddy, *It's All about the Benjamins,* 1997.
3. Cohen and Benney 2014.
4. Mulder 2022, 49–54.
5. Eichengreen and Flandreau 2009.
6. Carter and Farha 2013, 905.
7. Auboin 2009, 1.
8. Farrell and Newman 2019.
9. Payment data available from SWIFT at https://www.swift.com/about-us/discover-swift/fin-traffic-figures.
10. "SWIFT Wire Transfers: What Compliance Needs To Know" 2021.
11. Data were collected from documents available on SWIFT's RMB tracker website available at https://www.swift.com/our-solutions/compliance-and-shared-services/business-intelligence/renminbi/rmb-tracker.
12. SWIFT 2015, 6.
13. For the traditional taxonomy of the various roles of international money, see Cohen 1971.
14. Foreign exchange reserve data are from the International Monetary Fund's Currency Composition of Official Foreign Exchange Reserves database, available at https://www.imf.org/en/Data. International debt securities and banking data are from the Bank for International Settlements (BIS) database, available at https://www.bis.org/statistics/. The securities data presented reflect the dollar's share of the total outstanding stock of international debt securities. The banking data presented reflect the dollar's share of total outstanding bank liabilities as reported by the BIS locational banking statistics.
15. Equity market share data according to Statista, available at https://www.statista.com/statistics/710680/global-stock-markets-by-country/.
16. Winecoff 2015.
17. Federal Reserve Bank of New York 2002.
18. A list of CHIPS participants is available at https://www.theclearinghouse.org/payment-systems/chips.
19. Current and historical data on CHIPS transfers are available under the "Annual Statistics" link at https://www.theclearinghouse.org/payment-systems/chips.
20. Schularick 2011.
21. See https://www.treasurydirect.gov/instit/auctfund/held/held.htm.
22. Farrell and Newman 2019, 55–56.
23. US Treasury 2006, 62.
24. Carter and Farha 2013, 905.
25. Flitter 2019.
26. Raymond 2015.
27. Rosenberg et al. 2016, 36.
28. Carter and Farha 2013, 908.

29. Loeffler 2009.
30. Farrell and Newman 2019.
31. Farrell and Newman 2019, 55.
32. The "Travel" rule is the informal name for a funds transfer rule that was issued by US Treasury's Financial Crimes Enforcement Network in 1996 under the Bank Secrecy Act. The rule requires banks to pass on information about the identity of the transmitter and recipient of funds along with other information to all banks involved in the transaction. Thus, the information "travels" along with the transaction itself.
33. Scott and Gelpern 2016, 1422.
34. Scott 2010. This information would include the name, address, and account numbers of the originator, the amount and currency of the funds, the date of the transfer, the originator's financial institution, the beneficiary's financial institution, and the name, address, and account number of the beneficiary.
35. US Treasury 2016, 3; Scott and Gelpern 2016, 1426.
36. US Treasury 2014a.
37. There are four (legitimate) offshore dollar clearing centers: Hong Kong, Manila, Singapore, and Tokyo. In these locations, dollar transfers can be settled outside of US legal jurisdiction through the Clearing House Automated Transfer System (CHATS).
38. Farrell and Newman 2019.
39. Drezner 2011.
40. Drezner 2021, 142.
41. Each SREO includes a list of SDNs. The number of SDNs listed varies. Once issued, additional SDNs may be added to the list in the future, pursuant to the original order.
42. SREOs that revoke existing SREOs are not counted in these data. Only SREOs that add additional sanctions are included.
43. Of thirty-two active sanctions programs at the end of 2019, twenty-two directly or indirectly targeted foreign governments. The Treasury's list of sanctions programs is available at https://www.treasury.gov/resource-center/sanctions/Programs/Pages/Programs.aspx.
44. Gilsinan 2019; Drezner 2021.
45. A research assistant reviewed the text of all SREOs issued during the study period and hand coded the justification for each order. SREO texts are available from the US Treasury's website at https://www.treasury.gov/resource-center/sanctions/Programs/Pages/Programs.aspx.
46. Meyer 2009; Jack Lew directly addressed this point in his remarks on sanctions overuse, noting, "Secondary sanctions should be used only in the most exceptional circumstances." See Lew 2016.

Chapter 3

1. White House 2011.
2. Meo 2011.

3. Spencer 2011.

4. Zarate 2013, 343.

5. Zarate 2013, 347–348.

6. O'Harrow, Grimaldi, and Dennis 2011.

7. White House 2011.

8. Zarate 2013, 347–348.

9. The United States first froze the assets of a foreign central bank in 1979 when the US Treasury acted to prevent Iran's central bank from accessing $14 billion following the Iranian hostage crisis. See Alerassool 1993.

10. White House 2012. While the total value of the assets frozen has not been reported, it is likely far smaller than the Libyan freeze since Iran has faced US sanctions since 1979.

11. White House 2019.

12. US Treasury 2022.

13. IMF 2015.

14. Moghadam, Ostry, and Sheehy 2011, 4.

15. He, Krishnamurthy, and Milbradt 2016.

16. Clark and Mann 2016.

17. A government may wish to convert a bond into cash for a variety of reasons. For example, if it wanted to intervene in foreign exchange markets, it would need to liquidate some of its Treasury bonds. Alternatively, if a government needed to finance domestic servicing of foreign dollar-denominated debts, it may have to sell off some of its Treasuries.

18. For a brief discussion of how a weak dollar might influence its attractiveness as a reserve currency, see Liao and McDowell 2016, 280.

19. Federal Reserve Bank of New York 2018.

20. This technique is referred to as a "most-likely" case design. This method is based on the premise that "it is easier to disconfirm an inference than to confirm that same inference." Such designs implicitly rely on Bayesian logic in which evidence is appraised in relation to a priori theoretical expectations. If our priors indicate that a case should fit a theory and yet the evidence suggests otherwise, then we have little confidence the theory can "make it" anywhere else. However, if the case evidence is in line with the theory, then we gain additional confidence in its plausibility. See Gerring 2007, 120; Levy 2008, 12.

21. Johnson 2008.

22. Sputnik News 2014.

23. See Table A.1 in Appendix A for details on each of the SREOs targeting Russia.

24. US Treasury 2018a.

25. Agence France Presse 2018.

26. Ostroukh and Gumrukcu 2018; Yeung 2018.

27. Keynes 1923, 138.

28. Data were obtained from the World Gold Council, available at https://www.gold.org/goldhub/data/monthly-central-bank-statistics.

29. Cooper 2011.

30. Much of the CBR's additional gold holdings were acquired through domestic purchases. However, in 2018, Russian gold buying exceeded the mining supply. Thus, in order to implement its diversification plan, Russia became a net importer of gold. Much of this gold was imported from conflict-ridden African countries, like Sudan and Central African Republic, where a Russian mercenary force masquerading as a company called Wagner Group provided security services in exchange for gold. See Walsh 2022; Collins 2022.

31. Foreign exchange reserves data are from the IMF's International Financial Statistics database available at https://www.imf.org/en/Data; data on foreign holdings of US government securities are from the US Treasury's "Treasury International Capital System" and are available at https://www.treasury.gov/resource-center/data-chart-center/tic/Pages/ticsec2.aspx.

32. See Reuters 2016.

33. Data were collected from quarterly CBR Foreign Exchange and Gold Asset Management Reports. They are available, dating back to 2014, at http://www.cbr.ru/eng/analytics/exchange-gold-report/exchange-gold-report/.

34. Khachaturov 2019.

35. *Sputnik News* 2019b; Doff and Andrianova 2019.

36. Golubova 2019a, emphasis added.

37. DW 2019.

38. Silchenko 2019; This and all other quotes in the book from foreign language sources were translated into English using Google Translate, sometimes with additional help from a research assistant.

39. Polunin 2019.

40. Khachaturov 2019.

41. Danilov 2019.

42. Andrianova, Pismennaya, and Tanas 2018.

43. *Sputnik News* 2019b.

44. Gosteva 2019.

45. *Sputnik News* 2019a.

46. Andrianova 2018.

47. Hanna 2017.

48. Jovanovski 2018.

49. US Treasury 2018b.

50. As of the end of 2019, Magnitsky had been used to target actors in or closely associated with governments in Burma (Myanmar), Cambodia, Russia, Turkey, Saudi Arabia, and South Sudan.

51. Radio Free Europe 2018; Pamuk 2019.

52. Saraçoğlu 2018.

53. Dembinskaya 2018; Golubova 2018.

54. Iancu et al. 2020; Ito and McCauley 2020.

55. Christensen 2019.

56. Golubova 2018.

57. Reid 2018.

Chapter 4

1. Byron 1856, 666.
2. Monnet and Puy 2019.
3. O'Callaghan 1993, 1.
4. HM Treasury 2002.
5. Day 1998.
6. The initial agreement included the European Central Bank representing the then eleven central banks of countries participating in the new European currency, plus Sweden, Switzerland, and the United Kingdom. It lasted for five years. The deal was renewed in 2004, 2009, and 2014 before being allowed to lapse in 2019 due to limited gold sales.
7. World Gold Council 2020; the only reason that received more agreement in the survey was monetary authorities citing their "historical positions" in gold as a reason for holding it (83 percent agreed this was somewhat or highly relevant).
8. Blodget 2009.
9. For a review of these policies, see Santor and Suchanek 2016.
10. Gopalakrishnan and Mohapatra 2018.
11. IMF 2012, 82.
12. A safe asset is simply any asset viewed as likely to "preserve its value during adverse systemic events." See Caballero, Farhi, and Gourinchas 2017, 29.
13. Council 2010, 2.
14. Eichengreen 2011, 51–53; Gavin 2004, 73–75.
15. Pompeo 2019.
16. Banco Central de Venezuela 2011.
17. There were also reports that some of the gold may have been transferred to vaults in Russia, though the governor of the Central Bank of Russia denied these claims. See Ostroukh and Fabrichnaya 2019.
18. Bronner and Rosati 2018; Golubova 2019b; Laya 2019a; Pons and Armas 2019; Steinhauser and Bariyo 2019.
19. Laya and Bartenstein 2020.
20. BBC 2020.
21. A Russian media report echoed this point, noting, "Our gold reserve, unlike the Venezuelan, is placed securely. . . . But the main gold reserves are located on the territory of our country." See Polunin 2019.
22. Watson and Tuysuz 2012; Reuters 2012.
23. Several recent central bank surveys mention that for most reserve managers polled, the "lack of political risk" associated with gold holdings was relevant or highly relevant to their decision to hold gold. This attitude was especially pronounced among emerging market central bankers. Since the survey question about political risk does not specifically reference sanctions, the responses likely capture concerns about other political factors as well. Yet the survey responses further illustrate that political considerations played a role in the post-2008 gold revival. In 2016, 65 percent of responding central banks cited the "lack of political risk" as being somewhat or

highly relevant to their decision to hold gold reserves. In 2019, this number dropped to 50 percent before increasing to 63 percent in 2020. The share was 66 percent among emerging market central banks in 2020. The samples across these surveys are not balanced as the number of monetary authorities responding increased each year from just twenty-one in 2018 to fifty-one in 2020. For survey details, see World Gold Council 2018; 2019; 2020.

24. Data available at https://www.gold.org/goldhub/data/monthly-central-bank-statistics.

25. Portions of China's gold reserves data were interpolated using the *ipolate* command in Stata because the country did not report gold reserves from the second quarter of 2009 until the second quarter of 2015. The reporting in 2015 indicated a 600-ton increase in gold holdings during the unreported period. While the main estimates below include these interpolated data, the results are not sensitive to their removal. In fact, the results are largely unchanged if China is dropped from the sample.

26. The total adds up to more than 100 because many SREOs mention more than one of these reasons. Other reasons are cited in just a small fraction of cases. The most common other reason is related to revoking or amending past measures.

27. Dunteman 1989; Groth et al. 2013.

28. Bailey, Strezhnev, and Voeten 2017.

29. Data from Bailey, Strezhnev, and Voeten 2017.

30. Marshall, Jaggers, and Gurr 2017.

31. FSI 2020.

32. This decision was based on an inspection of a Scree plot using Kaiser's criterion that prescribes dropping all principal components with Eigenvalues below 1. Please see Appendix B for a more detailed discussion of this decision. See also Bryant and Yarnold 1995.

33. Throughout the period considered here, the dollar accounts for roughly 60 percent of all allocated foreign exchange reserves according to the IMF's Currency Composition of Official Foreign Exchange Reserves (COFER) data, available at https://data.imf.org/.

34. Otero-Iglesias and Steinberg 2013, 317.

35. Survey conducted by UBS Asset Management cited in Greifeld 2019.

36. Liao and McDowell 2016, 279–280.

37. Pukthuanthong and Roll 2011.

38. Bhatia 2012.

39. Rogoff 2016.

40. Rowling 2019.

41. All estimates rely on the natural log of the aforementioned control variables given their otherwise skewed distributions.

42. Beck and Katz 1995.

43. The results are not sensitive to dropping the two biggest buyers of gold during this period, Russia and China, from the analysis; they also happen to have high values on the *sanctions risk* variable.

44. Average price calculated based on quarterly prices from Q1 2007 through Q4 2020 according to World Gold Council data available at gold.org.

45. Specifically, I employ the Treasury International Capital (TIC) System's Portfolio Holdings of US and Foreign Securities Data, Statistics: A.2.b. Data are available at https://home.treasury.gov/data/treasury-international-capital-tic-system-home-page/tic-forms-instructions/securities-b-portfolio-holdings-of-us-and-foreign-securities.

46. US Treasury 2021. Thanks to Colin Weiss for providing this information.

47. Data are from the World Bank's World Development Indicators database.

48. The first year in the data (2011) is lost since I cannot calculate the annual change in holdings from the previous year.

49. Indeed, a working paper by a Federal Reserve economist simulates a model where countries concerned about US sanctions diversify out of dollar reserves and still concludes that the currency would maintain its pre-eminent position. See Weiss 2022.

50. Prasad 2022.

Chapter 5

1. Vladimir Putin, quoted in Doff and Andrianova 2019.

2. Lyrchikova 2017.

3. Rapoza 2017.

4. *Aluminum Insider* 2017; Ng 2017.

5. US Treasury 2018a.

6. Galouchko and Fedorinova 2018.

7. "Fitch Revises Rusal's Rating Watch to Negative; Withdraws Ratings" 2018; Onstad 2018.

8. Ultimately, Rusal was able to secure cooperation from Dutch bank ING, which agreed to change settlement currency from dollars to euros under an existing financing agreement. See TASS 2018b.

9. Devitt and Kobzeva 2018.

10. Friberg and Wilander 2008; Koibuchi, Sato, and Shimizu 2018, 87.

11. Goldberg and Tille 2008.

12. For economic models considering the role of expectations and competition in currency invoicing decisions, see Fukuda and Ono 2006; Bacchetta and van Wincoop 2005.

13. For studies that emphasize the transaction cost argument, see Rey 2001; Goldberg and Tille 2008.

14. Krugman 1980.

15. The empirical strategy used in this chapter mirrors the "Most Likely" case design, also employed in Chapter 3. See Levy 2008.

16. Reuters 2014.

17. *Huanqiu (Global Times)* 2014.

18. *Financial Tribune* 2014.

19. *Finanz* 2018.

20. TASS (Russian News Agency) 2015; Hobson 2015.

21. Disinterest was partly due to difficulty in obtaining RMB to repay debts issued in the currency. As one Russian executive who decided against rolling over RMB debts explained, "If you export to China, then it's perfect. In this way, you can close the currency risk by earning revenue in RMB, and you attract debts in the same currency. If you do not [export to China], then this is a new risk that you need to take." See *Finanz* 2019a.

22. Baraulina and Rudnitsky 2017.

23. Denison's full quote is this: "We already have settlements with China in national currencies, there are more settlements in yuan [renminbi] than in rubles. We are interested in the conditions of all restrictions in direct payments without any intermediaries.... Our banks can open special correspondent accounts, and they are open and directly pay under contracts. The very thing turned out to be a quick, risk-free event. It is profitable for us, profitable for business. Ruble accounts in Chinese banks, yuan [renminbi] accounts in Russian banks." See *Russian Gazette* 2019.

24. RT 2019.

25. RT 2018; *The Moscow Times* 2019; BRICS refers to a group consisting of five major emerging market economies: Brazil, Russia, India, China, and South Africa.

26. Ostroukh and Gumrukcu 2018.

27. Andrei Kostin, Chairman of VTB Bank, one of the largest financial institutions in Russia, was quoted in Russian media explaining that he "recently met with the president [Putin], I told him the proposals of our bank to reduce the dollar in the calculations, in general, in the economy of our country." VTB was the bank that facilitated Alrosa's initial ruble-based commercial transaction with a Chinese buyer. See RIA 2018.

28. Polina 2018a.

29. Polina 2018b.

30. *Nikkei* 2019; Zhou and Li 2019.

31. Ma 2019.

32. Yeung 2018.

33. Grinkevich 2019.

34. Reuters 2019a.

35. Kida, Kubota, and Cho 2019.

36. Grinkevich 2020; per press releases issued by CIPS, Russian members include GLOBEX Commercial Bank, Expobank Limited Liability Company, Gazprombank, and Credit Bank of Moscow.

37. The US Treasury eventually added Rosneft to the SDN list on February 18, 2020, in EO 13850 for its business dealings with Venezuela. For more on its decision to price and settle its sales in euros, see Astakhova, Fabrichnaya, and Ostroukh 2019.

38. Russia's economy minister, Maxim Oreshkin, described the ruble as such in an interview found here: Seddon and Foy 2019.

39. Yagova 2018; *Gazeta Ru* 2018.

40. *Agence France Presse* 2021.
41. These actions by Treasury expanded EO 13622. See US Treasury 2014b.
42. Slack 2017.
43. *Finanz* 2019b; Bipindra and Pismennaya 2019.
44. Reuters 2017a.
45. Gould 2019.
46. Aydinlik 2018.
47. In 2016, as the lira was under pressure, Erdoğan noted that promoting trade settlement in local currencies "would bring the price of the dollar down" and help stabilize the lira's exchange rate; see *Al Monitor* 2017. For details on the benefits of settling trade in national currency, see McDowell 2019a, 453–458.
48. Haber Turk 2018.
49. The swap line was activated for the first time, for the purpose of issuing a letter of credit for trade settlement, in April 2018. See Kalhor 2018.
50. Xinhua 2018, emphasis added.
51. *Daily Sabah* 2018a.
52. O'Byrne 2018.
53. *Daily Sabah* 2018b.
54. *Yeni Safak* 2018.
55. BBC Turkce 2018.
56. Biryukov and Baraulina 2019.
57. *Reuters* 2019b.
58. Data are from the Turkish Statistical Institute and can be found at https://data.tuik. gov.tr/Kategori/GetKategori?p=dis-ticaret-104&dil=2.
59. Reuters 2017b.
60. *El Reportero* 2017.
61. Kurmanaev 2017.
62. Rudnitsky 2019.
63. Shortly after reports implicated Evrofinance in its illicit ties to the Venezuelan economy, the US Treasury designated the bank in March 2019. See US Treasury 2019.
64. According to reporting by *Time*, the petro project was overseen by senior Kremlin advisors. Russia's interest in aiding Venezuela in the petro's development stemmed from Russia's own interest in developing a national cryptocurrency aimed at evading US sanctions. However, the Russian central bank was reluctant to launch its own coin because of concerns that it could destabilize the ruble. Rather than risk its own currency, Russia sought to use Venezuela—an economy with nothing to lose—as an experimental case that could prove, or disprove, the concept and inform future Russian policy. For more, see Shuster 2018.
65. Popper, Matsnev, and Herrero 2018; Bloomberg 2018.
66. Banco Central de Venezuela 2018.
67. TeleSur 2018.
68. Álvarez 2018, 2.
69. Bracci 2019; Karsten and West 2018.
70. Vasquez and Laya 2019; Laya 2019b.

71. Armas and Pons 2019.
72. "Meeting with Heads of International News Agencies" 2021.
73. For data on SWIFT messages processed by date, see https://www.swift.com/about-us/discover-swift/fin-traffic-figures.
74. TASS 2018a.

Chapter 6

1. Krämer 2018.
2. Kennedy 1962.
3. WTO 2020.
4. For helpful background on the basics of trade finance, see Auboin 2009.
5. Bank for International Settlements 2014, 13.
6. Gopinath and Stein 2021.
7. US purchases of Venezuelan oil ended abruptly following these additional US sanctions. However, China, India, and Malaysia continued to buy Maduro's crude outside the US financial system. See US Energy Information Administration 2020.
8. Local currency swap agreements are distinct from dollar-swap deals. While the former allows collaborating central banks to swap one local currency for another, the latter lets participating countries swap their local currency for US dollars. For more details on the difference, see McDowell 2019a.
9. Swap agreements are only one potential anti-dollar policy that governments may pursue in response to sanctions. The case studies in Chapter 5 illustrated that in some cases, targeted governments made other formal commitments to use local currencies in trade. In other cases, they launched or explored national cryptocurrencies to avoid the US banking system, or used alternative major currencies—like the euro or renminbi—in their cross-border payments. Since the outcome of interest here is a rather narrowly defined proxy for anti-dollar trade policies, focusing on local swaps agreements causes us to undercount the number of anti-dollar payments policies being pursued in trade settlement today. Thus, modeling the link between sanctions and swaps alone likely presents a harder test of the book's argument.
10. An emerging strand of the literature examines China's local currency swap deals. McDowell 2019c, which relied on direct communication with central banks with Chinese swap lines, found that most were never activated, even after being in place for several years. The study also concluded that significant barriers to RMB-based trade settlement remain, even in countries with access to the currency. Conversely, several other studies found that Chinese swap lines were associated with an increase in RMB-based trade settlement, suggesting they may promote de-dollarization in trade. See Georgiadis et al. 2021; Song and Xia 2020; Bahaj and Reis 2020.
11. McDowell 2019c, 131, 136.
12. Central Bank of Russia 2018, 224.
13. US House of Representatives 2018, 43–44.

14. For more on the Federal Reserve's use of swap lines to address the global dollar shortage, see: Allen 2013; McDowell 2017.

15. For a detailed discussion of the reasons countries have pursued local currency swap agreements, and the distinction between US dollar swaps and local currency swaps, see McDowell 2019a.

16. Cohen 2015; Liao and McDowell 2015.

17. Trade data are from the UN Comtrade database. GDP data are from the World Bank's World Development Indicators (WDI) database.

18. McDowell 2017; Schneider and Tobin 2020.

19. McDowell 2019c.

20. All remaining control variables are from the World Bank's WDI database with one exception. Foreign exchange reserves data for Iran, which were missing from the WDI database, were drawn from the Federal Reserve Economic Database, available at https://fred.stlouisfed.org/.

21. Because the outcome variable takes the form of count data, expressed as only positive integer values, I present Poisson regression results in Table D.1 in Appendix D. The results are substantively unchanged.

22. The author submitted a formal request to SWIFT in October 2019 to access payments data. SWIFT declined to provide the data, citing a policy change to no longer provide data to researchers, which was implemented in 2020. For studies that examine SWIFT data prior to this policy change, see Bahaj and Reis 2020; Song and Xia 2020.

23. Boz et al. 2022, 4.

24. These data come from Boz et al. 2022. The authors compile their data from a variety of official sources, including central bank websites and customs authorities. Some countries report currency invoicing patterns in trade while others report currency settlement patterns. The authors discuss the challenges related to compiling these data at length (see especially pages 6–7). Due to differences in reporting by country, the data are unbalanced. They are not updated through 2019 in all cases. Regressions use all available observations.

25. Friberg and Wilander 2008; Koibuchi, Sato, and Shimizu 2018, 87.

26. I employ these separately because there is no way to combine the values without biasing the measure since absolute trade values are not reported. However, there are benefits of these data being disaggregated. For example, in the Russia case study presented in Chapter 5, the evidence suggests that Moscow's de-dollarization efforts were most successful on the export payment side of the ledger. Thus, being able to estimate separate models enables us to probe the potential for systematic differences in the relationship between US sanctions and currency use in trade, contingent on the direction of the flow of goods.

27. See, for example, Kamps 2006; Koibuchi, Sato, and Shimizu 2012; Georgiadis et al. 2021.

28. Trade data is from the UN Comtrade database, reflecting a country's total imports and exports of goods to the United States and the rest of the world.

29. I use UN Comtrade's definition of oil imports/exports: "Petroleum oils and oils obtained from bituminous minerals; crude." Data are available at http://comtrade. un.org/.
30. GDP and GDP per capita data are from the World Bank's WDI database.
31. Gopinath and Stein 2021.
32. The PCI is produced by a partnership between the Vietnam Chamber of Commerce and Industry and the US Agency for International Development. Its primary function is to conduct annual surveys of the Vietnamese business climate. The experiment discussed here appeared in the Foreign Investor Module. I am indebted to Eddy Malesky for making room for my experiment in this module.
33. Malesky and Mosley 2018, 17.
34. Le and Tran-Nam 2018.
35. Barklie 2019.
36. The actual text presented to firm managers used "RMB," a common abbreviation for the Chinese renminbi.
37. American MNCs were excluded because the treatment about the US should not induce political risk perceptions among a group of firms that shares the nationality of the sanctioning state. Excluding these sixteen firms does not substantively change the results.

Chapter 7

1. Xi 2022.
2. Cœuré 2019.
3. Bernstein 1982; Kindleberger 1985; Horii 1986.
4. Morse 1979.
5. Kindleberger 1985, 308.
6. Eichengreen 2011, 8.
7. Kirshner 2014, 18.
8. Roubini 2009; Griesse and Kellermann 2008.
9. Oatley et al. 2013; Winecoff 2015.
10. Cohen 2020.
11. Keown 2020; Cox 2021; Stankiewicz 2021.
12. Ainger and McCormick 2020.
13. Srslanalp, Eichengreen, and Simpson-Bell 2021.
14. Cohen 2015, 186.
15. For a more detailed discussion of these limitations, see McDowell and Steinberg 2017; Germain and Schwartz 2014; Cohen 2015.
16. Gavin 2004, 77.
17. For an example of de Gaulle's anti-dollar rhetoric, see United Press International 1967. For a general discussion of de Gaulle's position, see Cohen 2019, 152.
18. Gros and Thygesen 1998, 373.

19. Cohen 2015, 184.

20. Cohen 2015, 120.

21. Germain and Schwartz 2014, 1096.

22. "The International Role of the Euro" 1999, 31.

23. *World Market Intelligence News* 2014.

24. Schaer 2018; Maas 2018.

25. Turak 2018.

26. Amir-Aslani 2018.

27. Bourdillon 2019b; Grandi 2019.

28. Bruggmann 2019; Bourdillon 2019a.

29. Stearns and Fouquet 2019.

30. *Gov.Uk* 2020.

31. Koch 2020.

32. Fischer, Koch, and Munchrath 2019.

33. Junker 2018.

34. European Commission 2018b, 12.

35. European Commission 2018a.

36. European Commission 2021.

37. European Commission 2021.

38. Berard et al. 2021, 4; Papadia and Efstathiou 2018, 3.

39. Hackenbroich et al. 2020, 39.

40. Dooley, Folkerts-Landau, and Garber 2004, 308.

41. For a full discussion of the risks facing China, see McDowell 2019c, 127–130.

42. Wines, Bradsher, and Landler 2009.

43. X. Zhou 2009.

44. Within Chinese politics, the bureaucratic fault lines of renminbi internationalization divide those institutions. For instance, the People's Bank of China supports liberal policy reforms that would free up the currency to take on a larger international role, while the National Development and Reform Commission prefers to keep policies like capital controls in place that generally constrain internationalization efforts. For a discussion of the internal politics of renminbi internationalization, see McDowell and Steinberg 2017. For a related discussion of the politics of capital controls in China, see Steinberg, McDowell, and Gueorguiev 2021.

45. For a detailed discussion of the Chinese policy response to outflows in 2015, see McDowell 2019b. For more on the effect of China's capital controls on the renminbi's international use, see Harada 2017.

46. Reserves data are from the IMF COFER database; payments data is from SWIFT'S RMB Tracker database.

47. After initial resistance, China agreed to join the multilateral sanctions regime organized by the Obama administration in 2010.

48. *Huanqiu (Global Times)* 2014.

49. *QQ (Tencent)* 2014.

50. Xiong 2014.

51. Siqing 2014.

52. Weijia 2017.
53. *Financial Tribune* 2017.
54. Yin 2018.
55. Hu 2018.
56. Harney 2018.
57. Yu 2018.
58. W. Hu 2019.
59. Harada and Ogawa 2019.
60. Zhu, Guan, and Liu 2020; Zhang 2020; *Reuters* 2020; Gao 2020.
61. Wang 2021.
62. Huang 2019; Chen 2020.
63. Zhou 2019.
64. Shen, Zhou, and Yao 2020; *Bloomberg* 2020.
65. Fang 2020.
66. Gentiloni 2021.

Chapter 8

1. Gao 2020.
2. Google 2011.
3. Martínez 2016.
4. "Inside the Failure of Google+, a Very Expensive Attempt to Unseat Facebook" 2015.
5. Fang 2020.
6. China Construction Bank 2021, 9.
7. The Clearing House Interbank Payments System (CHIPS) is the incorporated correspondent banking network in which major US-based banks operate as financial hubs, connecting all other banks participating in the dollar system. Nearly all international dollar transfers are cleared through the elite group of CHIPS institutions. The Society for Worldwide Interbank Financial Telecommunications (SWIFT) is the communication platform used by banks to request the debiting of one account and the crediting of another. SWIFT handles nearly all cross-border dollar payment requests as well as most payment instructions for non-dollar currencies.
8. Farrell and Newman 2019, 66.
9. Eavis 2018.
10. Blenkinsop 2022.
11. Discussed in detail in Chapter 2, secondary sanctions are extraterritorial measures that threaten consequences for banks *without* US operations doing business with entities blacklisted by US Treasury.
12. The panopticon effect refers to situations where states that control critical network hubs have unrivaled access to information flows within the network, which gives them valuable insights into their adversaries' behavior and tactics. The chokepoint effect refers to a circumstance where a state controls a critical hub through which most

network traffic flows, giving the state the capacity to cut targets out of the network by denying them access to the hub. See Farrell and Newman 2019.

13. See Eichengreen 2022 for a detailed discussion of these points.
14. "China Government Bond Market—Too Big to Ignore" 2021; Ming 2018.
15. McDowell 2022.
16. While the dollar has generally maintained the top spot, it is followed by the euro, the British pound, the Japanese yen, and then finally the Chinese renminbi.
17. People's Bank of China 2015.
18. Approximately 40 percent of SWIFT's business is in dollars.
19. Eichengreen 2022, 4.
20. Tang 2020.
21. Zhu, Guan, and Liu 2020.
22. Liu 2021.
23. What is unknown is whether the missing country-level data are randomly distributed by countries' relationship to US sanctions and sanctions risk. If the missing data are systematically associated with a low US sanctions risk, then the analysis presented here would be biased in favor of finding a statistical relationship between sanctions and CIPS participation. If the missing data are systematically associated with a high sanctions risk, the results presented here would underestimate the link.
24. CIPS announced on October 19, 2018, that the Turkish bank Kuveyt Turk Katlim Bankasi A.S. had joined CIPS. On November 23, 2018, CIPS reported that three additional banks in Turkey—Bank of China Turkey AS, Fibabanka AS, and Yapi Ve Kredi Bankasi AS—had also joined as indirect participants.
25. Gasper 2019.
26. Interfax 2022.
27. Kida, Kubota, and Cho 2019.
28. Finextra 2016.
29. Gannes 2011.

Conclusion

1. Widakuswara and Bredemeier 2022.
2. White House 2022.
3. This does not mean the threat is zero, since every new sanctions target is likely to develop anti-dollar policy preferences that increase aggregate demand for alternative currency systems. In time, as the number of financially aggrieved states rises, the incentives for a state like China to create such an alternative system grows. Still, small states' capacity to adapt to US financial pressure is likely to depend on assistance from a more powerful geopolitical benefactor.

References

@zeitonline. 2018. "Donald #Trump Zerstört Die Liberale Weltordnung. Der Ausstieg Aus Dem #Iran-Abkommen Ist Dabei Nur Ein Weiterer Schritt." Twitter. https://twitter.com/zeitonline/status/994092257346244609?s=20&t=A231GdPn0QTBoyp xTFRg4g.

AFP. 2018. "Putin Says 'Political Disputes' Damaging Dollar as Reserve Currency." *Agence France-Presse*, July 27. https://www.business-standard.com/article/pti-stories/putin-says-political-disputes-damaging-dollar-as-reserve-currency-118072701135_1.html.

Agence France Presse. 2021. "Putin Urges Europe to Pay for Gas in Euros, Not Dollars," June 4. https://www.barrons.com/news/putin-urges-europe-to-pay-for-gas-in-euros-not-dollars-01622814314.

Ainger, John, and Liz McCormick. 2020. "Goldman Warns the Dollar's Grip on Global Markets Might Be Over." Bloomberg, July 28. https://www.bloomberg.com/news/artic les/2020-07-28/goldman-warns-dollar-s-role-as-world-reserve-currency-is-at-risk.

Alerassool, Mahvash. 1993. *Freezing Assets: The USA and the Most Effetive Economic Sanction*. New York: St. Martin's Press.

Allen, William A. 2013. *International Liquidity and the Financial Crisis*. New York: Cambridge University Press.

Alloway, Tracy, and Joe Weisenthal. 2022. "Zoltan Pozsar on Russia, Gold, and a Turning Point for the U.S. Dollar." Bloomberg, March 2. https://www.bloomberg.com/news/articles/2022-03-02/zoltan-pozsar-on-russia-gold-and-a-turning-point-for-the-u-s-dollar.

Aluminum Insider. 2017. "Rusal Sets New Standard in Low-Carbon Aluminium with ALLOW," November 2. https://aluminiuminsider.com/rusal-sets-new-standard-low-carbon-aluminium-allow/.

Álvarez, Ricardo. 2018. "Las Criptomonedas y Los Sistemas de Pago [Cryptocurrencies and Payment Systems]." Banco Central de Venezuela. http://bcv.org.ve/bcv/public aciones.

Amir-Aslani, Ardavan. 2018. "Pourquoi l'Europe n'a Pas Les Moyens de Contrecarrer Les États-Unis Sur l'Iran [Why Europe Cannot Afford to Thwart the United States over Iran]." *Le Nouvel Economiste*, November 20. https://www.lenouveleconomiste.fr/pourq uoi-leurope-na-pas-les-moyens-de-contrecarrer-les-etats-unis-sur-liran-66074/.

Andrianova, Anna. 2018. "Russia's Shield Against Sanctions Draws Praise from Moody's." Bloomberg, August 5. https://www.bloomberg.com/news/articles/2018-08-05/russia-s-shield-against-u-s-sanctions-draws-praise-from-moody-s.

Andrianova, Anna, Evgenia Pismennaya, and Olga Tanas. 2018. "Putin Hedges Trump Bet by Dumping Treasuries to Safeguard Assets." Bloomberg, June 20. https://www.bloomberg.com/news/articles/2018-07-20/putin-hedges-trump-bet-by-dumping-tre asuries-to-safeguard-assets.

"Announcement of Expanded Treasury Sanctions within the Russian Financial Services, Energy and Defense or Related Materiel Sectors." 2014. US Treasury. https://www.treas ury.gov/press-center/press-releases/Pages/jl2629.aspx.

Armas, Mayela, and Corina Pons. 2019. "Exclusive: Facing U.S. Sanctions, Venezuela Offers Suppliers Payment in Chinese Yuan—Sources." Reuters, November 28. https:// www.reuters.com/article/us-venezuela-china-yuan-exclusive/exclusive-facing-u-s- sanctions-venezuela-offers-suppliers-payment-in-chinese-yuan-sources-idUSKB N1Y20FA.

Ashford, Emma. 2016. "Not-so-Smart Sanctions the Failure of Western Restrictions against Russia." *Foreign Affairs* 95 (1): 114–123.

Associated Press. 2018. "The Latest: Macron Calls US Exit from Iran Deal a 'Mistake.'" Associated Press, May 9. https://www.apnews.com/bb6dd8120b824d529132bcd9b a9e612b.

Astakhova, Olesya, Elena Fabrichnaya, and Andrey Ostroukh. 2019. "Rosneft Switches Contracts to Euros from Dollars due to U.S. Sanctions." Reuters, October 24. https:// www.reuters.com/article/us-rosneft-contracts-euro/rosneft-switches-contracts-to- euros-from-dollars-due-to-u-s-sanctions-idUSKBN1X31JT.

Auboin, Marc. 2009. "Boosting the Availability of Trade Finance in the Current Crisis: Background Analysis for a Substantial G20 Package." *Centre for Economic Policy Research, Policy Insights No. 35* (June): 1–7. http://www.cepr.org/sites/default/files/poli cy_insights/PolicyInsight35.pdf.

Aydinlik. 2018. "ABD'nin Korkulu Rüyası Yerel Para Birimi Havuzu [The United States' Fearful Dream Local Currency Pool]." *Aydinlik*, February 7. https://www.aydinlik.com. tr/abd-nin-korkulu-ruyasi-yerel-para-birimi-havuzu-turkiye-temmuz-2018.

Bacchetta, Philippe, and Eric van Wincoop. 2005. "A Theory of the Currency Denomination of International Trade." *Journal of International Economics* 67 (2): 295–319.

Bahaj, Saleem, and Ricardo Reis. 2020. "Jumpstarting an International Currency." Bank of England, London. https://www.bankofengland.co.uk/-/media/boe/files/working- paper/2020/jumpstarting-an-international-currency.pdf.

Bailey, Michael A., Anton Strezhnev, and Erik Voeten. 2017. "Estimating Dynamic State Preferences from United Nations Voting Data." *Journal of Conflict Resolution* 61 (2): 430–456.

Baker, Stephanie. 2018. "Deripaska's Two-Decade Wooing of U.S. Ends in Financial Meltdown." Bloomberg, April 11. https://www.bloomberg.com/news/articles/2018- 04-11/deripaska-s-two-decade-wooing-of-u-s-ends-in-financial-meltdown?

Banco Central de Venezuela. 2011. "BCV Inició La Repatriación Del Oro Monetario de La República." http://www.bcv.org.ve/notas-de-prensa/bcv-inicio-la-repatriacion-del- oro-monetario-de-la-republica.

Banco Central de Venezuela. 2018. "Presidente Maduro Autorizó Compras y Ventas Con El Petro [President Maduro Authorized Purchases and Sales with El Petro]." Banco Central de Venezuela. http://bcv.org.ve/notas-de-prensa/presidente-maduro-autor izo-compras-y-ventas-con-el-petro.

Bank for International Settlements. 2014. "Trade Finance: Developments and Issues." *Committee on the Global Financial System Papers*, January. https://www.bis.org/publ/ cgfs50.pdf.

Central Bank of Russia. 2018. "Bank of Russia Annual Report for 2017." http://www.cbr. ru/eng/publ/god/.

Baraulina, Anna, and Jake Rudnitsky. 2017. "So Much for Putin's China Pivot as Sberbank Sours on Yuan." Bloomberg, March 8. https://www.bloomberg.com/news/articles/2017-03-08/so-much-for-putin-s-china-pivot-as-sberbank-loses-taste-for-yuan.

Barklie, Glenn. 2019. "Greenfield FDI Performance Index 2019: Serbia Storms to Top." FDI Intelligence. https://www.fdiintelligence.com/article/75351.

BBC. 2020. "Venezuela Gold: UK High Court Rules against Nicolás Maduro," July 2. https://www.bbc.com/news/world-latin-america-53262767.

BBC Turkce. 2018. "Cumhurbaşkanı Erdoğan: Mesele Dolar, Euro Değil; Bunlar Ekonomik Savaşın Kurşunları, Füzeleri [President Erdoğan: The Issue Is Not the Dollar; They Are the Bullets of Economic War, Missiles]." BBC Turkce, August 13. https://www.bbc.com/turkce/haberler-turkiye-45157718.

Beck, Nathaniel, and Jonathan N. Katz. 1995. "What to Do (and Not to Do) with Time-Series Cross-Section Data." American Political Science Review 89 (3): 634–647.

Berard, Marie-Helene, Elvire Fabry, Farid Fatah, Edward Knudsen, Pascal Lamy, Genevieve Pons, Louis Schweitzer, and Pierre Vimont. 2021. "American Extraterritorial Sanctions: Did Someone Say European Strategic Autonomy?" Paris. https://www.delorscentre.eu/en/publications/detail/publication/american-extraterritorial-sanctions-did-someone-say-european-strategic-autonomy.

Bernstein, Edward M. 1982. "The Future of the Dollar and Other Reserve Assets." In The International Monetary System: A Time of Turbulence, edited by Jacob S. Dreyer, Gottfried Haberler, and Thomas D. Willett, 410–429. Washington, DC: American Enterprise Institute for Public Policy Research.

Bhatia, Ashish. 2012. "Optimal Gold Allocation for Emerging-Market Central Banks." In RBS Reserve Management Trends, 71–89. London: Central Banking Publications.

Bipindra, Nc, and Evgenia Pismennaya. 2019. "India, Russia Seek to Skirt U.S. Sanctions Threat to Arms Deals." July 15. https://www.bloomberg.com/news/articles/2019-07-15/india-russia-seek-to-skirt-u-s-sanctions-threat-to-arms-deals.

Biryukov, Andrey, and Anna Baraulina. 2019. "Trash Discovery Shows Turkey Eyes Putin's Anti-Sanctions Network." Bloomberg, August 21. https://www.bloomberg.com/news/articles/2019-08-21/trash-discovery-shows-turkey-eyes-putin-s-anti-sanctions-network.

Blenkinsop, Philip. 2022. "EU Bars 7 Russian Banks from SWIFT, but Spares Those in Energy." Reuters, March 2. https://www.reuters.com/business/finance/eu-excludes-seven-russian-banks-swift-official-journal-2022-03-02/.

Blodget, Henry. 2009. "Obama to China: U.S. Won't Default on $1 Trillion Loan." Business Insider, March 14. https://www.businessinsider.com/henry-blodget-obama-to-china-us-wont-default-on-1-trillion-loan-2009-3.

Bloomberg. 2018. "Venezuela to Issue Oil-Backed Cryptocurrency in 'Coming Days.'" Bloomberg 2, January 6. https://www.bloomberg.com/news/articles/2018-01-06/venezuela-to-issue-oil-backed-cryptocurrency-in-coming-days.

Bloomberg. 2020. "China Renews Push for Increased Global Role for the Yuan," July 12. https://www.bloomberg.com/news/articles/2020-07-12/china-presses-global-yuan-role-as-u-s-tensions-explode-into-fx.

Bolton, John. 2020. The Room Where It Happened: A White House Memoir. New York: Simon & Schuster.

Bourdillon, Yves. 2019a. "L'Europe Mise Sur Instex Pour Commercer Avec l'Iran [Europe Relies on Instex to Trade with Iran]." Les Echos, February 8. https://www.lesechos.fr/monde/europe/leurope-mise-sur-instex-pour-commercer-avec-liran-962972.

Bourdillon, Yves. 2019b. "Moscou Plaide Pour Du Troc Avec Téhéran [Moscow Pleads for Bartering with Tehran]." *Les Echos*, July 18. https://www.lesechos.fr/monde/europe/moscou-plaide-pour-du-troc-avec-teheran-1038986.

Boz, Emine, Camila Casas, Georgios Georgiadis, Gita Gopinath, Helena Le Mezo, Arnaud Mehl, and Tra Nguyen. 2020. "Patterns in Invoicing Currency in Global Trade." WP/20/126. Washington, DC.

Bracci, Luigino. 2019. "The Petro: Is It a 'Shuddering Failure' and a 'Laughing Stock'? What Can We Expect?" *Venezuela Analysis*, August 30. https://venezuelanalysis.com/analysis/14642.

Bronner, Ethan, and Andrew Rosati. 2018. "Maduro Got a Salt Bae Feast, But Turkey Gets Venezuela's Gold." Bloomberg, October 11. https://www.bloomberg.com/news/articles/2018-10-11/why-erdogan-is-maduro-s-new-bff.

Bruggmann, Mathias. 2019. "Wie Die EU Das Iran-Abkommen Noch Retten Kann [Nuclear Deal: How the EU Can Still Save the Iran Agreement]." *Handelsblatt*, May 9. https://www.handelsblatt.com/politik/international/atomdeal-wie-die-eu-das-iran-abkommen-noch-retten-kann/24322890.html.

Bryant, Fred B., and Paul R. Yarnold. 1995. "Principal-Components Analysis and Confirmatory Factor Analysis." In *Reading and Understanding Multivariate Statistics*, edited by L. G. Grimm and P. R. Yarnold, 99–136. Washington, DC: American Psychological Association.

Byron, Lord. 1856. *The Works of Lord Byron*. Edited by J. W. Lake. Philadelphia: J. B. Lippincott.

Caballero, Ricardo J., Emmanuel Farhi, and Pierre Olivier Gourinchas. 2017. "The Safe Assets Shortage Conundrum." *Journal of Economic Perspectives* 31 (3): 29–46.

Carter, Barry E., and Ryan M. Farha. 2013. "Overview and Operation of the Evolving U.S. Financial Sanctions, Including the Example of Iran." *Georgetown University of International Law* 107: 315–322.

Chen, Frank. 2020. "Frank Chen, Beijing to Bypass US Systems with e-RMB Drive." *Asia Times*, June 4. https://asiatimes.com/2020/06/beijing-to-bypass-us-systems-with-e-rmb-drive/.

China Construction Bank. 2021. "2021 Renminbi Internationalisation Report." Beijing. http://group1.ccb.com/cn/ccbtoday/news/upload/20211022_1634866375/2021102200 92955802527.pdf.

"China Government Bond Market—Too Big to Ignore." 2021. https://www.gsam.com/content/gsam/uk/en/advisers/market-insights/gsam-connect/2021/China-Government-Bond-Market-Too-Big-to-Ignore.html.

Christensen, Neils. 2019. "Romania Proposes to Repatriate 95% of Its Gold." *Kitco News*, February 28. https://www.kitco.com/news/2019-02-28/Romania-Proposes-to-Repatriate-95-Of-Its-Gold.html.

Clark, James, and Gabriel Mann. 2016. "A Deeper Look at Liquidity Conditions in the Treasury Market." US Treasury. https://www.treasury.gov/connect/blog/Pages/A-Deeper-Look-at-Liquidity-Conditions-in-the-Treasury-Market.aspx.

Cœuré, Benoît. 2019. "The Euro's Global Role in a Changing World: A Monetary Policy Perspective." European Central Bank. February 15. https://www.ecb.europa.eu/press/key/date/2019/html/ecb.sp190215~15c89d887b.en.html.

Cohen, Benjamin J. 1971. *The Future of Sterling as an International Currency*. London: Macmillan.

Cohen, Benjamin J . 2011. *The Future of Global Currency*. Abingdon, UK: Routledge.

Cohen, Benjamin J. 2015. *Currency Power: Understanding Monetary Rivalry*. Princeton, NJ: Princeton University Press.

Cohen, Benjamin J. 2016. "Will the Dollar Be Trumped?" *Project Syndicate*, November 23. https://www.project-syndicate.org/commentary/trump-dollar-longer-term-value-by-benjamin-j--cohen-2016-11.

Cohen, Benjamin J. 2019. *Currency Statecraft: Monetary Rivalry and Geopolitical Ambition*. Chicago: University of Chicago Press.

Cohen, Benjamin J. 2020. "The Pandemic Is Shaking the Dollar's Supremacy." Project Syndicate. May 18. https://www.project-syndicate.org/commentary/covid19-trump-failures-shaking-dollar-supremacy-by-benjamin-cohen-2020-05.

Cohen, Benjamin J., and Tabitha M. Benney. 2014. "What Does the International Currency System Really Look Like?" *Review of International Political Economy* 21 (5): 1017–1041.

Collins, Tom. 2022. "How Putin Prepared for Sanctions with Tonnes of African Gold." *Telegraph*, March 3. https://www.telegraph.co.uk/global-health/terror-and-security/putin-prepared-sanctions-tonnes-african-gold/.

Cooper, Amanda. 2011. "Emerging World Buys $10 Billion in Gold as West Wobbles." Reuters 2, August 3. https://www.reuters.com/article/businesspro-us-gold-reserves/emerging-world-buys-10-billion-in-gold-as-west-wobbles-idUSTRE7722IK20110803.

Cox, Jeff. 2021. "Stanley Druckenmiller Says the Fed Is Endangering the Dollar's Global Reserve Status." CNBC, May 11. https://www.cnbc.com/2021/05/11/stanley-druckenmiller-says-the-fed-is-endangering-the-dollars-global-reserve-status.html.

Cramer, Jim. 2015. "Does the Secretary Know Anything about the Dollar?" Twitter. https://twitter.com/jimcramer/status/631269287022436352.

Daddy, Puff. 1997. *It's All About the Benjamins*. Bad Boy, Arista Records.

Daily Sabah. 2018a. "Turkey, Qatar Central Banks Sign Currency Swap Deal." *Daily Sabah*, August 20. https://www.dailysabah.com/economy/2018/08/20/turkey-qatar-central-banks-sign-currency-swap-deal.

Daily Sabah. 2018b. "China Reiterates Support for Turkey's Call to Use National Currencies in Trade." *Daily Sabah*, September 16. https://www.dailysabah.com/economy/2018/09/17/china-reiterates-support-for-turkeys-call-to-use-national-currencies-in-trade.

Danilov, Ivan. 2019. "'Санкции Из Ада' Возвращаются. Нас Спасут Золото и Ракеты ['Sanctions from Hell' Are Back. Gold and Missiles Will Save Us]." *RIA*, April 5. https://ria.ru/20190405/1552398560.html.

Day, Timon. 1998. "Gold: The Asset No-One Seems to Want." *Investors Chronicle*, February 20.

Dembinskaya, Natalia. 2018. "Strategic Asset: Why Do States Buy Up Gold and Export It from the US. [Стратегический Актив: Зачем Государства Скупают Золото и Вывозят Его Из США]." *RIA*, April 21. https://ria.ru/economy/20180421/1519107937.html?inj=1.

Devitt, Polina, and Anastasia Lyrchikova Oksana Kobzeva. 2018. "How Russian Tycoon Deripaska Might Try to Navigate Sanctions." Reuters, April 11. https://www.reuters.com/article/us-usa-russia-sanctions-deripaska-explai-idUSKBN1HI1UJ.

Doff, Natahsa, and Anna Andrianova. 2019. "Russia Buys Quarter of World Yuan Reserves in Shift from Dollar." Bloomberg, January 9. https://www.bloomberg.com/news/articles/2019-01-09/russia-boosted-yuan-euro-holdings-as-it-dumped-dollars-in-2018.

Donahue, Patrick. 2018. "Merkel Says Trump's Iran Deal Withdrawal Harms Trust in Global Order." Bloomberg, May 11. https://www.bloomberg.com/news/articles/2018-05-11/merkel-says-trump-s-iran-pullout-harms-trust-in-global-order.

Dooley, Michael P., David Folkerts-Landau, and Peter Garber. 2004. "The Revived Bretton Woods System." *International Journal of Finance and Economics* 9 (4): 307–313.

Drezner, Daniel W. 2003. "The Hidden Hand of Economic Coercion." *International Organization* 57 (3): 643–659.

Drezner, Daniel W. 2011. "Sanctions Sometimes Smart: Targeted Sanctions in Theory and Practice." *International Studies Review* 13 (1): 96–108.

Drezner, Daniel W. 2015. "Targeted Sanctions in a World of Global Finance." *International Interactions* 41 (4): 755–764.

Drezner, Daniel W. 2021. "The United States of Sanctions: The Use and Abuse of Economic Coercion." *Foreign Affairs* 100 (5): 142–154.

Dunteman, George H. 1989. *Principal Components Analysis.* New York: Sage.

DW. 2019. "Trump Boost for Gold at Dollar's Expense." *DW,* June 11. https://www.dw.com/en/trumps-policies-add-luster-to-gold-at-dollars-expense/a-49135607.

Eavis, Peter. 2018. "Important European Financial Firm Bows to Trump's Iran Sanctions." *New York Times,* November 5. https://www.nytimes.com/2018/11/05/business/dealbook/swift-iran-sanctions.html.

Eichengreen, Barry. 2011. *Exorbitant Privilege: The Rise and Fall of the Dollar and the Future of the International Monetary System.* New York: Oxford University Press.

Eichengreen, Barry. 2016. "Three Ways to Make Sense of the Dollar's Uncertain Prospects." *Financial Times,* November 16. https://www.ft.com/content/b26509d2-aa9c-11e6-ba7d-76378e4fef24.

Eichengreen, Barry. 2022. "Sanctions, SWIFT, and China's Cross-Border Interbank Payments System." Washington, DC. https://www.csis.org/analysis/sanctions-swift-and-chinas-cross-border-interbank-payments-system.

Eichengreen, Barry, and Marc Flandreau. 2009. "The Rise and Fall of the Dollar (or When Did the Dollar Replace Sterling as the Leading Reserve Currency?)." *European Review of Economic History* 13 (3): 377–411.

Elliott, Kimberly Ann. 1998. "The Sanctions Glass: Half Full or Completely Empty?" *International Security* 23 (1): 50–65.

European Commission. 2018a. "Deepening Europe's Economic and Monetary Union." https://ec.europa.eu/info/sites/default/files/factsheet-strengthen-euro-global-role-05122018_en.pdf.

European Commission. 2018b. "Towards a Stronger International Role of the Euro: Commission Contribution to the European Council and the Euro Summit." https://commission.europa.eu/publications/towards-stronger-international-role-euro-commission-contribution-european-council-and-euro-summit-13_en.

European Commission. 2021. "Commission Takes Further Steps to Foster the Openness, Strength and Resilience of Europe's Economic and Financial System." https://ec.europa.eu/commission/presscorner/detail/en/ip_21_108.

Fang, Xinghai. 2020. "Global Economy and Prospects under the Covid-19 Pandemic 疫情下的全球经济及前瞻." *Caixin,* June 23. http://video.caixin.com/2020-06-23/101571271.html.

Farrell, Henry, and Abraham L. Newman. 2019. "Weaponized Interdependence: How Global Economic Networks Shape State Coercion." *International Security* 44 (1): 42–79.

Farrell, Henry, and Abraham L. Newman. 2020. "The Twilight of America's Financial Empire." *Foreign Affairs*. https://www.foreignaffairs.com/articles/2020-01-24/twilight-americas-financial-empire.

Federal Reserve Bank of New York. 2002. "CHIPS." https://www.newyorkfed.org/abou tthefed/fedpoint/fed36.html.

Federal Reserve Bank of New York. 2018. "Services for Central Banks and International Institutions." Federal Reserve Bank of New York. https://www.newyorkfed.org/abou tthefed/fedpoint/fed20.

Financial Tribune. 2014. "Russia to Launch Alternative to SWIFT," November 12. https://financialtribune.com/articles/world-economy/4527/russia-to-launch-alternat ive-to-swift.

Financial Tribune. 2017. "Iran-China Traders Agree to Sideline US Dollar." *Financial Tribune*, December 7. https://financialtribune.com/articles/economy-business-and-markets/77359/iran-china-traders-agree-to-sideline-us-dollar.

Finanz. 2018. "Китай Отверг Соглашение о Дедолларизации Торговли с Россией [China Rejected de-Dollarization Agreement with Russia]." *Finanz*, December 25. https://www.finanz.ru/novosti/valyuty/kitay-otverg-soglashenie-o-dedollarizacii-torgovli-s-rossiey-1027831859.

Finanz. 2019a. "ВЭБ Не Нашел Спасения От Санкций в Китае [VEB Did Not Find Salvation from Sanctions in China]." *Finanz*, February 18. https://www.finanz.ru/novo sti/obligatsii/veb-ne-nashel-spaseniya-ot-sankciy-v-kitae-1027960539.

Finanz. 2019b. "Russia Announced the Creation of a Secret Mechanism for Payments for Weapons." *Finanz*, July 9. https://www.finanz.ru/novosti/aktsii/rossiya-obyavila-o-sozdanii-sekretnogo-mekhanizma-raschetov-za-oruzhie-1028337712.

Finextra. 2016. "VTB Bank Connects to CIPS." *Finextra*, March 10. https://www.finextra. com/pressarticle/63508/vtb-bank-connects-to-cips.

Fischer, Eva, Mortiz Koch, and Jens Munchrath. 2019. "Die Selbstverzwergung Europas [Europe Weakens Itself]." *Handelsblatt*, May 20. https://www.handelsblatt.com/poli tik/international/europawahl/aussenpolitik-die-selbstverzwergung-europas/24354 088.html.

"Fitch Revises Rusal's Rating Watch to Negative; Withdraws Ratings." 2018. Fitch Ratings.

Flitter, Emily. 2019. "Standard Chartered Fined $1.1 Billion for Violating Sanctions and Anti-Money Laundering Laws." *New York Times*, April 9. https://www.nytimes.com/ 2019/04/09/business/standard-chartered-sanctions-violations.html.

Francis, David, and Lara Jakes. 2016. "Sanctions Are a Failure . . . Let's Admit That." *Foreign Policy*, April 28. https://foreignpolicy.com/2016/04/28/sanctions-are-a-failurel ets-admit-that/.

Friberg, Richard, and Fredrik Wilander. 2008. "The Currency Denomination of Exports—A Questionnaire Study." *Journal of International Economics* 75 (1): 54–69.

FSI. 2020. "Fragile States Index." https://fragilestatesindex.org/.

Fukuda, Shin Ichi, and Masanori Ono. 2006. "On the Determinants of Exporters' Currency Pricing: History vs. Expectations." *Journal of the Japanese and International Economies* 20 (4): 548–568.

Galouchko, Ksenia, and Yuliya Fedorinova. "Russian Markets Slide after US Ups Ante with the Worst Sanctions Yet." Bloomberg, April 9. https://www.bloomberg.com/ news/articles/2018-04-09/russia-government-said-to-seek-ways-to-help-sanctioned-oligarchs?

Gannes, Liz. 2011. "Zuckerberg on Google+: Been There, Done That." *All Things D*, July 6. https://allthingsd.com/20110706/zuckerberg-on-google-been-there-done-that/.

Gao, Desheng. 2020. "美国可以布下这些金融陷阱 中国企业和政府如何应对（详解）[The U.S. Can Set Up These Financial Traps. How Can Chinese Companies and Governments Respond (Detailed)]." *China Finance 40 Forum*, September 10. https://finance.sina.com.cn/china/gncj/2020-09-10/doc-iivhvpwy6008602.shtml.

Gasper, Donald. 2019. "Pain of Tariffs and Sanctions behind China and Russia's Push to Dethrone the US Dollar." *South China Morning Post*, June 16. https://www.scmp.com/comment/opinion/article/3014258/pain-tariffs-and-sanctions-behind-china-and-russias-push-dethrone.

Gavin, Francis. 2004. *Gold, Dollars, and Power: The Politics of International Monetary Relations*. Chapel Hill: University of North Carolina Press.

Gazeta.Ru. 2018. "Доллар Не Нужен: Какую Валюту Выберет Россия [The Dollar Is Not Needed: What Currency Will Russia Choose]." *Gazeta.Ru*, October 29. https://www.gazeta.ru/business/2018/10/20/12028693.shtml.

Gentiloni, Paolo. 2021. "Remarks by Commissioner Gentiloni at the Press Conference on Fostering the Openness, Strength and Resilience of Europe's Economic and Financial System." European Commission, January 19. https://ec.europa.eu/commission/presscorner/detail/en/speech_21_162.

Georgiadis, Georgios, Helena Le Mezo, Arnaud Mehl, and Cédric Tille. 2021. "Fundamentals vs. Policies: Can the US Dollar's Dominance in Global Trade Be Dented?" London.

Germain, Randall, and Herman Schwartz. 2014. "The Political Economy of Failure: The Euro as an International Currency." *Review of International Political Economy* 21 (5): 1095–1122.

Gerring, John. 2007. *Case Study Research: Principles and Practices*. New York: Cambridge University Press.

Gilsinan, Kathy. 2019. "A Boom Time for U.S. Sanctions." *The Atlantic*, May 3. https://www.theatlantic.com/politics/archive/2019/05/why-united-states-uses-sanctions-so-much/588625/.

Goldberg, Linda S., and Cédric Tille. 2008. "Vehicle Currency Use in International Trade." *Journal of International Economics* 76 (2): 177–192.

Golubova, Anna. 2018. "Is Gold Repatriation a Trend? Turkey Gets Its Reserves Back from the US—Reports." *Kitco News*, April 20. https://www.kitco.com/news/2018-04-20/Is-Gold-Repatriation-A-Trend-Now-Turkey-Wants-Its-Gold-Back-From-The-U-S.html.

Golubova, Anna. 2019a. "Russia's Central Bank Chief: Love Of Gold Stems from Need to Diversify." *Kitco News*, April 28. https://www.kitco.com/news/2019-04-28/Russia-s-Central-Bank-Chief-Love-Of-Gold-Stems-From-Need-To-Diversify.html.

Golubova, Anna. 2019b. "Venezuela Gold Saga Continues: 20 Tonnes of Gold to Be Shipped to Unknown Location—Reports." *Kitco News*, January 30. https://www.kitco.com/news/2019-01-30/Venezuela-Gold-Saga-Continues-20-Tonnes-Of-Gold-To-Be-Shipped-To-Unknown-Location-Reports.html.

Gopalakrishnan, Balagopal, and Sanket Mohapatra. 2018. "Turning over a Golden Leaf? Global Liquidity and Emerging Market Central Banks' Demand for Gold after the Financial Crisis." *Journal of International Financial Markets, Institutions and Money* 57: 94–109.

Gopinath, Gita, and Jeremy C. Stein. 2021. "Banking, Trade, and the Making of a Dominant Currency." *Quarterly Journal of Economics* 136 (2): 783–830.

Gosteva, Elena. 2019. "«У Кого Золото, у Того и Власть»: Чем Россия Пугает Запад ["Who Has the Gold, and the One Has the Power": Why Does Russia Scare the West]." *Gazeta.Ru*, May 22. https://www.gazeta.ru/business/2019/05/22/12369397.shtml.

Gould, Joe. 2019. "Pompeo: With S-400, Turkey Won't Get F-35, May Get Sanctions." *Defense News*, April 10. https://www.defensenews.com/congress/budget/2019/04/10/pompeo-with-s-400-turkey-wont-get-f-35-may-get-sanctions/.

Gov.Uk. 2020. "INSTEX Successfully Concludes First Transaction," March 31. https://www.gov.uk/government/news/instex-successfully-concludes-first-transaction.

Grandi, Michel de. 2019. "Les Echos, L'Union Européenne Veut Aider Cuba à s'affranchir Des Sanctions Américaines [The European Union Wants to Help Cuba Get Rid of American Sanctions]." *Les Echos*, September 10. https://www.lesechos.fr/monde/ameriques/lunion-europeenne-veut-aider-cuba-a-saffranchir-des-sanctions-americaines-1130123.

Greifeld, Katherine. 2019. "Central Banks Expect Dollar to Reign Supreme for Another 25 Years." Bloomberg, October 16. https://www.bloomberg.com/news/articles/2019-10-16/central-banks-expect-king-dollar-to-reign-for-another-25-years?srnd=markets-vp.

Grice, Dylan. 2022. "Never Seen Weaponization of Money on This Scale Before . . . You Only Get to Play the Card Once. China Will Make It a Priority to Need No USD before Going for Taiwan. It's a Turning Point in Monetary History: The End of USD Hegemony & the Acceleration towards a Bipolar Monetary Order." Twitter, February 27, 2022. https://twitter.com/dylangrice/status/1497916658433810434?s=20&t=GOGQpbcs4UZHAvnD5tSqKA.

Griesse, Jörn, and Christian Kellermann. 2008. "What Comes after the Dollar?" Berlin. https://library.fes.de/pdf-files/id/ipa/05257.pdf.

Grinkevich, Dmitry. 2019. "Шелковый Курс: Россия и Китай Договорились о Расчетах в Рублях и Юанях [Silk Course: Russia and China Have Agreed on Settlements in Rubles and Yuan]." *Izvestia*, June 28. https://iz.ru/893613/dmitrii-grinkevich/shelkovyi-kurs-rossiia-i-kitai-dogovorilis-o-raschetakh-v-rubliakh-i-iuaniakh.

Grinkevich, Dmitry. 2020. "Юань Брал: Доллар Впервые Занял Менее 50% в Торговле России с КНР [The Yuan Took: The Dollar for the First Time Took Less than 50% in Russia's Trade with the PRC]." *Izvestia*, July 29. https://iz.ru/1041188/dmitrii-grinkevich/iuan-bral-dollar-vpervye-zanial-menee-50-v-torgovle-rossii-s-knr.

Gros, Daniel, and Niels Thygesen. 1998. *European Monetary Integration: From the European Monetary System to European Monetary Union*. London: Longman.

Groth, Detlef, Stefanie Hartmann, Sebastian Klie, and Joachim Selbig. 2013. "Principal Components Analysis." *Computational Toxicology* 930: 527–547.

Haber Turk. 2018. "Cumhurbaşkanı Erdoğan: Uluslararası Ticarette Dolar Egemenliğine Son Verilmeli [President Erdoğan: The Hegemony of Dollar in International Trade Should Be Terminated]." *Haber Turk*. https://www.haberturk.com/cumhurbaskani-erdogan-uluslararasi-ticarette-dolar-egemenligine-son-verilmeli-2128351.

Hackenbroich, Jonathan, Janka Oertel, Philipp Sander, and Pawel Zerka. 2020. "Defending Europe's Economic Sovereignty: New Ways to Resist Economic Coercion." Berlin. https://ecfr.eu/publication/defending_europe_economic_sovereignty_new_ways_to_resist_economic_coercion/.

Hanna, Andrew. 2017. "Cardin: Turkey's Purchase of Russian Missile System May Trigger Sanctions." *Politico*, September 14. https://www.politico.com/story/2017/09/14/turkey-russia-purchase-may-trigger-sanctions-242725.

Harada, Issaku. 2017. "Yuan Falling Out of Favor in Global Trade." *Nikkei*, May 7. https://asia.nikkei.com/Economy/Yuan-falling-out-of-favor-in-global-trade.

Harada, Issaku, and Tomoyo Ogawa. 2019. "China Builds Up Gold Reserves in Shift Away from Dollar." *Nikkei*, January 24. https://asia.nikkei.com/Business/Markets/Commodities/China-builds-up-gold-reserves-in-shift-away-from-dollar.

Harney, Alexandra. 2018. "Former Central Bank Governor: Yuan's Internationalization Is Progressing." Reuters, August 11, 2018. https://www.reuters.com/article/us-china-forex-yuan/former-central-bank-governor-yuans-internationalization-is-progressing-idUSKBN1KW08W.

He, Zhiguo, Arvind Krishnamurthy, and Konstantin Milbradt. 2016. "What Makes US Government Bonds Safe Assets?" *American Economic Review* 106 (5): 519–523.

Heavey, Susan, and Nathan Layne. 2019. "Russian Metals Tycoon Deripaska Sues U.S. over Sanctions." Reuters, March 15. https://www.reuters.com/article/us-usa-trump-russia-deripaska/russian-metals-tycoon-deripaska-sues-u-s-over-sanctions-idUSKCN1QW2CA.

Helleiner, Eric. 2008. "Political Determinants of International Currencies: What Future for the US Dollar?" *Review of International Political Economy* 15 (3): 354–378.

Helleiner, Eric. 2017. "Downsizing the Dollar in the Age of Trump? The Ambiguities of Key Currency Status." *Brown Journal of World Affairs* 23 (2): 9.

Helleiner, Eric, and Jonathan Kirshner, eds. 2009. *The Future of the Dollar: Wither the Key Currency?* Ithaca, NY: Cornell University Press.

HM Treasury. 2002. "Review of the Sale of Part of the UK Gold Reserves." Bank of England, London.

Hobson, Peter. 2015. "Russia Embraces Yuan in Move Against US Dollar Hegemony." *Moscow Times*, June 15. https://themoscowtimes.com/articles/russia-embraces-yuan-in-ove-against-us-dollar-hegemony-47404.

Horii, Akinari. 1986. "The Evolution of Reserve Currency Diversification." 18. *BIS Economic Papers*. Basel.

Hu, Weijia. 2019. "Nation Must Guard Financial Security amid Trade War." *Global Times*, May 20. http://www.globaltimes.cn/content/1150787.shtml.

Hu, Xiaolian. 2018. "贸易战为中国关上一扇门，但也打开一扇推进人民币国际化的窗 [The Trade War Has Closed a Door for China, but It Has Also Opened a Window for the Internationalization of the Renminbi]." *China Finance 40 Forum*, August 14. http://www.cf40.org.cn/plus/view.php?aid=12917.

Huang, Qifan. 2019. "Qifan Huang, 数字化重塑全球金融生态 [Digital Reshaping the Global Financial Ecosystem]." *China Finance 40 Forum*, October 29. http://www.cf40.org.cn/plus/view.php?aid=13729.

Huanqiu (Global Times). 2014. "西方制裁拉近中俄关系 人民币结算正成替代方案 [Western Sanctions Draw Closer to China-Russia Relationship, RMB Settlement Is Becoming an Alternative]," September 1. https://world.huanqiu.com/article/9CaKrnJFuRa.

Iancu, Alina, Gareth Anderson, Sakai Ando, Ethan Boswell, Andrea Gamba, Shushanik Hakobyan, Lusine Lusinyan, Neil Meads, and Yiqun Wu. 2020. "Reserve Currencies in an Evolving International Monetary System." International Monetary Fund, Washington, DC. https://www.imf.org/en/Publications/Departmental-Papers-Policy-Papers/Issues/2020/11/17/Reserve-Currencies-in-an-Evolving-International-Monetary-System-49864.

IMF. 2012. "Global Financial Stability Report: The Quest for Lasting Stability." Washington, DC.

IMF. 2015. "Assessing Reserve Adequacy—Specific Proposals." Washington, DC. https://www.imf.org/external/np/pp/eng/2014/121914.pdf.

"Inside the Failure of Google+, a Very Expensive Attempt to Unseat Facebook." 2015. Reddit. https://www.reddit.com/r/technology/comments/3fijps/inside_the_failure_of_google_a_very_expensive/.

Interfax. 2022. "Belarus Finalizing Connection to Chinese Version of SWIFT." Interfax. April 26. https://interfax.com/newsroom/top-stories/78612/.

"International Role of the Euro." 1999. *Monthly Bulletin*. Frankfurt. https://www.ecb.europa.eu/pub/pdf/mobu/mb199908en.pdf.

International, United Press. 1967. "De Gaulle Launches Big Attack on U.S. Dollar." *Madera Tribune*, November 27.

"Introducing the Google+ Project: Real-Life Sharing, Rethought for the Web." 2011. Google Official Blog. https://googleblog.blogspot.com/2011/06/introducing-google-project-real-life.html.

Investor's Business Daily. 2015. "Ignore John Kerry's Fear-Mongering about the Dollar and Iran." *Investor's Business Daily*, August 12. https://www.investors.com/politics/editorials/john-kerry-is-wrong-to-say-dollar-will-lose-reserve-status-if-iran-deal-is-rejected/.

Ito, Hiro, and Robert N. McCauley. 2020. "Currency Composition of Foreign Exchange Reserves." *Journal of International Money and Finance* 102 (April).

Johnson, Juliet. 2008. "Forbidden Fruit: Russia's Uneasy Relationship with the US Dollar." *Review of International Political Economy* 15 (3): 379–398.

Jovanovski, Kristina. 2018. "Senators Warn of 'Measures' against Turkey over Andrew Brunson Case." NBC News, April 20. https://www.nbcnews.com/news/world/senators-warn-measures-against-turkey-andrew-brunson-case-n867721.

Junker, Jean-Claude. 2018. "President Jean-Claude Junker's State of the Union Address 2018." European Commission, September 12. http://europa.eu/rapid/press-release_SPEECH-18-5808_en.htm.

Kalhor, Navid. 2018. "Turkey, Iran Implement First Forex Swap." *Daily Sabah*, April 18. https://www.dailysabah.com/economy/2018/04/18/turkey-iran-implement-first-forex-swap.

Kamps, Annette. 2006. "The Euro as Invoicing Currency in International Trade." European Central Bank, Working Paper Series, no. 665.

Karsten, Jack, and Darrell M. West. 2018. "Venezuela's 'Petro' Undermines Other Cryptocurrencies—and International Sanctions." Brookings Institution, Washington, DC. https://www.brookings.edu/blog/techtank/2018/03/09/venezuelas-petro-undermines-other-cryptocurrencies-and-international-sanctions/.

Kennedy, John F. 1962. "Address to the Economic Club of New York." John F. Kennedy Presidential Library. December 14. https://www.jfklibrary.org/asset-viewer/archives/JFKWHA/1962/JFKWHA-148/JFKWHA-148.

Keown, Callum. 2020. "Billionaire Investor Ray Dalio Fears for the Dollar and the 'Soundness of Our Money,' and Here's Why." *Market Watch*, July 28. https://www.marketwatch.com/story/billionaire-investor-ray-dalio-warns-us-china-conflict-could-become-a-capital-war-that-hits-the-dollar-2020-07-27.

Keynes, John Maynard. 1923. *A Tract on Monetary Reform*. Cambridge: Cambridge University Press.

Khachaturov, Arnold. 2019. "Наличные Деньги и Золото Хороши Тем, Что Их Сложно Заблокировать [Why the Russian Central Bank Is Increasing Its Gold Reserves? Explains RSE Finance Professor Oleg Shibanov]." *Novaya Gazeta*, May 17. https://www.novayagazeta.ru/articles/2019/05/07/80451-nalichnye-dengi-i-zoloto-horoshi-tem-chto-ih-slozhno-zablokirovat.

Kida, Kazuhiro, Masayuki Kubota, and Yusho Cho. 2019. "Rise of the Yuan: China-Based Payment Settlements Jump 80%." *Nikkei*, March 20. https://asia.nikkei.com/Business/Markets/Rise-of-the-yuan-China-based-payment-settlements-jump-80.

Kindleberger, Charles P. 1985. "The Dollar Yesterday, Today, and Tomorrow." *Quarterly Review*. Rome.

Kirshner, Jonathan. 2008. "Dollar Primacy and American Power: What's at Stake?" *Review of International Political Economy* 15 (3): 418–438.

Kirshner, Jonathan. 2014. *American Power after the Financial Crisis*. Ithaca, NY: Cornell University Press.

Koch, Mortiz. 2020. "Die EU Schlägt Zurück: Wie Sich Die Staatengemeinschaft Gegen Sanktionen Wehren Will [The EU Strikes Back: How the International Community Wants to Defend Itself against Sanctions]." *Handelsblatt*, October 21, 2020. https://amp2.handelsblatt.com/politik/international/welthandel-die-eu-schlaegt-zurueck-wie-sich-die-staatengemeinschaft-gegen-sanktionen-wehren-will/26290552.html.

Koibuchi, Satoshi, Kiyotaka Sato, and Junko Shimizu. 2012. "The Choice of an Invoicing Currency by Globally Operating Firms: A Firm-Level Analysis of Japanese Exporters." *International Journal of Finance & Economics* 17 (4): 305–320.

Koibuchi, Satoshi, Kiyotaka Sato, and Junko Shimizu. 2018. *Managing Currency Risk: How Japanese Firms Choose Invoicing Currency*. Northampton, MA: Edward Elgar Publishing.

Krämer, Jörg. 2018. "Trump's Sanctions—End of the Dollar's Reign as Leading World Currency?" Commerzbank. YouTube, May 18. https://www.youtube.com/watch?v=ECXsWh7DT30.

Krugman, Paul. 1980. "Vehicle Currencies and the Structure of International Trade." *Journal of Money, Credit and Banking* 12 (3): 513–526.

Kurmanaev, Anatoly. 2017. "Venezuela Stops Accepting Dollars for Oil Payments Following U.S. Sanctions." *Wall Street Journal*, September 13. https://www.wsj.com/articles/venezuela-stops-accepting-dollars-for-oil-payments-following-u-s-sancti ons-1505343161.

Laya, Patricia. 2019a. "Venezuela Sells $570 Million From Gold Reserve Despite Sanctions." Bloomberg, May 17. https://www.bloomberg.com/news/articles/2019-05-17/venezuela-sells-570-million-from-gold-reserves-despite-sanction.

Laya, Patricia. 2019b. "Venezuelan Reserves Jump on PDVSA Cash Transfer." Bloomberg, August 28. https://www.bloomberg.com/news/articles/2019-08-28/venezuelan-reser ves-are-said-to-jump-on-pdvsa-cash-transfer.

Laya, Patricia, and Ben Bartenstein. 2020. "Iran Is Hauling Gold Bars Out of Venezuela's Almost-Empty Vaults." Bloomberg, July 30. https://www.bloomberg.com/news/artic les/2020-04-30/iran-is-hauling-gold-bars-out-of-venezuela-s-almost-empty-vaults.

Le, Thai Ha, and Binh Tran-Nam. 2018. "Relative Costs and FDI: Why Did Vietnam Forge so Far Ahead?" *Economic Analysis and Policy* 59 (September): 1–13.

Levy, Jack S. 2008. "Case Studies: Types, Designs, and Logics of Inference." *Conflict Management and Peace Science* 25 (1): 1–18.

Lew, Jack. 2016. "Remarks of Secretary Lew on the Evolution of Sanctions and Lessons for the Future at the Carnegie Endowment for International Peace." U.S. Treasury. https://home.treasury.gov/news/press-releases/jl0397.

Liao, Steven, and Daniel McDowell. 2015. "Redback Rising: China's Bilateral Swap Agreements and Renminbi Internationalization." *International Studies Quarterly* 59 (3): 401–422.

Liao, Steven, and Daniel McDowell. 2016. "No Reservations: International Order and Demand for the Renminbi as a Reserve Currency." *International Studies Quarterly* 60 (2): 272–293.

Liu, Xiaochung. 2021. "In Response to the Risk of Financial Sanctions, China Needs to Consider Building a New Cross-Border Clearing System with Multiple Levels and Multiple Schemes [刘晓春：应对金融制裁风险，中国需考虑多层次、多方案建设新型跨境清算系统]." *China Finance 40 Forum*, January 13. http://finance.sina.com.cn/zl/china/2021-01-13/zl-ikftssan5387632.shtml.

Loeffler, Rachel L. 2009. "Bank Shots: How the Financial System Can Isolate Rogues." *Foreign Affairs* 88: 101–110.

Lyrchikova, Anastasia. 2017. "Rusal Resumes Taishet Aluminum Project, Sees Deeper Global Deficit." Reuters, July 12, 2017. https://www.reuters.com/article/us-russia-rusal-idUSKBN19X1M0.

Ma, Josephine. 2019. "Russia, China Keen to Increase Use of Yuan, Rouble in Trade Settlement, Ambassador Andrey Denisov Says." *South China Morning Post*, April 20. https://www.scmp.com/news/china/diplomacy/article/3006988/russia-china-keen-increase-use-yuan-rouble-trade-settlement.

Maas, Heiko. 2018. "Wir Lassen Nicht Zu, Dass Die USA Über Unsere Köpfe Hinweg Handeln [We Do Not Allow the US to Act beyond Our Heads]." *Handelsblatt*, August 21. https://www.handelsblatt.com/meinung/gastbeitraege/gastkommentar-wir-lassen-nicht-zu-dass-die-usa-ueber-unsere-koepfe-hinweg-handeln/22933006.html?ticket=ST-1702787-VKqUls5ETaBdUGtaxrea-ap2.

Malesky, Edmund J., and Layna Mosley. 2018. "Chains of Love? Global Production and the Firm-Level Diffusion of Labor Standards." *American Journal of Political Science* 62 (3): 712–728.

Marshall, Monty G., Keith Jaggers, and Ted Robert Gurr. 2017. "Polity IV," 2017. http://www.systemicpeace.org/polityproject.html.

Martínez, Antonio García. 2016. "How Mark Zuckerberg Led Facebook's War to Crush Google Plus." *Vanity Fair*, June. https://www.vanityfair.com/news/2016/06/how-mark-zuckerberg-led-facebooks-war-to-crush-google-plus.

McDowell, Daniel. 2017. *Brother, Can You Spare a Billion? The United States, the IMF, and the International Lender of Last Resort*. New York: Oxford University Press.

McDowell, Daniel. 2019a. "Emergent International Liquidity Agreements: Central Bank Cooperation after the Global Financial Crisis." *Journal of International Relations and Development* 22 (2): 441–467.

McDowell, Daniel. 2019b. "From Tailwinds to Headwinds: The Troubled Internationalization of the Renminbi." In *Handbook on the International Political Economy of China*, edited by Ka Zeng, 190–202. Northampton, MA: Edward Elgar.

McDowell, Daniel. 2019c. "The (Ineffective) Financial Statecraft of China's Bilateral Swap Agreements." *Development and Change* 50 (1): 122–143.

McDowell, Daniel. 2022. "What Is Holding the Yuan Back? Xi Is." *Georgetown Journal of International Affairs*, February 11. https://gjia.georgetown.edu/2022/02/11/what-is-holding-the-yuan-back-xi-is/.

McDowell, Daniel, and David Steinberg. 2017. "Systemic Strengths, Domestic Deficiencies: The Renminbi's Future as a Reserve Currency." *Journal of Contemporary China* 26 (108): 801–819.

"Meeting with Heads of International News Agencies." 2021. The Kremlin, 2021. http://en.kremlin.ru/events/president/news/65749.

Mehreen, Khan, and Jim Brunsden. 2018. "Junker Vows to Turn Euro into Reserve Currency to Rival US Dollar." *Financial Times*, September 12. https://www.ft.com/content/7358f396-b66d-11e8-bbc3-ccd7de085ffe.

Meo, Nick. 2011. "Libya Protests: 140 'Massacred' as Gaddafi Sends in Snipers to Crush Dissent." *The Telegraph*, February 20. https://www.telegraph.co.uk/news/worldnews/africaandindianocean/libya/8335934/Libya-protests-140-massacred-as-Gaddafi-sends-in-snipers-to-crush-dissent.html.

Meyer, Jeffrey A. 2009. "Second Thoughts on Secondary Sanctions." *University of Pennsylvania Journal of International Law* 30 (3): 905–968.

Ming, Cheang. 2018. "Index Giant MSCI Announces 234 China A Shares to Be Added to Indexes." *CNBC*, May 14. https://www.cnbc.com/2018/05/14/msci-announces-234-china-a-shares-to-be-added-to-equity-indexes.html.

Moghadam, Reza, Jonathan D. Ostry, and Robert Sheehy. 2011. "Assessing Reserve Adequacy." IMF Policy Papers, Washington, DC.

Mogherini, Federica, Jean-Yves Le Drian, Heiko Maas, Jeremy Hunt, Bruno Le Maire, Olaf Scholz, and Philip Hammond. 2018. "Iran Nuclear Deal: Joint Statement by UK, France and Germany." UK.Gov. https://www.gov.uk/government/news/joint-statement-by-the-uk-france-and-germany-on-the-iran-nuclear-deal.

Monitor, Al. 2017. "Deal with Iran Boosts Turkey's Hopes of Trading in National Currency." *Al Monitor*, October 18. https://www.al-monitor.com/pulse/originals/2017/10/turkey-iran-may-boost-hopes-of-trading-in-national-currency.html.

Monnet, Eric, and Damien Puy. 2019. "Do Old Habits Die Hard? Central Banks and the Bretton Woods Gold Puzzle." *NBER Working Paper*. https://www.imf.org/en/Publications/WP/Issues/2019/07/24/Do-Old-Habits-Die-Hard-Central-Banks-and-the-Bretton-Woods-Gold-Puzzle-47121?cid=em-COM-123-39235.

Morse, Jeremy. 1979. "The Dollar as a Reserve Currency." *International Affairs* 55 (3): 359–366.

Moscow Times. 2019. "Russia Says BRICS Nations Favor Idea of Common Payment System," November 14. https://www.themoscowtimes.com/2019/11/14/putin-to-invite-china-and-india-to-join-anti-sanctions-bank-network-a68172.

Mulder, Nicholas. 2022. *The Economic Weapon: The Rise of Sanctions as a Tool of Modern War*. New Haven, CT: Yale University Press.

Murphy, Taggart. 2006. "East Asia's Dollars." *New Left Review* 4 (8): 1–19.

Ng, Eric. 2017. "Rusal Plans to Power Its Smelters Wholly on Hydro Electricity by 2020." *South China Morning Post*, June 25. https://www.scmp.com/business/companies/article/2099773/rusal-plans-power-its-smelters-wholly-hydro-electricity-2020.

Nikkei. 2019. "人民币结算手段扩大的背后是美国的制裁 [U.S. Sanctions behind the Expansion of RMB Settlement]," May 22. https://cn.nikkei.com/politicsaeconomy/efinance/35666-2019-05-22-05-00-50.html.

Norrlof, Carla. 2010. *America's Global Advantage: US Hegemony and International Cooperation*. Cambridge University Press.

Norrlof, Carla. 2014. "Dollar Hegemony: A Power Analysis." *Review of International Political Economy* 21 (5): 1042–1070.

Norrlof, Carla, Paul Poast, Benjamin J. Cohen, Sabreena Croteau, Aashna Khanna, Daniel McDowell, Hongying Wang, and W Kindred Winecoff. 2020. "Global Monetary Order and the Liberal Order Debate." *International Studies Perspectives* 21 (2): 109–153.

O'Byrne, David. 2018. "Turkey, Russia, Iran to Trade Using Local Currencies: Report." S&P Global Platts. https://www.spglobal.com/platts/en/market-insights/latest-news/oil/091018-turkey-russia-iran-to-trade-using-local-currencies-report.

O'Callaghan, Gary. 1993. "The Structure and Operation of the World Gold Market." Washington, DC: International Monetary Fund.

O'Harrow Jr., Robert, James V. Grimaldi, and Brady Dennis. 2011. "How the U.S. Pulled off a Major Freeze of Libyan Assets." *Washington Post*, March 11. https://www.washingtonpost.com/investigations/sanctions-in-72-hours-how-the-us-pulled-off-a-major-freeze-of-libyan-assets/2011/03/11/ABBckxJB_story.html?utm_term=.363931e12227.

Oatley, Thomas. 2015. *A Political Economy of American Hegemony: Buildups, Booms, and Busts*. New York: Cambridge University Press.

Oatley, Thomas, W. Winecoff Kindred, Andrew Pennock, and Sarah Bauerle Danzman. 2013. "The Political Economy of Global Finance: A Network Model." *Perspectives on Politics* 11 (1): 133–153.

Obama, Barak. 2015. "Remarks by the President on the Iran Nuclear Deal." White House, August 5. https://obamawhitehouse.archives.gov/the-press-office/2015/08/05/remarks-president-iran-nuclear-deal.

Onstad, Eric. 2018. "Rusal Removed from Share, Debt Indexes; Moscow Mulls Response." Reuters, April 11. https://www.reuters.com/article/usa-russia-sanctions-rusal-idINKBN1HI1UF.

Ordoñez, Franco, Jacqueline Charles, and Alex Daugherty. 2019. "Trump Response to Guaidó Aide Arrest: New Financial Sanctions on Venezuela." McClatchy, March 22. https://www.mcclatchydc.com/news/politics-government/white-house/article228254319.html.

Ostroukh, Andrey, and Elena Fabrichnaya. 2019. "Russia c.Bank Lowered Gold Purchase Price to Encourage Exports—Governor." Reuters, July 3. https://www.reuters.com/article/russia-cenbank-gold/russia-cbank-lowered-gold-purchase-price-to-encourage-exports-governor-idUSL8N2433O7.

Ostroukh, Andrey, and Tuvan Gumrukcu. 2018. "Russia Says Dollar's Days Numbered as Global Trade Currency." Nasdaq, August 14. https://www.nasdaq.com/article/russia-says-dollars-days-numbered-as-global-trade-currency-20180814-00278.

Otero-Iglesias, Miguel, and Federico Steinberg. 2013. "Is the Dollar Becoming a Negotiated Currency? Evidence from the Emerging Markets." *New Political Economy* 18 (3): 309–336.

Pacheco Pardo, Ramon, Jan Knoerich, and Yuanfang Li. 2019. "The Role of London and Frankfurt in Supporting the Internationalisation of the Chinese Renminbi." *New Political Economy* 24 (4): 530–545.

Palma, Brian De. 1983. *Scarface*. Universal Pictures.

Pamuk, Humeyra. 2019. "Turkey Should Scrap Russian Missile System or Face U.S. Sanctions: White House Official." Reuters, November 10. https://www.reuters.com/arti

cle/us-turkey-security-usa/turkey-should-scrap-russian-missile-system-or-face-us-sanctions-white-house-official-idUSKBN1XK0JS.

Papadia, Francesco, and Konstantinos Efstathiou. 2018. "The Euro as an International Currency." *Policy Contribution*. https://www.bruegel.org/2018/12/the-euro-as-an-international-currency/.

Pape, Robert A. 1997. "Why Economic Sanctions Do Not Work." *International Security* 22 (2): 90–136.

Pengelly, Martin. 2018. "Fox & Friends Diplomacy: Boris Johnson Urges Trump to Stay in Iran Deal." *The Guardian*, May 7. https://www.theguardian.com/us-news/2018/may/07/boris-johnson-fox-friends-trump-iran-deal.

People's Bank of China. 2015. "The People's Bank of China Issued the 'Renminbi Cross-Border Payment System (Phase I) Answers to Reporters'' Questions.'"

Polina, Ivanova. 2018a. "Rusal Bonds Slump, Customers Review Contracts as US Sanctions Bite." Reuters, April 10. https://www.reuters.com/article/us-usa-russia-sanctions-rusal/rusal-bonds-slump-customers-review-contracts-as-u-s-sanctions-bite-idUSKBN1HH2MG.

Polina, Ivanova. 2018b. "Russian Miners Explore Payment Schemes Eschewing Dollar." Reuters, August 15. https://www.cnbc.com/2018/08/15/reuters-america-update-1-russian-miners-explore-payment-schemes-eschewing-dollar.html.

Polunin, Andrey. 2019. "Кремль Скупает Золото На «Судный День» [The Kremlin Is Buying Gold Ahead of the Judgment Day]." *Свободная Пресса [Free Press]*, March 22. https://svpressa.ru/economy/article/233334/.

Pompeo, Michael R. 2019. "The United States Imposes Maximum Pressure on Former Maduro Regime." US Department of State, 2019. https://www.state.gov/the-united-states-imposes-maximum-pressure-on-former-maduro-regime/.

Pons, Corina, and Mayela Armas. 2019. "Exclusive: Venezuela Plans to Fly Central Bank Gold Reserves to UAE—Source." Reuters, January 31. https://www.reuters.com/article/us-venezuela-politics-gold-exclusive/exclusive-venezuela-plans-to-fly-central-bank-gold-reserves-to-uae-source-idUSKCN1PP2QR.

Popper, Nathaniel, Oleg Matsnev, and Ana Vanessa Herrero. 2018. "Russia and Venezuela's Plan to Sidestep Sanctions: Virtual Currencies." *New York Times*, January 4. https://www.nytimes.com/2018/01/03/technology/russia-venezuela-virtual-currencies.html?ref=nyt-es&mcid=nyt-es&subid=article.

Posen, Adam S. 2008. "Why the Euro Will Not Rival the Dollar." *International Finance* 11 (1): 75–100.

Prasad, Eswar. 2022. "Enduring Preeminence." *Finance & Development*, June, 12–15. https://www.imf.org/en/Publications/fandd/issues/2022/06/enduring-preeminence-eswar-prasad.

Pukthuanthong, Kuntara, and Richard Roll. 2011. "Gold and the Dollar (and the Euro, Pound, and Yen)." *Journal of Banking and Finance* 35 (8): 2070–2083.

QQ (Tencent). 2014. "制裁攻防战再度升级中俄同意以本币进行贸易结算; [Sanctions Offensive and Defensive War Escalated Once Again China and Russia Agree to Trade Settlement in Local Currency]," September 9. https://new.qq.com/rain/a/20140910010500.

Radio Free Europe. 2018. "Turkey Dismisses U.S. Warning Against Buying Russian Missile System," April 28. https://www.rferl.org/a/turkey-cavusoglu-dismisses-us-warning-against-buying-russian-2-400-missile-system-pompeo-done-deal/29197261.html.

Rapoza, Kenneth. 2017. "Russian Tycoon Deripaska Launches One of London's Largest IPOs." *Forbes*, November 3. https://www.forbes.com/sites/kenrapoza/2017/11/03/russian-tycoon-deripaska-launches-one-of-londons-largest-ipos/?sh=26cf6bf33c30.

Raymond, Nate. 2015. "BNP Paribas Sentenced in $8.9 Billion Accord over Sanctions Violations." Reuters, May 1. https://www.reuters.com/article/us-bnp-paribas-settlement-sentencing-idUSKBN0NM41K20150501.

Reid, David. 2018. "Turkey's Erdogan Claims US Sanctions Are a Stab in the Back." CNBC, August 20. https://www.dailysabah.com/economy/2018/08/20/turkey-qatar-central-banks-sign-currency-swap-deal.

Reportero, El. 2017. "Maduro de Venezuela Sugiere Comercio de Petróleo En Rublo Ruso y Yuan Chino [Maduro de Venezuela Suggests Oil Trade in Russian Ruble and Chinese Yuan]." *El Reportero*, October 6. http://elreporterosf.com/maduro-de-venezuela-sugiere-comercio-de-petroleo-en-rublo-ruso-y-yuan-chino/.

Reuters. 2012. "Iran to Accept Payment in Gold from Trading Partners," February 29. https://www.reuters.com/article/us-iran-oil-payment/iran-to-accept-payment-in-gold-from-trading-partners-idUSTRE81S0GU20120229.

Reuters. 2014. "Kremlin Aide Warns US of Response if Sanctions Imposed: RIA." Reuters, March 4. https://www.yahoo.com/news/kremlin-aide-says-u-may-face-consequences-sanctions-081601584—finance.html.

Reuters. 2016. "Russian Central Bank Bought Chinese Government Bonds in 2015," May 6. https://www.reuters.com/article/russia-cenbank-chinese-bonds-idUSL5N183392.

Reuters. 2017a. "Russian Minister Says Companies Would Prefer Borrowing in Roubles," July 13. https://www.reuters.com/article/russia-economy-funding/russian-minister-says-companies-would-prefer-borrowing-in-roubles-idUSR4N1JW07Q.

Reuters. 2017b. "Venezuela's Maduro Says Will Shun U.S. Dollar in Favor of Yuan, Others." Reuters, September 7. https://www.reuters.com/article/us-venezuela-forex/venezuelas-maduro-says-will-shun-us-dollar-in-favor-of-yuan-others-idUSKCN1BJ06O.

Reuters. 2019a. "Russia Relaxes Rules for Companies Wanting to Raise Funds in China," April 2. https://www.reuters.com/article/us-russia-china-borrowing-idUSKCN1RE1BV.

Reuters. 2019b. "Russia, Turkey Agree on Using Rouble, Lira in Mutual Settlements," October 8. https://www.reuters.com/article/russia-turkey-forex/russia-turkey-agree-on-using-rouble-lira-in-mutual-settlements-idUSR4N26O04T.

Reuters. 2020. "Chinese Banks Urged to Switch Away from SWIFT as U.S. Sanctions Loom," July 29. https://www.reuters.com/article/us-china-banks-usa-sanctions-idUSKCN24U0SN.

Rey, H. 2001. "International Trade Currency Exchange." *Review of Economic Studies* 68 (2): 443–464.

RIA. 2018. "Глава ВТБ Прокомментировал Снижение Доли России в Госдолге США [The Head of VTB Commented on the Decline in the Share of Russia in the US National Debt]." *RIA*, July 18. https://ria.ru/20180718/1524891493.html?inj=1.

Roche, Darragh. 2022. "Will U.S. Sanctions Be 'Suicide of the Dollar?' Spanish Newspaper Asks." *Newsweek*, March 29. https://www.newsweek.com/american-sanctions-suicide-dollar-spanish-newspaper-russia-ukraine-1692838.

Rogoff, Kenneth. 2016. "Kenneth Rogoff: Emerging Economies Should Buy Gold." *World Economic Forum*, May 4. https://www.weforum.org/agenda/2016/05/kenneth-rogoff-emerging-economies-should-buy-gold/.

Rosenberg, Elizabeth, Zachary K. Goldman, Daniel Drezner, and Julia Solomon-Strauss. 2016. "The New Tools of Economic Warfare." Washington, DC. https://www.cnas.org/publications/reports/the-new-tools-of-economic-warfare-effects-and-effectiveness-of-contemporary-u-s-financial-sanctions.

Roubini, Nouriel. 2009. "The Almighty Renminbi?" *New York Times*, May 14. https://www.nytimes.com/2009/05/14/opinion/14Roubini.html.

Rowling, Rupert. 2019. "Rupert Rowling, Central Banks Are Ditching the Dollar for Gold." Bloomberg, May 2. https://www.bloomberg.com/news/articles/2019-05-02/central-bank-first-quarter-gold-buying-at-highest-since-2013.

RT. 2018. "As World Turns Away from US Dollar, Role of Russian Ruble Is Growing—Putin." RT, December 20. https://www.rt.com/business/447032-ruble-role-growing-putin/.

RT. 2019. "Russia Bringing Back the Gold Standard May Kill US Dollar & Solve Main Problem of Cryptocurrencies," June 13. https://www.rt.com/business/461752-russia-gold-dollar-cryptocurrencies/.

Rudnitsky, Jake. 2019. "Venezuela's Russian Bank Grows Assets as U.S. Sanctions Hit Home." Bloomberg, January 31. https://www.bloomberg.com/news/articles/2019-01-31/venezuela-s-russian-bank-grows-assets-as-u-s-sanctions-hit-home.

Russian Gazette. "Россия и Китай Расширяют Взаиморасчеты в Нацвалютах [Russia and China Expand Mutual Settlements in National Currencies]," January. https://rg.ru/2019/01/09/rossiia-i-kitaj-rasshiriaiut-vzaimoraschety-v-nacvaliutah.html.

Santor, Eric, and Lena Suchanek. 2016. "A New Era of Central Banking: Unconventional Monetary Policies." *Bank of Canada Review* Spring.

Saraçoğlu, Cahit. 2018. "220 Ton Altın Türkiye'ye Geldi [220 Tons of Gold Arrived in Turkey]." *Yeni Safak*, April 19. https://www.yenisafak.com/ekonomi/220-ton-altin-turkiyeye-geldi-3245946.

Schaer, Cathrin. 2018. "Making Europe Financially Independent, One Transaction at a Time." *Handelsblatt*, August 28. https://www.handelsblatt.com/today/politics/heikos-dream-making-europe-financially-independent-one-transaction-at-a-time/23583146.html?ticket=ST-29503-6dpueyXkVTbwbG5UW6iz-ap3.

Schneider, Christina J., and Jennifer L. Tobin. 2020. "The Political Economy of Bilateral Bailouts." *International Organization* 74 (1): 1–29.

Schularick, Moritz. 2011. "Managing the World's Dollar Dependency." Washington, DC. https://www.cfr.org/report/managing-worlds-dollar-dependency.

Scott, Hal S., and Anna Gelpern. 2016. *International Finance: Transactions, Policy, and Regulation; Twenty-First Edition*. St. Paul, MN: Foundation Press.

Scott, Kathleen A. 2010. "US to Require Reporting of Cross-Border Funds Transfers." *New York Law Journal* 244 (92).

Seddon, Max, and Henry Foy. 2019. "Russia Looks at Alternatives to Dollar for Energy Transactions." *Financial Times*, October 13. https://www.ft.com/content/704cde6c-eb53-11e9-a240-3b065ef5fc55.

Shen, Samuel, Winni Zhou, and Kevin Yao. 2020. "In China, Fears of Financial Iron Curtain as U.S. Tensions Rise." Reuters, August 13. https://www.reuters.com/article/us-usa-china-decoupling-analysis-idUSKCN2590NJ.

Shuster, Simon. 2018. "Exclusive: Russia Secretly Helped Venezuela Launch a Cryptocurrency to Evade U.S. Sanctions." *Time*, March 20. http://time.com/5206835/exclusive-russia-petro-venezuela-cryptocurrency/.

Silchenko, Sergey. 2019. "США Своими Санкциями Помогли России Накопить 450 Млрд Долларов [US Sanctions Helped Russia Save $450 Billion]." *Financial Gazette*, February 19. https://fingazeta.ru/finance/budget/454441/.

Siqing, Chen. 2014. "中国银行行长陈四清出席第九届中俄经济工商界高峰论坛并发言 [President of Bank of China Chen Siqing Attended and Spoke at the 9th China-Russia Economic, Business and Industrial Summit]." Bank of China, October 13. https://www.boc.cn/ABOUTBOC/BI1/201410/t20141013_3993346.html.

Slack, Robert. 2017. "Secondary Sanctions Targeting Russia's Defense and Intelligence Sectors Move Closer to Implementation." Kelley Drye and Warren, LLP, October 30. https://www.ustrademonitor.com/2017/10/secondary-sanctions-targeting-russias-defense-and-intelligence-sectors-move-closer-to-implementation/.

Song, Ke, and Le Xia. 2020. "Bilateral Swap Agreement and Renminbi Settlement in Cross-Border Trade." *Economic and Political Studies* 8 (3): 355–373.

Spencer, Richard. 2011. "Libya: Muammar Gaddafi Fires on His Own People." *The Telegraph*, February 21. https://www.telegraph.co.uk/news/worldnews/africaandindianocean/libya/8339347/Libya-Muammar-Gaddafi-fires-on-his-own-people.html.

Spiro, David. 1999. *The Hidden Hand of American Hegemony*. Ithaca, NY: Cornell University Press.

Sputnik News. 2014. "Putin Adviser Urges Dumping US Bonds in Reaction to Sanctions." *Sputnik News*, March 4. https://sputniknews.com/business/20140304188081405-Putin-Adviser-Urges-Dumping-US-Bonds-In-Reaction-to-Sanctions/.

Sputnik News. 2019a. "Four Good Reasons Why Russia Is Purging the Dollar from Its Reserves." *Sputnik News*, January 12. https://sputniknews.com/business/201901121071420576-russia-dollar-dump-analysis/.

Sputnik News. 2019b. "Russia Buys Yuan Reserves: Still Long Way to Go on Ditching Dollar—Pundits." *Sputnik News*, January 17. https://sputniknews.com/analysis/201901171071543542-russia-economy-intl-trade-reserves-dollar/.

Srslanalp, Serkan, Barry Eichengreen, and Chima Simpson-Bell. 2021. "The Stealth Erosion of Dollar Dominance: Active Diversifiers and the Rise of Nontraditional Reserve Currencies." WP/22/58. Washington, DC. https://www.imf.org/en/Publications/WP/Issues/2022/03/24/The-Stealth-Erosion-of-Dollar-Dominance-Active-Diversifiers-and-the-Rise-of-Nontraditional-515150.

Stankiewicz, Kevin. 2021. "Gundlach Says the Dollar Is 'Doomed' over the Long Term Because of Rising U.S. Deficits." CNBC, July 15. https://www.cnbc.com/2021/07/15/doubleline-ceo-jeffrey-gundlach-says-dollar-doomed-over-the-long-term.html.

Stearns, Jonathan, and Helene Fouquet. 2019. "U.S. Warns Europe That Its Iran Workaround Could Face Sanctions." Bloomberg, May 29. https://www.bloomberg.com/news/articles/2019-05-29/u-s-warns-europe-that-its-iran-workaround-could-face-sanctions.

Steinberg, David, Daniel McDowell, and Dimitar Gueorguiev. 2022. "Inside Looking Out: How International Policy Trends Shape the Politics of Capital Controls in China." *Pacific Review*, July 5.

Steinhauser, Gabriele, and Nicholas Bariyo. 2019. "How 7.4 Tons of Venezuela's Gold Landed in Africa—and Vanished." *Wall Street Journal*, June 18. https://www.wsj.com/articles/how-7-4-tons-of-venezuelas-gold-landed-in-africaand-vanished-11560867792.

Strange, Susan. 1971a. *Sterling and British Policy: A Political Study of an International Currency in Decline*. London: Oxford University Press.

Strange, Susan. 1971b. "Sterling and British Policy: A Political View." *International Affairs* 47 (2): 302–315.

Strobel, Warren. 2015. "Dollar Could Suffer If U.S. Walks Away from Iran Deal: John Kerry." Reuters, August 11. https://www.reuters.com/article/us-iran-nuclear-kerry/dollar-could-suffer-if-u-s-walks-away-from-iran-deal-john-kerry-idUSKCN0QG1V02 0150811.

SWIFT. 2015. "Worldwide Currency Usage and Trends: Information Paper Prepared by SWIFT in Collaboration with City of London and Paris EUROPLACE." https://www.swift.com/news-events/news/new-research-highlights-currency-usage-and-trends-in-global-payments.

"SWIFT Wire Transfers: What Compliance Needs to Know." 2021. Tier1 Financial Solutions. https://tier1fin.com/alessa/blog/swift-wire-transfers-an-overview-for-compliance-professionals/#_edn1.

Tang, Frank. 2020. "China Urged to Develop Its Own International Payment System to Counter Risk of US Financial Sanctions." *South China Morning Post*, July 30. https://www.scmp.com/economy/china-economy/article/3095374/china-urged-develop-its-own-international-payment-system.

TASS (Russian News Agency). 2015. "Два Китайских Банка Отрыли Кредиты Сбербанку, ВТБ, Внешэкономбанку и ВЭБу [Two Chinese Banks Opened Loans to Sberbank, VTB, Vnesheconombank and VEB]," May 8. https://tass.ru/ekonomika/1956850.

TASS. 2018a. "Что Известно о Российской Дедолларизации [All You Need to Know about Russian Dedollarization]," October 16. https://tass.ru/ekonomika/5679286.

TASS. 2018b. "Голландский Банк Согласился Перевести Расчеты По Кредиту 'Русалу' в Евро [Dutch Bank Agreed to Transfer the Calculations for the Loan 'Rusal' in the Euro," November.

TeleSur. 2018. "Venezuela Venderá Petróleo En Criptomoneda Petro En 2019 [Venezuela Will Sell Oil in Cryptocurrency Petro in 2019]." TeleSur, December 6. https://www.telesurtv.net/news/venezuela-venta-compra-petroleo-criptomoneda-petro—20181 206-0023.html.

White House. 2011. "Executive Order 13566—Libya." 2011. https://obamawhitehouse.archives.gov/the-press-office/2011/02/25/executive-order-13566-libya.

White House . 2012. "Executive Order—Blocking Property of the Government of Iran and Iranian Financial Institutions." White House, February 6. https://obamawhitehouse.archives.gov/the-press-office/2012/02/06/executive-order-blocking-property-government-iran-and-iranian-financial-.

White House. 2019. "Treasury Sanctions Central Bank of Venezuela and Director of the Central Bank of Venezuela." White House, April 17. https://home.treasury.gov/news/press-releases/sm661.

White House. 2022. "Press Briefing by Press Secretary Jen Psaki and National Security Advisor Jake Sullivan, January 13, 2022." https://www.whitehouse.gov/briefing-room/press-briefings/2022/01/13/press-briefing-by-press-secretary-jen-psaki-and-national-security-advisor-jake-sullivan-january-13-2022/.

"Treasury Sanctions Russia-Based Bank Attempting to Circumvent U.S. Sanctions on Venezuela." 2019. US Treasury, March 11. https://home.treasury.gov/news/press-releases/sm622.

Turak, Natasha. 2018. "Europe, Russia and China Join Forces with a New Mechanism to Dodge Iran Sanctions." CNBC, September 25. https://www.cnbc.com/2018/09/25/eu-russia-and-china-join-forces-to-dodge-iran-sanctions.html.

US Energy Information Administration. 2020. "Country Analysis Executive Summary: Venezuela." Washington, DC, November 30. https://www.eia.gov/intern ational/analysis/country/VEN.

US House of Representatives. 2018. "Oversight of US Sanctions Policy," September 13.

US Treasury. 2006. "Feasibility of a Cross-Border Electronic Funds Transfer Reporting System Under the Bank Secrecy Act." U.S. Treasury, October. https://www.fincen.gov/sites/default/files/shared/CBFTFS_Complete.pdf.

US Treasury. 2014. "Revised Guidance on Entities Owned by Persons Whose Property and Interests in Property Are Blocked." Washington, DC, August 13. https://home.treasury.gov/system/files/126/licensing_guidance.pdf.

US Treasury. 2016. "'Frequently Asked Questions Regarding Customer Due Diligence Requirements for Financial Institutions.'" US Treasury, July 19. https://www.fincen.gov/resources/statutes-regulations/guidance/frequently-asked-questions-regarding-customer-due-diligence.

US Treasury. 2018a. "Treasury Designates Russian Oligarchs, Officials, and Entities in Response to Worldwide Malign Activity." US Treasury, April 6. https://home.treasury.gov/news/press-releases/sm0338.

US Treasury. 2018b. "Treasury Sanctions Turkish Officials with Leading Roles in Unjust Detention of U.S. Pastor Andrew Brunson." US Treasury, August 1. https://home.treasury.gov/news/press-releases/sm453.

US Treasury. 2021. "Foreign Portfolio Holdings of U.S. Securities." US Treasury, June 30. https://ticdata.treasury.gov/resource-center/data-chart-center/tic/Documents/shla2021r.pdf.

US Treasury. 2022. "Treasury Prohibits Transactions with Central Bank of Russia and Imposes Sanctions on Key Sources of Russia's Wealth." US Treasury. February 28. https://home.treasury.gov/news/press-releases/jy0612.

Vasquez, Alex, and Patricia Laya. 2019. "Venezuela Has Bitcoin Stash and Doesn't Know What to Do with It." Bloomberg, September 26. https://www.bloomberg.com/news/articles/2019-09-26/venezuela-has-bitcoin-stash-and-doesn-t-know-what-to-do-with-it.

Walsh, Declan. 2022. "'From Russia with Love': A Putin Ally Mines Gold and Plays Favorites in Sudan." New York Times, June 5, https://www.nytimes.com/2022/06/05/world/africa/wagner-russia-sudan-gold-putin.html.

Wang, Cong. 2022. "Biden Takes Victory Lap over Russia Sanctions but US Dollar Hegemony Shows Cracks." Global Times, March 17. https://www.globaltimes.cn/page/202203/1255191.shtml.

Wang, Yongli. 2021. "人民币国际化的目标与行动 [The Goals and Actions of RMB Internationalization]." Sina, February 6. http://finance.sina.com.cn/zl/bank/2021-02-06/zl-ikftpnny5450942.shtml.

Watson, Ivan, and Gul Tuysuz. 2012. "Iran Importing Gold to Evade Economic Sanctions, Turkish Official Says." CNN, November 29. https://www.cnn.com/2012/11/29/world/meast/turkey-iran-gold-for-oil/index.html.

Weijia, Hu. 2017. "Helping Russia Cope with Impact of Proposed US Sanctions Can Benefit All Parties." Global Times, July 27. https://www.globaltimes.cn/content/1058400.shtml.

Weiss, Colin. 2022. "Geopolitics and the U.S. Dollar's Future as a Reserve Currency." Board of Governors of the Federal Reserve, Division of International Finance, Washington, DC.

Wheatley, Jonathan, and Colby Smith. 2022. "Russia Sanctions Threaten to Chip Away at Dominance of US Dollar, Says IMF." *Financial Times*, March 31. https://www.ft.com/content/3e0760d4-8127-41db-9546-e62b6f8f5773.

Widakuswara, Patsy, and Ken Bredemeier. 2022. "Biden Warns of 'Severe' Actions if Russia Invades Ukraine." *Voice of America News*, January 26. https://www.voanews.com/a/us-warns-russia-economic-sanctions-would-be-sharper-than-in-2014/6411902.html.

Winecoff, William Kindred. 2015. "Structural Power and the Global Financial Crisis: A Network Analytical Approach." *Business and Politics* 17 (3): 495–525.

Wines, Michael, Keith Bradsher, and Mark Landler. 2009. "China's Leader Says He Is 'Worried' over U.S. Treasuries." *New York Times*, March 13. https://www.nytimes.com/2009/03/14/world/asia/14china.html.

Wolf, Martin. 2022. "A New World of Currency Disorder Looms." *Financial Times*, March 29. https://www.ft.com/content/f18cf835-02a0-44ff-875f-7de7facba54e.

Wong, Andrea. 2016. "The Untold Story Behind Saudi Arabia's 41-Year U.S. Debt Secret." Bloomberg, May 30. https://www.bloomberg.com/news/features/2016-05-30/the-untold-story-behind-saudi-arabia-s-41-year-u-s-debt-secret.

World Gold Council. 2010. "The Importance of Gold in Reserve Asset Management." London.

World Gold Council. 2018. "2018 Central Bank Gold Reserves Survey." https://www.gold.org/goldhub/data/world-gold-council-survey-central-bank-gold-reserves-2018.World Gold Council. 2019. "2019 Central Bank Gold Reserves Survey." *World Gold Council.* https://www.gold.org/goldhub/data/2019-central-bank-gold-reserve-survey.

World Gold Council. 2020. "2020 Central Bank Gold Reserves Survey." *World Gold Council.* https://www.gold.org/goldhub/data/2020-central-bank-gold-reserve-survey.

World Market Intelligence News. 2014. "BNP May Prompt Shift Away from Dollar, Says Bank of France Governor," June 16.

WTO. 2020. "Evolution of Trade under the WTO: Handy Statistics." 2020. https://www.wto.org/english/res_e/statis_e/trade_evolution_e/evolution_trade_wto_e.htm.

Xi, Jinping. 2022. "Full Text: Chinese President Xi Jinping's Keynote Speech at the Opening Ceremony of the BRICS Business Forum." *Xinhua*, June 6. https://english.news.cn/20220622/2531b1cc563d4f59b11a3f2f42eea908/c.html.

Xinhua. 2018. "Iran, Turkey's Senior Officials Discussing Banking Ties." *Xinhua*, January 16. http://www.xinhuanet.com/english/2018-01/16/c_136900384.htm.

Xiong, Aizong. 2014. "熊爱宗：欧美对俄制裁利好中俄贸易 [Xiong Aizong: European and US Sanctions on Russia Benefit Sino-Russian Trade]." *QQ (Tencent Finance)*, April 12. https://finance.qq.com/original/caijingguancha/f1111.html.

Yagova, Olga. 2018. "Exclusive: Rosneft in Stand-off with Oil Buyers as It Seeks Sanctions Protection." Reuters, November 6. https://www.reuters.com/article/us-rosneft-sanctions-exclusive/exclusive-rosneft-in-stand-off-with-oil-buyers-as-it-seeks-sanctions-protection-idUSKCN1NB1V4.

Yeni Safak. 2018. "The Kingdom of the Dollar Collapses," May 20. https://www.yenisafak.com/ekonomi/dolarin-kralligi-cokuyor-3332526.

Yeung, Karen. 2018. "China and Russia Look to Ditch Dollar with New Payments System in Move to Avoid Sanctions." *South China Morning Post*, November 22. https://www.scmp.com/economy/china-economy/article/2174453/china-and-russia-look-ditch-dollar-new-payments-system-move.

Yin, Yong. 2018. "Promote the Internationalisation of RMB and Better Serve the New Pattern of All-Round Opening Up." *China Finance 40 Forum*, July 13. http://www.cf40.org.cn/html/RESEARCH-REPORTS/201807/13-12843.html.

Yu, Yongding. 2018. "China Should Not Underestimate the Long-Term and Complex Nature of Renminbi Internationalization." *China Finance 40 Forum*, August 31. http://www.cf40.org.cn/html/RESEARCH-REPORTS/201812/07-13153.html.

Zarate, Juan C. 2013. *Treasury's War: The Unleashing of a New Era of Financial Warfare.* New York: PublicAffairs.

Zhang, Dan. 2020. "US Unlikely to Play Debt Game with China: Analysts." *Global Times*, May 7. https://www.globaltimes.cn/content/1187703.shtml.

Zhou, Hai, and Yanling Li. 2019. "China and Russia Have a Long Way to Go in Cross-Border RMB Business [周中俄人民币跨境业务任重道远]." *Sina*, September 27. https://finance.sina.cn/forex/hsxw/2019-07-19/detail-ihytcerm4766411.d.html?cre=tianyi&mod=wpage&loc=8&r=32&rfunc=0&tj=none&tr=32&cref=cj.

Zhou, Xiaochuan. 2009. "Reform the International Monetary System," March 23. https://www.bis.org/review/r090402c.pdf.

Zhou, Xiaochuan. 2019. "Response Must Pay High Attention to RMB Internationalization [应对须高度关注人民币国际化]." *China Finance 40 Forum*, December 12. http://www.cf40.org.cn/plus/view.php?aid=13613.

Zhu, Qibin, Tao Guan, and Liping Liu. 2020. "If the US Imposes Financial Sanctions on Chinese Banks, How Should We Respond? [若美国对中资银行实施金融制裁，我们当如何应对？]." Hong Kong. http://pg.jrj.com.cn/acc/Res/CN_RES/MAC/2020/7/28/7d5689fd-3507-4f38-8560-41229e0f8253.pdf.

Zhu, Zibin, Tao Guan, and Liping Liu. 2020. "若美国对中资银行实施金融制裁，我们当如何应对? [If the US Imposes Financial Sanctions on Chinese Banks, How Should We Respond?]." Beijing. http://pg.jrj.com.cn/acc/Res/CN_RES/MAC/2020/7/28/7d5689fd-3507-4f38-8560-41229e0f8253.pdf.

Zimmermann, Hubert. 2002. *Money and Security: Troops, Monetary Policy, and West Germany's Relations with the United States and Britain, 1950-1971.* Cambridge, UK: Cambridge University Press.

Index